I Wish I'd Been There®, Book Two

I Wish I'd Been There®

Book Two

EUROPEAN HISTORY

———◆———

Edited by

BYRON HOLLINSHEAD
and **THEODORE K. RABB**

DOUBLEDAY

NEW YORK LONDON TORONTO SYDNEY AUCKLAND

Published in the United States by Doubleday, an imprint of The Doubleday Broadway Publishing Group, a division of Random House, Inc., New York.

www.doubleday.com

DOUBLEDAY and the portrayal of an anchor with a dolphin are registered trademarks of Random House, Inc.

Book design by Diane Hobbing of Snap-Haus Graphics

Cataloging-in-Publication Data is on file with the Library of Congress.

ISBN 978-0-385-51908-3

PRINTED IN THE UNITED STATES OF AMERICA

10 9 8 7 6 5 4 3 2 1

First Edition

CONTENTS

———————➤●◄———————

History is an ambiguous word. It refers both to what happened and to the process of telling what happened. In both cases the central problem is that the subject at hand is at best only partially recoverable. Even the deepest research and the highest imagination cannot bring the past fully back to life. Yet that is the ideal that historians find themselves pursuing. They marshal their sharpest insights, their shrewdest arguments, and their most evocative words in the hope that, somehow, they can re-create (and thus create) history.

Essential to that aim is the ability to think oneself into a situation long gone. Historians may shape narratives and explanations to suit their own predilections, but they will never carry their readers or listeners with them unless the pictures they draw are persuasive—unless their history is indeed, in Ranke's famous phrase, *"wie es eigentlich gewesen,"* as it actually was. Ranke was not advocating an imperturbable objectivity. His phrase assumed a *subjective* fashioning of the past by historians, but with a special purpose: After completing a comprehensive examination of the surviving evidence, they had to try to make sure that the result would be accepted as the actuality itself. History is, after all, a daughter of rhetoric.

All of which is merely to say that putting themselves into the past, and bringing their audience with them, is what historians have to do if their work is to be effective and convincing. The epitome of that effort is the mental leap that enables the scholars of today to become so attuned to the way that historical actors thought and behaved that it is almost as if they were there. That, one can say with some confidence, is the heart of the historian's enterprise.

From that statement of basic purpose, it is but a small step to the seemingly artificial, but in fact profoundly natural, exercise that asks scholars to pick a moment in the past which they believe they can inhabit. They do that implicitly all the time. What this exercise requires is that they do so explicitly. At that point, however, the question arises that every contributor to this volume had to face: If I have to pick a moment, which will it be? Clearly, it ought to be an occasion of some significance or broad interest, and to give it meaning one has to explain the context and tease out the implications. But in the end there has to be a scene, or a succession of scenes, to which the writer is particularly drawn—an unfolding of events that can bring clarity and perhaps even new levels of comprehensibility if one imagines what a fly on the wall might have seen and heard.

To some extent, the appeal is the frisson of proximity to a famous event. Probably more people than the entire population of Paris later claimed to have joined in the storming of the Bastille. For the historian, however, the exercise goes well beyond prurience; it becomes a means of understanding the past. When one throws oneself into a sharply defined occasion, scouring every available source of information and determinedly seeking to engage with the dramatis personae directly, one is forced to make decisions about what happened that the usual sober, distant, scholarly appraisal may not demand. *I Wish I'd Been There*® is not just a way of evoking history; it requires a degree of concentration and informed speculation that the historian may otherwise not venture. Again and again in the essays that follow, as the authors take their close looks at moments in the past, they are led to new and original readings of history.

That outcome could hardly have been expected. The presiding assumption was that historians, as they imagined what a witness might have seen, would add immediacy, color, and vibrancy to well-known events. In most cases, however, vital information either is missing or can be interpreted in more than one way, and so these journeys across time required a fresh illumination or a rethinking of vital moments in the history of Europe. As a result, these essays are not only engaging and suggestive, they are also telling contributions to historical understanding.

What is particularly fascinating is the range that they cover. We have politics, law, religion, peace and war, science and the arts, rebellion and social change. We move across a wide geography for over two millennia. And above all, we gain a sense of the excitement, the passion, the drama, and the joys and tragedies that are the essence of history.

I Wish I'd Been There®, Book Two

JOSIAH OBER

At the Deathbed of Alexander the Great

Josiah Ober is the Constantine Mitsotakis Professor in the School of Humanities and Sciences at Stanford University, where he holds appointments in Political Science, Classics, and Philosophy. After teaching at Montana State University, he joined the Classics Department at Princeton University in 1990, where he was the David Magie Professor of Classics from 1993 to 2006. Professor Ober has written extensively on military history, classical political thought, and ancient and modern democracy. He is the author of a number of books, including *Mass and Elite in Democratic Athens*, *The Athenian Revolution*, *Political Dissent in Democratic Athens*, and, most recently, *Athenian Legacies: Essays on the Politics of Going On Together* (2005). He is currently completing a new book on participatory democracy, knowledge organization, and innovation. He spends as much of his spare time as possible wading the streams near Bozeman, Montana, fly-fishing for trout.

To start this volume, he takes us back to the last days of the greatest conqueror in history.

At the Deathbed of Alexander the Great

The last days of Alexander the Great have been obsessively studied since antiquity and much is known; the numerous Greek literary sources can be complemented by precious cuneiform texts
and the evidence of archaeology. We know when and where he
died: June 11, 323 B.C., between 4:00 and 5:00 P.M., on the
banks of the Euphrates River in the fabled city of Babylon, in a
palace built by the great and notorious Nebuchadnezzar a quarter millennium before. At the moment of his death, Alexander
was surrounded by his lieutenants, soldiers, wives, and eunuchs;
by Macedonians, Greeks, Persians, and Babylonians; along with
petitioners, ambassadors, admirers, and gawkers from across
three continents. The cause of death was fever. The symptoms
began several days before, after a long night of heavy drinking.
The fever abated briefly, then became increasingly severe. At the
end Alexander could barely move and could not speak clearly,
but he retained enough strength to press his signet ring into the
hand of one of his generals. When asked to whom his spear-won
realm should pass, the king, it was said, managed to whisper "to
the strongest."

Few ancient death scenes are as well documented, yet so
much remains mysterious. Upon Alexander's demise, a rumor
circulated that he had been poisoned. Fingers pointed to Antipater, the veteran commander who had been left in charge of
Macedon when the twenty-year-old Alexander set out to conquer Asia. Antipater's son Cassander arrived in Babylon just a
few days before the onset of the king's fever and had quarreled
violently with Alexander. Cassander's brother Iolaus was the
king's cupbearer; the story held that Cassander had smuggled

Alexander's Conquest Route

Only nine years after becoming King of Macedon, Alexander the Great had conquered the entire Persian Empire and spread the influence of Greek civilization as far as India. The map shows his astonishing route of conquest. Alexander's vast empire, however, did not survive his death.

into Babylon a poison so deadly that it corroded all metal and could only be contained by a mule's hoof. Had Cassander passed a hoof-full of death to Iolaus, fearing that the king planned to strip Antipater of his command? But if so, what was the poison? Ancient and modern pharmacologists have struggled to correlate the reported symptoms with the action of poisons known in Alexander's day.

The rumors about the cause of Alexander's death are intertwined with reports of his plans for the future: Having conquered Greece, Egypt, and Asia as far east as India, what lands would the Undefeated God, as the king had recently designated himself, choose to conquer next? A massive fleet of warships had recently gathered at Babylon, and the rivers had been cleared of obstructing dams: The waterway was open to the Persian Gulf. At the least, it seemed, Alexander's plans included circumnavigation of the Arabian Peninsula. That would be a notable feat of navigation—and allow him to acquire the spice and incense-producing coastal zones of Arabia. But those in the know said that the king had his eye on restive city-states in Greece, and on fresh conquests in Africa, Italy, and even Spain. Close to hand, the city-state of Athens had recently (if only briefly) offered asylum to Alexander's onetime chief treasurer, Harpalus, who had absconded with thousands of talents of silver. Farther west, on the northern shore of Africa, lay the hugely wealthy Afro-Phoenician state of Carthage, and then there were the luxury-loving Etruscans of central Italy and their neighbor, the fast-rising state of Rome. Mineral riches were there for the taking in Spain. To the north lay Thrace and Scythia, rich in gold and grain. According to the rumor mill, no part of the civilized world lay outside the king's ambit of desire. Which of these rumors were true?

And by what system of governance and what social policies did Alexander intend to rule his vast kingdom? Would he continue to reign as his father Philip had before him, as king of the Macedonians and constitutional hegemon of the Greek city-states? Would he bring all of his realm under one government, lording over the world from Babylon as the legitimate successor of a long line of Persian Kings of Kings, on the model of Cyrus, Xerxes, and Darius? Had he reinvented himself as the greatest of the Central Asian warlords during the challenging Indo-Bactrian campaigns of the last several years? Would he return to Egypt, to rule as a divine conqueror-pharaoh on the model of Ramses the Great?

We could frame an answer to these questions if only we could observe how Alexander chose to dress in public and in private. Dress mattered a lot in the ancient world: How you dressed was an indication of who you were. It is certain that the king had taken to wearing selected items of Persian garb, at least on certain occasions: gorgeous purple robes, but not trousers; the diadem, but not the tiara. How often and in what circumstances did Alexander choose to costume himself as Persian royalty? As

Macedonian soldier or rough-riding warlord? How widely and deeply were oriental court customs being adopted by his Macedonian followers? Some were happy to adopt Persian protocol by prostrating themselves before the king. Other men, who openly scorned the Persian custom of *proskinesis,* had recently lost their lives: Callisthenes, the philosopher and nephew of Alexander's teacher Aristotle, died in prison. Cleitus the Black, whose quick work with a sword had saved Alexander's life at the start of the Asian adventure, had been stabbed to death by Alexander in a drunken quarrel. The squabble had been over the king's growing passion for the trappings of what Cleitus despised as orientalism. How important was it to the son of Philip of Macedon that he be humbly acknowledged by one and all by obsequies traditionally accorded the Persian Great King?

Even more pressingly: How would he treat his subjects—and how would they relate to one another? A few months before his death, Alexander had held a military review of thirty thousand Persian youths who had just completed four years of training in the arts of fighting in the Greek style. Apparently Macedonians and Greeks would no longer hold a monopoly on military service; Persians were being incorporated into the cavalry and into the infantry phalanx. Were these the first moves toward a unified empire, whose diverse ethnic groups would be equal in the eyes of their king?

Perhaps the key to understanding the king's intentions lay with the new cities populated by mustered-out veterans, recently founded by and named for Alexander. Many new cities had been planned, but were they to be culturally purely Greek, as the king's old tutor, Aristotle, advised? Or semi-Greek? Or some exciting hybrid form as yet unknown? The port city of Egyptian Alexandria was becoming a cosmopolitan center of trade, culture, and government. But what of the others? At the farthest northeast frontier of the empire, at the modern site of

Ai Khanoum on the Afghan border, archaeologists were amazed to discover a major town featuring a startling mix of Hellenic and Asian cultural features; it was apparently founded by Alexander during his Afghan campaign. How many *other* new cities had been planned for the lands between Egypt and India? What role were they to play in the king's schemes for governing his vast realm?

The answers to at least some of these questions must have been known and recorded. For modern historians, some of the most tantalizing mysteries about the last days of Alexander concern documents. What records were being kept and by whom? Authors of the Roman era believed that Royal Diaries were maintained by Alexander's official staff. The diaries supposedly recorded the details of what the king did and said day by day, from the beginning of his reign to the end. What would a modern historian give to travel back in time, to study those records at leisure, perhaps with a helpful archivist nearby to pull the papyrus scrolls from their cedarwood cabinets? Did Alexander have the foresight to prepare a final testament that would clarify the succession and the distribution of power among the many ambitious and able men who had fought by his side and who must now manage the gigantic and diverse empire? A detailed version of Alexander's will has come down to us, but it is attached to the fantasy-filled *Romance of Alexander.* The will seems to be earlier than the rest of the *Romance,* but does it have any bearing on the king's actual intentions?

Every historian wants to know what really happened in the past. That means—at a minimum—gaining access to records, the more detailed and accurate, the closer to the actual events, the better. But in our hearts we always want more than we can ever have: We want to read documents that are lost forever; to interview people long dead; to be eyewitness to the great events that changed the course of history. We want that in part because we want to solve mysteries, we do want to know the truth about the past. But in honesty, the search for the truth about events and historical trends is only one of the reasons I would choose to experience *this* moment of past time above all others. What I really want to know is what it *felt like* to be at the center of the world, at a moment when human history had reached one of its great turning points.

A turning point it certainly was: Thirty years before, when the baby Alexander was just beginning to walk and talk, the world had seemed set in its course. The Greeks would fight endless wars over the meaningless question of which city-state would exercise brief hegemony. An ossified but operational Persian Empire would continue to dominate an extensive core. People at the fringes of the empire—western Anatolia, Egypt, and India—would continue to find ways to avoid Persian domination, and ambitious local governors would periodically assert a tenuous independence. Macedon would continue in its role as underperforming giant with great human and natural resources, but lacking effective central government.

Some of those assumptions began to change as Alexander's father, Philip, consolidated royal power in Macedon, brought the mainland Greeks under his control, and laid plans for an Asian expedition that would add the rich provinces of western Anatolia to his burgeoning Macedonian Empire. But in the dozen years since Alexander had inherited the throne of Macedon, the pace had accelerated wildly. So much had changed for an unimaginable number of people across Europe and Asia, as long-entrenched systems of government had been suddenly overturned. The treasure-houses of the Persian Empire, packed with the carefully hoarded loot of two centuries of plunder and efficient taxation, had been thrown open. Tons of silver and gold spilled into the Euro-Asian economy. The Greek language, and the rich cultural heritage it brought with it, was becoming the new lingua franca. Everything, it seemed, would be made anew.

In the days before the news of Alexander's death was broadcast, everything was still possible. I want to experience the vertigo of gazing at the unlimited horizons that had opened virtually overnight. Alexander had done the unthinkable by toppling the greatest empire in the Mediterranean and western Asian world in three great battles. He burned down the great Persian capital of Persepolis, giving the Greek world revenge for all the temples burned by Xerxes during the Greco-Persian wars of a century and a half past. Then he ruthlessly hunted down the killer of his enemy, Persia's last Great King. He went on to defeat the bellicose tribes of Central Asia and honored the pride of the Afghans, his toughest opponents, by taking as his first wife Roxane, daughter of a local warlord. Alexander had met the challenge of the giant rajah Porus's war elephants on a tributary of the Indus River, and then survived the extraordinary rigors of a desert crossing upon his return east.

I want to hear the war stories of soldiers who had answered the call of a teenage king, marched out as raw recruits from their home villages in the Macedonian highlands, and were now wealthy, weary, battle-scarred veterans of the greatest expedition in human history. By their terrifying prowess with spear and sword, many tens of thousands of Greeks and Asians had died. But, meanwhile, once-insular worlds of thought were opened to one another as Indian religious adepts, priestly Egyptian temple archivists, Babylonian astronomers and mathematicians, and Greek historians and philosophers rubbed shoulders in the imperial capitals. I want to listen to their conversations, to attend the birth of a new and cosmopolitan world of knowledge.

The conviction that everything had changed and anything might be possible was intensified by the blurring of the bound-

ary between the realm of the gods and mortals. After his conquest of Egypt, Alexander had been welcomed as a divine son
by the great god Ammon in the desert oasis Siwa. He had enthusiastically been adopted by the native populace of Egypt as
a legitimate successor to the dynastic god-kings of the Old, Middle, and New Kingdoms. Shortly before his death, Alexander sent
a request (which was taken as an order) to the Greeks assembled
for the games at Olympia: They were to offer their king divine
rights, as if he were a living god. The divinity of the man Alexander was only one new religious idea among many now cascading
through the world. The Greeks, long used to offering sacrifices
to a wide pantheon of anthropomorphized deities, found themselves confronted by highly sophisticated philosophical-religious
traditions founded by the Persian Zarathustra and by the Indian
Gautama Buddha; they were astonished by the practices of the
Indian "naked philosophers" and by the complex ritual rules of
Hinduism. Bold new religious syncretisms were blossoming;
new ways were being found to explore and honor the unseen
world of the divine. I want to hear tales of enlightenment, con-
version, and spiritual rebirth. I want to be in Babylon in the
spring of 323 B.C. to breathe in the potent atmosphere of hope
mixed with dread. The hope was stimulated by the miraculous
return of Alexander from the dead. Along with most of the
Macedonian army, he had set out from his base in India with
the plan of crossing what he supposed would be a reasonably
well inhabited zone to the west. Instead he had found the night-
marish Gedrosian Desert. Coordination between Alexander's
land army with his fleet broke down as the desolation of the
coastal zone became apparent; both fleet and army were cut off,
assumed lost. With the king's disappearance, imperial order began to break down: Men Alexander had set up as local governors began, tentatively, to consolidate authority in their own

names. Without Alexander they knew there could be no unified empire, but only spoils. Each was positioning himself to grab his share.

When Alexander did emerge from the desert with most of the army intact, and his admiral Nearchus appeared with the fleet, hope for a new world was reborn and the celebrations were extravagant. What were people hoping for? Alexander had already helped Greek cities in western Anatolia replace corrupt oligarchies with democracy. Some people would have been looking forward to lives as free citizens in democratic towns; others were imagining the cultural opportunities to be offered by the many new "Alexandrias." Yet others anticipated the huge potential for long-distance trade that would emerge with the expanded empire.

Yet Alexander had emerged from the desert with his dark side to the fore. He had always been volatile, but his displeasure now grew more violent. Governors who had shown too much independence were summoned to the king—some were summarily executed. Meanwhile, Alexander issued high-handed orders commanding Greek cities to accept back within their walls all persons who had been sent into exile. For democratic city-states, this could mean introducing terrorists and revolutionaries: embittered oligarchs who could be expected to plot against the existing governments.

More reasons for dread: The newly formed regiments of Persian youths had been a rude shock to the veterans. The Macedonian soldiers feared that they would now be summarily dismissed from service, and they rose up in vehement protest. They were brought back into the fold with munificent mustering-out bonuses, a splendid feast in which their ethnic pride was catered to, and their king's expansive declaration that he regarded all of his Macedonian soldiers as his kinsmen. But the unease remained—the veterans were more than ready to go home; they dreaded what would happen if they did.

Then, en route to Babylon, Alexander's closest friend and most trusted companion, Hephaestion, suddenly sickened and died. Alexander's grief was terrifying. The attending physician was crucified. The king's misery was nightmarishly expressed in a series of ferocious, near-genocidal military raids on horse-stealing tribal peoples in the Iranian highlands. What did this new level of combat savagery portend for the grand expeditions in the works?

I want to walk the steaming midsummer streets of Babylon in June of 323 B.C. to know what it feels like to live in a wildly heterogeneous society at the brink of a strange and wonderful and terrifying new world that had been opened by a man whose life now hung by a thread. But I also long to visit Babylon when it was, for the last time, the center of the world. Within fifty years after Alexander's death, Babylon's population was shipped away to new homes in an upstart town named for another of Alexander's lieutenants. The great city's temples, palaces, gardens, and houses slowly disappeared under the sand and would remain invisible until modern archaeologists began excavation.

But in 323 B.C., Babylon was still the greatest and most populous city in the world, and its history was unthinkably long by Greek standards—it had been a great urban center at the dawn of the second millennium B.C., when Hammurabi had made it the capital of his empire. With its huge and unruly population and its venerable religious tradition, Babylon had spelled trouble for the Assyrian Empire during the early first millennium; it had been sacked by the Assyrian kings Sennacherib and Assurbanipal. When the Assyrians were overthrown by a new Babylonian dynasty, the city was splendidly rebuilt by Nebuchadnezzar II—King Nebuchadnezzar of biblical infamy. Beginning at the turn of the sixth century B.C., Nebuchadnezzar dedicated much of his long reign to reconstructing the city in a fashion worthy of its long and glorious history. The massive old ziggurat temples were restored, and new temples of staggering opulence were dedicated to the Babylonian gods. Superb gardens (the famous Hanging Gardens recorded by Greek historians and geographers) imitated a mountain landscape in the midst of the flat and fertile plain. A stone bridge now spanned the Euphrates, connecting the two halves of the city.

In June 323 B.C., Alexander's attendants carried him over this bridge to a cool bathhouse on the west bank of the river in an attempt to quell his raging fever. At the center of the city, near the river, lay Nebuchadnezzar's palace—it was here that Alexander died.

How would Babylon strike the senses of a traveler in midsummer of 323 B.C.? The first impression would surely be one of immensity: The mighty fortification walls, wide enough at the top for two chariots to pass, enclosed some two hundred square miles, according to the measurements of the Greek historian Herodotus. After the fall of the neo-Babylonian dynasty to the Persians, Babylon had become one of the capital cities of the Persian Empire, but the Babylonians had not lost their stubborn independence of spirit: King Xerxes destroyed the great temple of Marduk to punish them for a revolt in 482 B.C. Later Persian kings allowed Babylon to go to seed, preferring to spend their winters at Susa near the Persian Gulf and their summers at the pleasantly cool royal residence at Ecbatana. By contrast, Alexander had announced great plans for the ancient city.

After his final and decisive defeat of the Persian King Darius III at Gaugamela in 331 B.C., Alexander had taken over Babylon without a fight. The Macedonian invader earned the affection of the Babylonians by forbidding his soldiers to enter private

In 331 B.C.E., after expanding his kingdom to encompass the eastern Mediterranean, Alexander turned his forces toward Babylon for a victory that would gain him sovereignty over western Asia. *The Triumph of Alexander*, a seventeenth-century painting by Charles Le Brun, captures Alexander's glorious entrance into the city. Only eight years later, the young king would die there surrounded by mourners from three continents.

homes without permission. Moreover, he had promised to rebuild the great temple of Marduk. When Alexander left Babylon to head east, he arranged for the city to serve as a primary resupply center and left it under the control of his chief treasurer, Harpalus. Before his treasonous defection in 324 B.C., the treasurer had set to work putting familiar Greek plants in the royal gardens and building a notoriously expensive monument to his favorite concubine. Had Harpalus also been preparing the city to become a worthy capital of the world empire—restoring the palace so that it would once again be fit for a King of Kings, repaving the boulevards for the victory parades to come? Alexander's plans for the city became even more extravagant in the early months of 323 B.C. After Hephaestion's untimely death, planning began for his gigantic tomb. Thousands of craftsmen flooded into the city, eager to work on the mausoleum that everyone expected would be one of the grandest architectural enterprises in human history.

In anticipation of Alexander's triumphant return to Babylon, we must suppose that the public areas, and especially the palace, were given a facelift. But did the generations of Persian neglect show through? Was the ancient city's degeneration disguised by a new coat of stucco and paint? Where and when did the decay show through? Was the magnificent Ishtar Gate still splendid, with its brilliant blue and golden tile mosaics of lions and winged griffins? What of the famous gardens—were they newly planted and irrigated by the ambitious Harpalus? Or overgrown tangles of weed and vine, only partially masked by potted plants? What of the ancient temples, and the private homes and workshops and wharves? Did Babylon smell of river, or of dust? Of animal and human waste, or of perfume, incense, and scented oil? Of ambition or desire? Walking through the crowded city at night, guided by the flickering orange light of naphtha-torches, would I hear the cough of a captive lion, the shriek of an ostrich, or the bark of jackals amidst the babble of multitudes of men and women speaking in myriad foreign tongues?

Who would I meet if I could move freely through the streets of the city, through the palace, into the private royal quarters and the homes of the great and the ordinary? Who was there in Babylon, at the center of the world, at the moment of Alexander's final breath? Along with the local Babylonians, there were camp followers, captives, and emissaries from all the lands Alexander had conquered: Anatolians, Cilicians, Syrians, Phoenicians, Jews, Egyptians, Medes, Persians, Bactrians, Indians, and a thousand other ethnicities. Ambassadors had flocked to the new capital from around the world, hoping for a private moment with the Great King. There were Greeks, of course: Athenians to complain about the exiles decree, Thebans to urge the rebuilding of the first great Greek city to be sacked by the young Alexander, Rhodians with plans for how their island could become a center of Mediterranean trade. But the Greeks were outnumbered by envoys from more distant and exotic lands: Scythians and Thracians, Italians—including, it was said, Roman senators—Carthaginians, Spaniards.

Dominating the throng were thousands of hard-fighting and hard-partying Macedonians. These included the great field marshals, regimental commanders, and generals, each with his retinue: men of extraordinary talent and ambition, steely-eyed specialists in violence who excelled in the arts of war, and diplomacy, treachery, and survival, all learned in the hard school of Alexander's camp. And with them were their concubines and Asian wives. In Susa, en route to Babylon, Alexander had officiated over a mass wedding: Scores of commanders were given huge dowries when, at the king's urging, they agreed to marry the daughters of Persian and Bactrian aristocrats. Alexander himself had added to his polygamous family: It was in Bactria that he had first married, and Roxane was now visible with child—it would be a boy, although no one knew that yet. More recently Alexander had wed the daughters of two former Persian kings, Artaxerxes III and Darius III. If the rumors were true, Alexander had far exceeded his father's total of seven wives. It was said that the Great King had followed Persian royal practice by gathering a proper harem and now had as many beautiful concubines as there were days in the year.

Thousands of ordinary Macedonian soldiers had taken camp wives on the long march across Asia. Alexander blessed these unions by offering his soldiers dowries and discharging the debts they had contracted in the course of the expedition. The king's apparently keen interest in legitimizing cross-cultural unions seemed to point to a vision of the future that transcended the narrowly Greco-Macedonian horizon of many of his closest associates. What was going through the minds of Alexander's veterans and their newly legalized wives, and the countless others who anxiously awaited news from the palace in the long, hot days while the king's illness worsened?

Finally, the suspense undid the veterans. They demanded to see their king. And here is the moment I most long to see: Alexander being taken from the palace on a litter, which was then set up in a high place in the city. His men filed by for a last moment of communion with the commander who had led them to glory. The communion was silent: The king could not speak, but acknowledged each of them with his eyes or a slight gesture. They had seen him so often before, but never like this, never in silence, never with the recognition that the adventure was over. It would end here, in Babylon, and I want to be there to see that moment as the curtain gently comes down, as the members of the audience realize that they will soon be alone in this vast and crumbling theater. I long for that last, intimate glimpse of Alexander, reduced to his human essence, slipping away into legend.

If I could be there, would I know if what the Roman chronicler Quintus Curtius wrote was true? "Wandering about and as if crazed, they filled that city, great as it was, with grief and sorrow, . . . those who had stood outside the royal quarters, Macedonians and foreigners alike, rushed together. And in their common sorrow the vanquished could not be distinguished from the victors. . . ." Did Macedonian and Persian, Babylonian and Greek weep together? Were they mourning the man Alexander, their all-too-mortal king and former master? Or had some of them already begun to grieve for the loss of their own dreams, and for a stillborn world in which an expansive Alexandrian identity might have overcome the deadly entrenched distinctions between Greek and barbarian, between Iranian and Babylonian, between pagan and Jew?

Further Reading

A. B. Bosworth, *Conquest and Empire: The Reign of Alexander the Great* (Cambridge, 1998).

Paul Cartledge, *Alexander the Great: The Hunt for a New Past* (Woodstock, NJ, 2004).

Peter Green, *Alexander of Macedon, 356–323 B.C.: A Historical Biography* (Berkeley, 1991).

TOM HOLLAND

Hannibal Crosses the Alps

Tom Holland lives in London and is the author of *Rubicon*, a study of the last days of the Roman Republic, and *Persian Fire*, a history of the Greco-Persian wars. He has also written a much-acclaimed series of adaptations of Herodotus's *Histories*, Virgil's *The Aeneid*, and Homer's *The Iliad* and *The Odyssey* for London's BBC Radio 4.

In this thought-provoking essay, we join the Carthaginian general Hannibal, 60,000 men, and 37 elephants as they begin their crossing of the Alps in 218 C.E.

Hannibal Crosses the Alps

Crossing mountains with an unfeasibly large army has been by no means a unique feat in the annals of military history. Alexander the Great did it; so too did Mao Tse Tung. In Europe alone, two A-list future emperors both invaded Italy by storming the Alps. Charlemagne's victorious expedition of A.D. 773 was long remembered as a peculiarly epic undertaking: "What an effort it cost him," wrote his earliest biographer, "to traverse the pathless ridges of the mountains, and the rocks which scrape the sky, and the sheer abysses." A thousand years later, and it was the turn of Napoleon to lead his men on an expedition across the steepling range: Indeed, so dramatic did it seem to his admirers, so daring, and so heroic, that it came to serve them as the perfect expression of his genius. In 1801, barely twelve months after the French had erupted from the Alps and routed the startled Austrians at the Battle of Marengo, Jacques-Louis David, the supreme artist of the revolutionary era in France, completed his most flamboyant masterpiece: *Napoleon Crossing the Saint-Bernard*. Despite the fact that Napoleon himself, somewhat embarrassingly, had made the entire journey on a mule, David opted to portray the youthful general astride a rearing white horse, possessed of the same ferocious sublimity of the jagged peaks behind him. More than any other single work of art, it served to define Napoleon as the quintessence of a romantic hero: restless, demonic, aiming for the skies.

Yet it is not the French crossing of the Alps that I would choose to watch, if I had a time machine and only the single ticket. Even David, when he painted his great portrait, was obliged to acknowledge that Napoleon's expedition, fired with a revolutionary ardor though it was, had merely been following in the footsteps of a very ancient predecessor indeed. Rocks at the foot of the painting are shown inscribed with three names. One is that of Napoleon himself: "Bonaparte." The second is that of Charlemagne, whose achievements as a conqueror of Europe, and ultimately as an emperor, the upstart Corsican would soon decisively emulate. The third name, despite belonging to a general whose career, like Napoleon's own, ended in catastrophic defeat, was endowed with such an immortality that it remains to this day indelibly associated with the crossing of the Alps, long after the mountain expeditions of other generals have faded from popular consciousness: "Hannibal."

It helped, of course, that he took elephants with him. Iconic moments in history are invariably distinguished by their strong qualities of visual drama—but can any compare for pure spectacle with the passage of Hannibal's army over the Alps? The ascent was made late in the campaigning season, in October, when snow had already begun to fall in the mountain passes and ice lay thick over the bare rocks of the trail. It was across this bleak landscape that the war elephants were obliged to slip and stumble: creatures from the heat of Africa* transplanted to the frozen roof of the world. Many, starved of food and exhausted by their terrible climb, sank to their knees with plaintive cries, immediately to be butchered for what little meat still clung to their mighty frames. Others, tormented by arrows and slingshot, perished in the ambushes that the mountain tribesmen, inveterately hostile to intruders, persisted in setting for Hannibal's snaking columns. Others yet, trustingly following wherever their mahouts guided them, somehow made their way along paths of

---

*Although the fact that Hannibal's favorite elephant was known as "Syrus," or "the Syrian," implies that at least one of them came from India.

fearsome narrowness and did not succumb to the cold, or the circling vultures, or the depths of the waiting ravines. Such were the exploits, when I was young and poring over illustrated histories of the world, that moved me more than any others; and they are exploits that continue to move me now.

Yet fond though I remain of elephants, I do not think that a desire to witness scenes of pachydermatous heroism would be sufficient on its own to have me setting the controls of my time machine to the Alps, 218 B.C. Just as, for the moviegoer, special effects are hardly an infallible imprimatur of quality, so similarly, for the discerning time traveler, the sheer spectacle of a historical episode would never on its own be a sufficient guarantee of its momentousness. Context, in the business of time-tourism, would be everything. Over the centuries, after all, many millions have crossed the Rubicon and the Delaware; made the journey from Mecca to Medina; been crucified. Many generals too have invaded Italy. Is the fact that Hannibal was the only one to do so with elephants the limit of his significance? If so, then the very drama and heroism of the undertaking would serve only to emphasize its ultimate futility. It would seem to illustrate nothing save the vanity of human wishes.

An ancient perspective. Juvenal, Rome's angriest satirist, was the first to make the point. Undercutting pretensions came naturally to him. Like any self-respecting talk-radio host today, he could work himself up into a lather of indignation about a whole host of issues, whether immigration, sexual deviancy, or the breakdown of law and order: All served to rouse him to apoplexy. Celebrities, however, were a particular bugbear: not only those, like gladiators, whom Juvenal felt did not deserve their fame, but even those who did. In the cause of excoriating them, his satire was capable of aiming stratospherically high.

The objects of his mockery included some of the most legendary figures in history: Alexander the Great, Julius Caesar—and Hannibal.

By the time that Juvenal came to write his satires, some three and a half centuries had passed since the celebrated crossing of the Alps. Rome, which had been brought to the verge of destruction in the war that followed Hannibal's descent into Italy, was by now at the very peak of her greatness and prosperity. Her dominion comprised the fairest portions of the known world. Roman arms had proved themselves triumphant from the moors of Scotland to the deserts of Iraq. Beyond the borders of the empire, there seemed to lurk only barbarous savages not worthy of being conquered. Certainly the notion that any foe might oppose the legions as their equal appeared a ludicrous one. Mothers, warning their naughty children that Hannibal was at the gates, might still use Rome's greatest enemy as a bogeyman—but Juvenal, at any rate, could afford to be witheringly unimpressed. "You're a lunatic," he wrote, addressing Hannibal's shade. "It's all very well, powering your way over the savage peaks of the Alps, but what are you good for now? Exciting small boys. Serving them as a theme for school recitations. Nothing else besides."

Two millennia on, and Hannibal—as my own youthful enthusiasm for him suggests—continues to excite small boys. But is that, as Juvenal mocked, the limit of his relevance? Hardly. Poets cocooned by the *Pax Romana* could afford, perhaps, to sneer; and yet there was, in the very iconoclasm of Juvenal's satire, a grudging acknowledgment of the shadow that Hannibal still cast over the city he had labored so heroically to destroy. Even at the very peak of their greatness, the Romans had not forgotten that it was the defeat of their most inveterate enemy, more than any other achievement, that had proved them fit to rule the world. If they had hated and dreaded him, then so too, albeit grudgingly, had they admired him: For by admiring him, they were, of course, admiring themselves. Centuries after his death, statues of Hannibal still stood in Rome. Juvenal, a great one for pacing the streets of the capital, would surely have known them well. The very force of his satire derived from the fact that it was so strikingly counterintuitive. Hannibal, the most brilliant general that the Romans had ever confronted, more than merited his fame.

And merits it to this day. It is not merely that his own life was one of the most remarkable in history: a narrative of incomparable daring and achievement, yet culminating in the bleakest ruin. For the tragedy was far from Hannibal's alone: A great empire was indeed destroyed by his exertions, but it was that of Carthage, his own native city, not Rome's. The battle between these two republics for the mastery of the western Mediterranean was the closest that the ancient world ever came to the style of total warfare as practiced in the twentieth century: the first conflict in history, perhaps, that can properly be titled a world war. Lasting, on and off, for more than a century, and embroiling not only the Romans and the Carthaginians, but Spaniards, Numidians, Macedonians, and Gauls as well, it was finally concluded only when a prostrated Carthage was utterly razed from the face of the earth.

Had Hannibal, as he prepared his invasion of Italy, appreciated that he was committing his city to a death struggle? Certainly he would have had few illusions as to the character of his enemy. Carthage and Rome were seasoned adversaries. The one a great naval power, the other the mistress of Italy, their ambitions had been bound to clash—and had duly done so, in 264 B.C., in Sicily. For two decades a deadly war of attrition had bled both cities white until, at last, thanks to a monstrous demonstration of their sheer bloody-mindedness, the Romans succeeded in dragging their exhausted enemy down to defeat. Not, however, to utter ruin—for even among the general wreckage of the Carthaginian war effort, one commander had remained unvanquished in open battle. This was Hamilcar, leader of Carthage's forces in Sicily, where the nickname he had won for himself—"Barca," or "Lightning"—was a fitting reflection of the scorching brilliance of his generalship.

Hamilcar, although obliged to return to Africa as commander of a defeated city, had remained confident that Carthage could reclaim her former preeminence. Restlessly, he had scouted about for new horizons. The Carthaginians, by the terms of the peace treaty forced on them by Rome, had undertaken a complete withdrawal from Sicily; and so it was, in 237 B.C., that Hamilcar Barca turned his attentions instead to Spain. Naturally, before leaving Carthage, he had made sure to offer up a sacrifice to Ba'al Hammon, greatest of the city's gods. Accompanying him to the shrine that day had been his eldest son: nine-year-old Hannibal. As the sacrifice reeked before them, Hamilcar asked the boy if he wished to sail for Spain as well. Hannibal nodded eagerly. Hamilcar had then ordered his son to lay his hands upon the bloody viscera of the sacrificial victim and swear a solemn oath. "Never to bear goodwill to the Romans."

Such, at any rate, was the story that Hannibal told many years later in his old age, as reported by Polybius, a Greek concerned to investigate the rise of Rome to empire. Two centuries on, and the great Roman historian of the wars with Carthage, Livy, decided that the oath had been insufficiently vengeful and opted to hype it up: In his account, Hamilcar makes his son swear always to be an enemy of Rome. Here, with a rare clarity, we can see Hannibal's legend in the process of its formation: blended of the great Carthaginian's own genius for self-promotion, Greek scholarship, and hatred of Romans. Whether the episode in Ba'al's temple really took place as Hannibal claimed it did is impossible to know, of course; yet even if it did not, it feels as though it should have, for certainly, as he grew up, it appeared as though his life did indeed have a single purpose. Leaving his native city, the young Hannibal's mastery of warfare was soon being forged in a succession of grueling frontier campaigns. Spain was a fearsome place, swarming with murderous tribes—but the mountains there were rich with precious metals. The Barca family, braving ceaseless risk, succeeded in carving out in less than two decades an entire new empire. Although Hamilcar himself was killed in 228 B.C., the victim of a tribal ambush, Hannibal was more than capable of keeping the flame of his father's ambitions alive. Over the following decade the flood of wealth from his new mines enabled him to recruit ever-larger forces. Hannibal knew that he would need them all if he were to renew the struggle with Rome. Total war would have to be met with total war. Victory would be impossible unless the enemy was utterly prostrated.

Here, then, was why the Romans were right to regard the assault that was finally launched against them in 218 B.C. as the supreme test of their national character. Hannibal's invasion of their homeland had been planned very consciously as an exploit designed to shake and astound the world. As such, it represented a marked break from the generally crabbed approach to overseas adventures that had long distinguished Carthaginian policy. Hannibal, a virtual stranger to his native city, looked farther afield for his inspiration. As with so many other areas of expertise, the cutting edge of international generalship was Greek. Ever since the reign of Alexander the Great and his spectacular conquest of the Persian Empire, his successors—the generals of what is known by historians today as the Hellenistic Age—had indulged themselves by thinking big. Big spending; big armies; big dreams. That none had remotely succeeded in emulating the great conqueror's own achievements had done little to dent the widespread enthusiasm for aping Alexander that flourished amid advanced military circles. Hannibal, who spoke Greek, worshiped Greek gods, and took Greek scholars with him on his campaigns, was also aiming to fight as a Greek might have done.

Hence the elephants. Compared to the other units under Hannibal's command—the carnage-hungry Libyan pikemen, say, or the Namidian cavalry, or the Balearic slingers, or the Gallic tribesmen, or the Spaniards with their deadly stabbing swords—the great beasts were of merely limited tactical value, "unsuited by their very nature," as one candid military analyst would later put it, "to the demands of combat." Nevertheless, in an age that had long since come to equate power with swaggering displays of gigantism, they represented the very ultimate in status symbols, an indispensable military brand, without which no Hellenistic general could hope to be regarded as a serious player. Hannibal, obliged as he was by Roman command of the sea to launch his invasion by land, took his elephants with him in order to mythologize what would otherwise have appeared all too obviously a strategy bred of weakness. As they lumbered over the Pyrenees or trampled the trails of southern Gaul, or bellowed their anxiety from makeshift rafts bobbing across the river Rhône, so also did they trumpet the godlike scale of their master's ambition. Not even Alexander had attempted anything quite so fabulously exotic as Hannibal was attempting now.

And then, of course, there came the crossing of the Alps. Hannibal's decision to take the mountain road into Italy rather than continue hugging the coast was a reflection, once again, of his obsession with winning victories that would resonate with the power of myth. Keeping to the lowlands, as the Romans expected him to do, would have obliged him to fight his first battle against the legions of the republic in neutral territory; but Hannibal, confident as he was in his own genius, wanted it won on Italian soil. So it was, as Polybius put it, that "he marched

According to the Roman historian Livy, "The elephants proved both a blessing and a curse: for though getting them along the narrow and precipitous tracks caused serious delay, they were nonetheless a protection to the troops, as the natives, never having seen such creatures before, were afraid to come near them."

away from the sea, in an easterly direction, as though heading for the center of Europe," leaving a Roman consul slack-jawed with astonishment in his wake, who scrabbled to lead his forces back to Italy. Even as the legions were being embarked, Hannibal was advancing some one hundred miles inland. Then, after ten days' march, he swung back southward. He and his army began their ascent. Ahead, white-crested, and towering ominously above them now—the Alps.

What followed was to prove one of the most celebrated and totemic of all military feats. In truth, however, as a strategic maneuver, it was little short of a catastrophe. Hannibal attempted it too late in the year; he had failed to win the mountain tribesmen to his side; he had so seriously miscalculated the likely number of casualties that his army, by the time it finally debouched into northern Italy, had been more than halved. Perhaps some 60,000 men had followed Hannibal across the Pyrenees that summer; of these, by the autumn, almost 35,000 had deserted or been killed, or fallen frozen by the wayside. Among the elephants, the rate of attrition was even worse. True, it had seemed at first as though sufficient numbers had survived the terrible expedition to constitute an operational unit; but by the spring of 217 B.C., only a single beast, out of the 37 that had originally left Spain, was still alive. Losses on such a scale must have been devastating to Hannibal. It had never been any part of his plans to destroy Rome with a mere 25,000 men. Although the local Gauls would soon add to his numbers, they could not entirely make up for the many skilled and battle-hardened troops he had lost. Hannibal would surely have dreaded that his invasion of Italy had failed almost before it had begun.

In the event, his achievements in the aftermath of his crossing of the Alps would be sufficient to establish him as one of the very greatest generals of all time, and bring Rome perilously close to total ruin. Between late 218 and the summer of 216 B.C., in a masterful display of strategy and tactics infinitely beyond his opponents, Hannibal brought three Roman armies to murderous defeat. In the third of his victories, at Cannae, he faced eight legions, the largest single army that Rome had ever put into the field. Monstrously outnumbered though he was, Hannibal enveloped some 70,000 of the enemy and wiped them out. It has been calculated that not until the Battle of the Somme would more combatants die in a single day of fighting. To this day, Hannibal's tactics at Cannae are taught at Sandhurst and West Point as the very model of how to fight the perfect battle.

Yet if his astounding victory had served to raise the benchmark of generalship to a new high, then so also, for Hannibal himself, did it represent an ultimately fateful tipping point. On the evening that followed the battle, with the moans of the wounded still rising from the blood-soaked fields that stretched beyond their camp, his lieutenants urged their commander to march on Rome. The prize, as Maharbal, the Numidian cavalry chief, was said to have put it, would be the chance to dine in triumph on the Capitol. And almost certainly, he was right. Swept with panic, overwhelmed by refugees, riven by rumors of treachery, the Roman people would surely have succumbed to an immediate advance by the Carthaginians against their city—and even if they had not, they would have been hard-pressed to withstand a sustained blockade. Yet Hannibal did not move. Why not? One factor, more than any other, must have preyed upon his mind: the nagging dread that his forces were too small to compel Rome's surrender. A bitter irony indeed: that at the very moment of his greatest triumph, and with ultimate victory almost at his fingertips, the consequences of his Alpine crossing should have come so damagingly home to roost.

Maharbal's supposed reproach has echoed down the ages. "Truly, Hannibal, you know how to win a victory—but not how to use one." And so it would prove. It had been Hannibal's hope—even his expectation—that the Romans, in the aftermath of the unprecedented slaughter he had inflicted upon their legions, would sue for peace. Instead, in the face of catastrophe, they showed only continued defiance. Stiffening every sinew, summoning up every last reserve of strength, they grimly began to haul themselves back from the brink. Fresh armies were raised; a second Carthaginian invasion of Italy, led by Hannibal's brother, was annihilated; an expeditionary force conquered the Barcid Empire in Spain. Still the Romans did not dare to confront Hannibal himself. For a decade and a half after Cannae, he was left to roam Italy unopposed; but what the legions no longer dared attempt, disease and desertion were progressively accomplishing. His numbers were running out for good at last. In 203 B.C. he was frantically summoned back to

Africa, there to confront a Roman army on his native soil. He lost.

This one defeat ended the war. Carthage, unlike Rome after Cannae, had no further reserves of manpower on which to draw. Predictably savage though the conquerors' terms were, Hannibal persuaded his countrymen that they had no choice but to accept them. Carthage, once the greatest power of the West, was reduced to an impotent, indemnity-bled rump. Still, though, the Romans could never forget, nor forgive, those responsible for the ordeal they had been forced to pass through. So it was that Hannibal was first driven into exile, and then, "like a poor bird stripped of its feathers by age," harried into committing suicide. So it was, too, in 146 B.C., that Carthage was stormed and burned, and a deadly interdiction was proclaimed, forbidding anyone ever again to build upon the site of the city. Rome's hatred had proved implacable. But such vengefulness was also, in a sense, the greatest compliment that the new mistress of the world could pay a foe. The Romans would never forget what they had been up against in Hannibal.

And nothing better exemplified it than Hannibal's crossing of the Alps. In the life of every great hero, the Romans believed, a crisis point was bound to come, a moment of supreme and agonizing tension, when the quality of the man would be tested to the very limit and his fullest potential revealed. That Hannibal had dared, like a god, to lead war elephants over mountains in the cause of his hatred was the surest measure of the examination that Rome herself had passed. To sit and watch his forces as they labored over the Alpine ice would be to gauge the future greatness of the most extraordinary empire in the history of the world.

But that is not the only reason why I wish I had been there. Not only would the Romans go on to defeat Hannibal, they would also keep the tightest of grips upon how the story of that defeat was told. The holocaust that obliterated Carthage obliterated countless records, too, for the conquerors, brutally pragmatic as ever, bothered to save only agricultural manuals from the flames. As a result, everything we know about Hannibal derives from his enemies, either the Romans themselves or their collaborators. To see his army in the flesh and consult with those who marched with it would be a precious opportunity indeed: the chance to hear voices that have been forever silenced, and glimpse what the world might have been like had it ended up, not Roman, but Carthaginian.

Further Reading

Adrian Goldsworthy, *The Fall of Carthage: The Punic Wars, 265–146 B.C.* (London, 2003).

Dexter Hoyos, *Hannibal's Dynasty: Power and Politics in the Western Mediterranean, 247–183 B.C.* (New York, 2003).

Richard Miles, *Punic Faith: The Rise and Fall of Carthage.*

THEODORE K. RABB

Christmas Day in the Year 800

Theodore K. Rabb is Emeritus Professor of History at Princeton University, where he taught for nearly forty years. He has also served on the faculties of Stanford, Northwestern, Harvard, and Johns Hopkins universities. Among his books are *The Struggle for Stability in Early Modern Europe*, *Renaissance Lives*, and *The Last Days of the Renaissance*. He was the principal historical adviser and writer of the five-part 1993 PBS television series *Renaissance*, which was nominated for an Emmy Award. He has directed a joint program between Princeton and New Jersey's community colleges, and he has served as Chair of the Trustees of the National Council for History Education, a national membership organization devoted to the improvement of history instruction in America's schools. Professor Rabb has also contributed to various general publications, including the *New York Times*, the *New York Review of Books*, and the *(London) Times Literary Supplement*.

In this essay he seeks to relive a moment that helped shape centuries of European political and religious history.

Christmas Day in the Year 800

The glitter of the knightly courts and splendid cathedrals we associate with medieval Europe tends to obscure how dim and fragmented that world still was in its early days, in the seventh and eighth centuries. The coherence and the confidence that had emanated from Rome were now but a distant memory, hundreds of years in the past. Both political and religious authority were so feeble as to be virtually nonexistent. The population of the area west of the Elbe and the Balkans had shrunk from over 40 million at the height of the Roman Empire to one-quarter that number. Even Rome itself, once home to over a million people, now had no more than 25,000 inhabitants. Dotted with isolated and largely defenseless communities, Europe was a grim and dangerous place. Its glories seemed entirely in the past.

And yet in the eighth century there were at last signs of hope for the future. The Muslims who had swept across the Mediterranean and through Spain during the previous century were finally stopped at the Battle of Tours near the Loire River in 732. The victor, Charles Martel, leader of the Franks, was the founder of a dynasty that at last created some continuity of political authority. And the great monasteries that were being founded across Europe—notably Bobbio in Italy, St. Gall in Switzerland, and Fulda in Germany—by monks from the far west, mainly Ireland, were becoming famous centers of religious devotion. Their example of holiness and charity, and their determination to uphold the traditions of Western culture, provided both an ideal of sanctity and a preservation of learning that were of vital importance in troubled times.

The contrast with the role of the Papacy could not have been sharper. From the death of Gregory I in 604, and for over four hundred years, the pontiff was a helpless figure, battered by rivals, by political leaders, and by the mobs and powerful families of Rome. Bribery, corruption, assaults by non-Christians—whether Lombards from the north or Saracens from the south—and futile negotiations with emperors and generals were constant themes. Some reigns lasted only days; others were disrupted by two or even three claimants to the throne of Saint Peter. A number of popes were condemned as heretics; others were put on trial, punished, imprisoned, or deposed for various crimes (in one case, the exhumed bones of a dead pope were tried); and none is remembered as being a visionary or powerful voice for the faith that he served.

With no city in Western Europe in flourishing condition, the Papacy in disarray, and cultural pursuits kept alive in only a handful of scattered monasteries, it was clear that the center of what had been Roman civilization had moved decisively to the east, to a still brilliant capital in Constantinople. Here the ruler continued to call himself the Roman Emperor, a title to which he had every right, as a successor to Constantine the Great. He was the upholder of Christianity, without whose approval no pope could take office, and a force to be reckoned with in matters of doctrine, though he exercised his control from afar. The last emperor to visit Rome arrived in 663, and although thereafter many of the popes were Greek or Syrian, they rarely traveled to the east. Only one in the eighth century made the trip, meeting the emperor in Nicomedia, a few miles from Constantinople, in 711. Within a few decades, however, this relationship—never easy, given the distances involved—was to change dramatically.

The shifts that sent Rome and Byzantium (the ancient Greek name for Constantinople) in different directions were many and deep, even though their full significance was not apparent at the time. The first was a sudden aggressiveness on the part of the Byzantine Emperor, Leo III. Around 730, he decided to ban holy images in worship. Attempts by emperors to shape Christian practice or belief were not new, but this iconoclasm was to split Christians into two warring camps for over a century. At the same time, Leo tried to impose harsh new taxes on Italy, but the Pope, Gregory II, showing more determination than usual in Rome, took the lead in opposing both iconoclasm and the taxes. His successor, Gregory III, proved to be the last pope to seek the emperor's approval for his elevation.

Meanwhile, the chief secular power in Italy, the Lombards, who had expelled the Byzantines from most of the peninsula, were also on the march. Faced with threats on all sides, Gregory III turned to the rising power of the north, Charles Martel, for help. For the time being the approach came to nothing, because Charles refused to move against the Lombards, who were his most important allies in his principal effort, driving the Muslims out of the large territory that is now France. But the pope's search for help from Charles Martel's Franks was another harbinger of a changing European world.

The rise of Charles Martel and the widening rupture in the relationship between Rome and Byzantium were developments of the second quarter of the eighth century. Over the next fifty years the implications of these events were to be extended until, by the end of the century, a dramatic reorientation of Europe's political and religious inclinations became possible.

• • •

Central to this transformation was the astonishing series of military successes won by Charles Martel's grandson, known to history as Charles the Great, or Charlemagne. From Germany to Spain, from Brittany to Hungary, his armies swept opponents aside, and the palace he built at Aachen, a site of hot springs that is now on the border between Germany and Belgium, became the most remarkable cultural center Northern Europe had ever seen. Over the course of his reign, from 768 to 814, not only did his armies triumph over Muslims, Lombards, Danes, Avars, and Saxons, but his court oversaw revolutions in education and learning—including even such interests as calligraphy and the calendar—that are often referred to as the Carolingian Renaissance. Although he could read, it is not clear that Charlemagne himself knew how to write, but his dedication to Europe's heritage and its religious faith was as powerful as his dedication to war.

Thanks to the growing might of the Franks in the second half of the eighth century, the Papacy at last had a serious alternative to the Byzantine Emperor when it ran into difficulties. This had become clear in the 750s, during one of its perennial conflicts with the Lombards. The Pope at the time was Stephen III (to some Stephen II, because his predecessor served for just three days). Instead of looking to Constantinople, Stephen asked the Franks for help, and their leader, Pepin, the father of Charlemagne, asked in exchange to be recognized as king. Pepin had been crowned by a papal legate in 751, but three years later Stephen traveled to Paris and himself anointed the monarch, thus ensuring a sacred endorsement for his title. A new alliance, linking Rome with the Franks, was being born.

In the early days of his rule, Charlemagne maintained the connection, but only as part of his ambitions in Italy and to establish his credentials as protector of the Church, not to validate his title. His father had divided his realm between his two sons, and when the younger died, in 771, the new king had been recognized by the acclamation of an assembly of Frankish nobles rather than by papal coronation. It certainly helped the Pope that one of Charlemagne's first wars brought an end to the Lombard kingdom and gave the Franks control of Italy. Yet it was not until the 790s that it became clear that more might be at stake.

Essential to the unfolding of this next stage in the relationship was a shocking turn of events in Constantinople. If ever a monarchy epitomized Shakespeare's "uneasy lies the head that wears a crown," it was Byzantium's. Revolted against, assassinated, or merely deposed, the emperors regularly lived dangerously, surrounded by palace intrigue. Trouble was only to be expected, therefore, when Constantine VI in 780 became sole emperor (he had previously shared the throne with his father) at the age of nine, and his mother, Irene, appointed regent, held on to her power with fierce determination. She broke off her son's engagement to a daughter of Charlemagne and refused to hand over authority when he reached the standard age of majority, sixteen. Finally, in 790, when Irene tried to have her position as empress formally recognized, revolt erupted, Constantine was at last able to break free, and he sent her into exile. Two years later, however, he relented, and though she never forgave him for his temerity, she did come back to court. And the plots persisted, prompting responses of appalling cruelty: Of Constantine's five uncles, four had their tongues cut off and the fifth was blinded. Eventually, in 797, Irene had Constantine seized, blinded, and hidden away so well that, to this day, scholars argue over whether he died shortly thereafter or as long as twenty years later. At this point Irene took over as sole empress and remained as ruler of the Byzantine Empire until her death in 802.

These events caused tremors that went far beyond the empire. Never before had a woman taken the imperial dignity on her own, and there was a widespread assumption that the throne was in fact vacant. Conspiracies seeking to restore false Constantines erupted, and in the West it was almost unanimously believed that there was no longer a Roman emperor in Constantinople. Thus was the stage set for the drama of the late 790s in Germany and Italy.

• • •

Both the opening scene and the denouement took place in Rome, but so much about what happened is uncertain that one has to wish to have been there so that the story—central to the history of the West—could be told without the usual evasions and hesitancies of the careful historian. We do know, however, that trouble began in 798, when leading Roman families who had been allied with the previous pope accused his successor, Leo III, of venality, fornication, and perjury. Alerted to the problem by one of his most trusted advisers and mentors— Alcuin, a cleric who had been the presiding intellectual figure at Aachen, and now in retirement was abbot of a monastery in Tours—Charlemagne decided to send an emissary, the Count Germaire, to Rome to learn more. As ruler of Italy, he thought of himself as the protector of its holy places. He had visited Rome three times and become a notable benefactor of Saint Peter's.

Before Germaire could arrive, however, the situation deteriorated. On April 25, 799, the Feast of Saint Mark, Leo left his palace on the Lateran Hill to lead the annual procession across Rome that was known as "the great litany," a supplication for the protection of spring crops. But Leo never completed the procession. As he was passing a monastery near the present-day Piazza San Silvestro and the Rinascente department store, he was attacked by a gang of ruffians who sought to sever his tongue and gouge out his eyes.

This was not uncommon behavior at the time—it was the way the emperor had treated his uncles in Constantinople; two prominent papal officials had suffered the same assault in Rome less than thirty years earlier; and ten years before that it had been the fate that befell Constantine, an unsuccessful claimant to the papal throne. As everyone knew, Leo would have been disqualified from the Papacy if the attack had succeeded, and it was soon clear that he was the victim of a plot by those who had accused him of immorality, including members of the innermost circle of his advisers. According to some accounts, they succeeded in their evil design: They "tore out his two eyes and his tongue; beating him with clubs, they mutilated him with various wounds and left him half-dead." Miraculously, however, the Lord "gave him back light and restored his tongue." Whatever the historian might wish to think of that recovery, there is no doubt that the Pope's supporters did manage to rescue him. They brought him to sanctuary at Saint Peter's, and the only long-term damage turned out to be a wound that left a disfiguring white scar across Leo's face.

The question was what to do next, because the Pope's enemies still insisted that he was morally unfit for office (an accusation that may not have been groundless, in view of the destruction by Alcuin, one of Leo's most ardent advocates, of a letter from a friend that explained the charges). It was now obvious that only outside intervention could resolve the issues, and this took the form of the leading political figure of the region, the Duke of Spoleto, who hurried to Rome with a small force and took the Pope back with him to his hilltop redoubt. The dukes had come under the sway of Charlemagne after the Franks defeated the Lombards, and it happened that Count Germaire had just arrived at Spoleto on his way to Rome. Who persuaded whom we will never know—had one been there, one would likely have seen the initiative coming from the Pope, a canny tactician who knew he would have to find allies wherever he could—but it was soon decided that Leo would accompany Germaire back to Germany to see Charlemagne.

The second act of the epic took place at a fortified palace

Charlemagne had built at Paderborn, some one hundred miles northeast of Aachen, as part of his campaign against the Saxons. Here Leo arrived in late July, only to find that some of his enemies from Rome had beaten him to it, and that the king was considering how to respond. Once again it would have been fascinating to sit in on the conversations that followed over the next few weeks, before Leo was sent back to Rome. But we do know that the Pope was received with full courtesy, and that Alcuin was sending Charlemagne some rather firm opinions about the role he ought now to play.

In Alcuin's view, the Pope stood above the judgment of men; no secular ruler could investigate his failings, let alone put him on trial. It was Charlemagne's duty to restore him to full authority. He was to do so, however, not merely because he was conveniently at hand. Rather, he had to act as the protector of the Church. This was a role that circumstances were pushing Charlemagne to assume, whether willingly or not, though the alacrity with which he took it up suggests that Alcuin did not have to do much persuading.

The opportunity arose because of the events in Constantinople. As a result of her coup, Irene had undermined the authority of the Byzantine throne. The chief power in the Middle East, the Abbasid caliph Harun al-Rashid, now regarded Charlemagne as the monarch who represented Christianity, and, more important, so too did the patriarch of Jerusalem. Indeed, an emissary from the patriarch, seeking his patronage of the holy places, arrived at Charlemagne's court not long after the Pope.

Nor did Alcuin have any doubt about the implications of the situation Christianity faced in 799. As he wrote to Charlemagne, "Until now there have been three persons of great eminence in the world." He listed first the Pope, and then the emperor, now deposed. "The third," in his view, was "the throne on which our Lord Jesus Christ has placed you to rule over the

Christian people, with greater power, keener insight, and a grander royalty than these other dignitaries." "On you alone," he continued, "the whole safety of the churches of Christ depends." To Alcuin, the right path was absolutely clear, and although he did not say so explicitly, the language of his letters suggests that he was aware that the situation held even more far-reaching implications.

It is notable that, from 798, the word "Empire" began to make a regular appearance in Alcuin's correspondence. He sent wishes to Charlemagne for his good health "which is so necessary for the entire Empire of the Christians." God gave Charlemagne power not only to glorify the Church, but also to maintain the government of "the most sacred Empire." And when heresy threatened, before it could engulf "the world of the Christian Empire," Charlemagne would rein it in. To do so, thundered Alcuin, "Rise up, you chosen of God; rise up, son of God, soldier of Christ, and defend the bride of the Lord your God with the power you have received from him to govern and protect her." This was heady language, thrusting upon Charlemagne a responsibility that had always belonged to another emperor, the one in Constantinople.

Whatever was said on those warm summer evenings in Paderborn before the Pope returned to Rome with all honors, we do know that Charlemagne promised to come to Rome to put an end to the conflict. Indeed, the emissaries who accompanied Leo brought back his chief accusers, who were sent to prison and then exile. But what did Charlemagne extract in return? It is hard not to believe that, with Alcuin's language fresh in his mind, he demanded that the Pope endorse a more exalted status for himself.

Papal sources later claimed that this was the Church's idea—that the deal was struck at Paderborn because Charlemagne had performed the classic imperial task of rescuing the Pope, and also as an acknowledgment of the Frankish king's political and military supremacy over much of Europe. Moreover, there is a hint that Alcuin was working both sides of the street. A friend of his, an archbishop who was seeing the Pope, wrote from Rome in 798 that "the plan" that Alcuin "ardently wanted to bring to fruition might in fact be realized"—a tantalizing reference that some have interpreted to mean that Alcuin put the idea in Leo's head, too.

Nevertheless, it stretches credulity to believe that the main impulse came from anyone but Charlemagne. He may have been influenced by Alcuin. The latter sent him a present of a Bible in 800, well before he arrived in Rome, and called it "a fully worthy gift for the splendor of your imperial power," which strongly implies that Alcuin knew exactly what was about to happen. But in the end we have to believe that the dominant figure on the scene, Charlemagne, was the one who controlled the action.

• • •

He certainly took his time getting to Rome. Leo had to wait for over a year, and one can imagine how nerve-racking the passing months must have been. Charlemagne spent the winter of 799–800 in Aachen, after which he inspected the defenses in northern France against the first Viking raids. He then headed south and spent time in Tours with Alcuin, who returned with him to Aachen for meetings that condemned a recent heresy. The two men doubtless had plenty of time to discuss imperial ambitions, but still the king remained north of the Alps. A general council of the leaders of his realm had been called for Mainz, and here at last Charlemagne announced that he was going to Rome to settle the matter of the accusations against the Pope. But even then he did not hurry. Once in Italy, he stopped for a while in Ravenna to hire some mosaic artists to come to Aachen, and not until November 23 did he reach a small town some twelve miles from Rome, where Leo came out to meet him.

That distance in itself was unprecedented. Traditionally, the Pope had traveled only six miles to greet an emperor. And what followed was equally remarkable. Instead of arriving at Saint Peter's by foot, as befitted a pilgrim, Charlemagne rode into the city in a magnificent procession, with banners flying and crowds cheering his passage. When he finally reached the Basilica, the Pope, who had gone ahead, greeted him and led him into Saint Peter's to the sound of psalms. One historian has likened the event to a triumphal entry by Caesar.

Eight days later Charlemagne convoked an assembly of prominent churchmen and nobles to hear the case that was the official purpose of his visit: the accusations against Leo. Notwithstanding Alcuin's strictures about judging a pope, which many people shared, Charlemagne felt that a formal process was necessary in order to clear the Papacy of wrongdoing and start the pontificate afresh. To that end, he came up with a compromise that was acceptable on all sides. At a climactic assembly, the Pope would make a solemn oath that the accusations were untrue. Given the weight that this society put upon the sacred power of oaths, that was an outcome nobody could question.

And so, on December 23, Leo made his way to Saint Peter's and, in the presence of a dazzling assembly of the leaders of Western Christendom, mounted the pulpit. Holding above his head a copy of the Gospels, he swore the oath that was required of him: that he had no knowledge either of the crimes of which he was accused or of having committed them. The process was at an end.

But the assembly did not dissolve. Remaining in session, it declared that, with Irene's usurpation in Constantinople, the imperial throne was empty. Since in ancient times the emperors had been associated with Rome, and Charlemagne ruled over

A lithograph after a French miniature shows Charlemagne (seated) being crowned the Holy Roman Emperor by Pope Leo III.

much of the territory that they had controlled, it was proper now to bestow the title on him.

There seems little doubt that this "election" had been planned in advance, and none of the accounts expressed surprise that Charlemagne agreed. Moreover, on this very same day, his emissaries to the Middle East returned to Rome, bringing with them two monks who represented the patriarch of Jerusalem. They brought with them the keys to the city, to the Church of the Holy Sepulchre, and to Mount Zion, which they handed to Charlemagne as a symbol of his new role as protector of the holy places. The combination of circumstances could not have been more telling. An awesome title had been added to Charlemagne's defense of the Church and his sway over the lands Rome had once ruled. There could be little question that a new emperor had now arisen in the West.

But there was a final twist in store. We know that, for Charlemagne, Christmas Day 800 had special meaning. There had been various ways of calculating the passing years in the ancient world, but one had been brought to prominence by the man who was arguably the most famous historian of the eighth century, Bede. In his history of England, Bede used the birth of Christ as his starting point and counted the years from that date. Alcuin, a fellow Englishman, knew Bede's work, and it was probably he who ensured that this form of dating became everyday practice at Aachen. Once adopted at so major a center of learning and culture, the usage spread throughout Europe and made Anno Domini the standard way of organizing the calendar throughout the West. For Charlemagne, therefore, December 25 would be exactly 800 years after the birth of Christ—clearly a day of vast significance.

Had one been in Saint Peter's that morning, as the Pope led a Christmas mass attended by the elite of the Christian West, one would have witnessed the event that determined assumptions about politics and the relations of Church and state for centuries to come. As Charlemagne rose after the confession, the Pope placed on his head a golden crown from the Church's treasury and consecrated his status with a blessing and possibly (though this remains controversial) by anointing his head with holy oil. The response was a shout of acclamation and loyalty to "the peace-loving emperor" by the entire assembly (in some accounts, repeated twice). All then made obeisance, led by Leo, who prostrated himself at Charlemagne's feet.

Crowning was a new idea in the West (the most famous precedent was Mark Antony's crowning of Caesar in the Forum). Moreover, contrary to Frankish custom, the acclamation followed the assumption of the title rather than being its cause. This breach of precedent may well have displeased Charlemagne, as was reported by his devoted biographer, Einhard, who was there that day. Indeed, Einhard himself demonstrated the court's attachment to precedent by modeling his biography on Suetonius's life of Augustus, the first emperor. Yet it is clear that Charlemagne's aim in coming to Rome was, at least in part, to cement the mutual support of Empire and Papacy. And that was what the ceremony accomplished. Moreover, nobody else noted Charlemagne's displeasure, and one cannot imagine Leo doing anything that might risk offending his patron, the most powerful man in Europe. To Einhard the reluctance may have been a fitting sign of modesty, but only those who were there can have known for sure.

That the ceremony changed the course of European history, however, there can be no doubt. It has been called a momentous nonevent, but the symbolic can have as much effect as the practical. Indeed, one could argue that the repercussions of that Christmas mass were no less far-reaching than the consequences of some of Europe's more glamorous "historic turning points," such as military victories or revolutions. It was the beginning of the split, formalized 250 years later, between the Western and Eastern churches. It set the basic precedent for the notion that emperor and Pope, reciprocally dependent on one another, were the twin supreme figures of Europe. It implied that Charlemagne and his successors were the heirs of the emperors of Rome, and thus the arbiters of Italy and many lands besides. And it created a concept of royal authority that laid the foundation for the territorial state. None of these implications were recognized for a very long time. Charlemagne's empire fell apart after his death; the Papacy went through more hard times for another 250 years. To someone who participated, the Christmas mass may well have seemed like a splendid and unusual occasion, but little more. It could be that only a historian, who knows what was to come, would wish to have been there.

Further Reading

Matthias Becher, *Charlemagne*, trans. David S. Bachrach (New Haven, CT, 2003).

Einhard the Frank, *The Life of Charlemagne*, ed. and trans. Lewis Thorpe (London, 1970).

Derek Wilson, *Charlemagne* (New York, 2006).

JOHN JULIUS NORWICH

Venice, July 24, 1177

John Julius Norwich is the author of histories of the Norman Kingdom of Sicily, the Republic of Venice, the Byzantine Empire, and, most recently, the Mediterranean. He has also written travel books on Mount Athos and the Sahara. His annual anthology, *A Christmas Cracker*, is now in its thirty-seventh year. For BBC Television he has written and presented over thirty historical documentaries on subjects including Napoleon's "hundred days," Cortés and Montezuma, Toussaint l'Ouverture of Haiti, and the Zulu War. He also made three programs to complement the Treasure Houses of Britain Exhibition at the Washington National Gallery of Art in 1985. On radio, he was chairman of the popular BBC panel game *My Word*. Lord Norwich is cochairman of the World Monuments Fund and honorary chairman of the Venice in Peril Fund. He is a regular lecturer on art, architecture, history, and music, and occasionally does one-man shows, reading from his "Christmas crackers" and singing to the piano.

Here he evokes one of the most colorful and dramatic moments in the long history of the Venetian republic.

Venice, July 24, 1177

Of the hundreds of thousands of tourists who now flock to
Venice every year, there can be few indeed who notice, set into
the pavement just in front of the central doorway of the Basilica of Saint Mark, a small porphyry lozenge two or three inches
across; and fewer still who know what it signifies. It marks the
spot where, on one of the most memorable days of the city's
history and after nearly a quarter of a century of bitter hostility,
the two most powerful men in Europe finally set the seal upon
their reconciliation.

Those two men were the Holy Roman Emperor, Frederick
Barbarossa, and Pope Alexander III. There was nothing new in
the contest between Emperor and Pope; it had been grumbling
on for the best part of four centuries—perhaps, it might be argued, ever since that fateful Christmas Day of the year 800
when Pope Leo III had laid the imperial crown on the head of
Charlemagne. The fundamental idea of a united Christendom
under two rulers, one temporal and one spiritual, sounded sen-
sible enough in theory; in practice, on the other hand, there
were innumerable areas of contention. To begin with, a document known as the Donation of Constantine alleged that the
Emperor Constantine the Great had granted to Pope Sylvester I
and his successors temporal dominion over Rome "and all the
provinces and places in Italy and the western regions." In 1440
this was shown to be a shameless forgery, cooked up in the papal curia in the eighth century or thereabouts; throughout the
Middle Ages, however, it was implicitly believed and was one of
the chief causes of the papal-imperial struggle.

Then, at least for the people of Italy, there was the anomaly that although they were technically subjects of the emperor, they had no say in his election: He was always a German prince, never an Italian; so too were his electors. On the other hand, though elected King of the Romans, he could assume the dignity of Emperor only after his coronation by the Pope in Rome; and his claim to the right of papal appointment was not accepted in Italy—least of all by the Curia and the Roman aristocracy. By the eleventh century the intervening cities of northern Italy were growing steadily stronger and more self-willed; even the journey to Rome for his coronation, through Lombardy, Tuscany, and the Papal States, could be made difficult for an unpopular candidate.

Already in 1075 matters had come to a head over the question of Church investitures. After an acrimonious dispute concerning the archbishopric of Milan, Pope Gregory VII had categorically condemned all ecclesiastical investiture by laymen, on pain of anathema—upon which a furious King Henry IV (he had not yet been crowned Emperor) had immediately invested two more German bishops to Italian sees, adding for good measure a further archbishop of Milan even though his former nominee was still alive. Refusing a papal summons to Rome to answer for his actions, he had then called a general council of all the German bishops and formally deposed Gregory from the Papacy.

Alas, he had badly overplayed his hand. The Pope's answering deposition, accompanied by the excommunication of the king and the release of all his subjects from their allegiance, led to revolts throughout Germany, which brought Henry literally to his knees. Crossing the Alps in the depth of winter with his wife and baby son, he found Gregory in January 1077 at the castle of Canossa where, after three days of abject humiliation, he at length was granted the absolution he needed. The story of Canossa, usually enlivened by an illustration of the king and his family, barefoot and in sackcloth, shivering in the snow before the locked gates of the castle, has been a perennial favorite with the authors of children's history books, where it is presented as an improving object-lesson in the vanity of temporal ambitions. In fact, Gregory's triumph was empty and ephemeral, and Henry knew it. He had no intention of keeping his promises of submission. Four years later he crossed into Italy again—this time at the head of an army. At first Rome held firm; but after two years' campaigning against the Pope's staunchest ally, Countess Matilda of Tuscany, Henry managed to break through its defenses. On Easter Day 1084 he had himself crowned emperor by his puppet, the anti-Pope Clement III.

Even now Gregory, entrenched in Castel Sant'Angelo, refused to surrender. Instead, he appealed to Robert Guiscard, the Norman Duke of Apulia; and in May 1084, Robert suddenly appeared with an army of thirty-six thousand at the walls of Rome. Henry, hopelessly outnumbered, withdrew just in time. The Normans broke through the Flaminian Gate, and for three days the city was given over to an orgy of pillage and slaughter. When at last peace was restored, the whole district between the Colosseum and Saint John Lateran had been burned to the ground. Rome had suffered more from the champions of the Pope than she had ever had to endure from Goth or Vandal. Robert Guiscard, not daring to leave the unhappy Gregory to the mercy of the populace, escorted him south to Salerno, where in the following year he died. His last words have come down to us: "I have loved righteousness and hated iniquity; therefore I die in exile."

It was a bitter valediction, but Gregory's achievement had been greater than he knew. He had finally established papal supremacy over the Church hierarchy—the practice of lay investitures, already losing ground, was to die out early in the following century—and even if he had not won a similar victory over the empire, he had at least asserted his claims in such a way that they could never again be ignored. The Church had shown its teeth; future emperors would defy it at their peril.

The emperor who most signally failed to learn this lesson was Henry's great-grandson, Frederick Barbarossa. Early in 1152 he was crowned with the Iron Crown of Lombardy—in a ceremony even more symbolic than usual since several of the Lombard towns, led by Milan, were now in open opposition to the empire—after which he headed south, with a considerable army, for his imperial coronation in Rome. The Pope at this time was Adrian IV, the former Nicholas Breakspear and the only Englishman ever to occupy the throne of Saint Peter; and not without difficulty—for neither party trusted the other an inch—a meeting was arranged between King and Pope near Sutri. It nearly ended in fiasco when for two days Barbarossa refused to perform the symbolical act of holding Adrian's bridle and stirrup as he dismounted; but at last agreement was reached and the two rode on south together. They were soon intercepted by envoys from the Roman commune; if Frederick wished to enter the city, he would have to pay tribute and guarantee all civic liberties. The king angrily refused, and the envoys returned to Rome; Adrian meanwhile, scenting trouble, quickly dispatched a heavy advance force to take over the Leonine City.*

The next morning at first light, he and Frederick slipped into Rome, and an hour or two later the new emperor was already crowned. The news reached the commune while they were discussing how best to prevent the coronation. Furious at having been tricked, mob and militia together attacked the Vatican. All day the fighting went on, with heavy slaughter on both sides;

---

*That part of Rome across the Tiber and including the present Vatican City that was enclosed with a defensive wall by Pope Leo IV in the ninth century.

but by evening the imperial forces had prevailed and the remaining attackers withdrew across the Tiber.

Frederick, having got what he wanted, now returned to Germany. Just six years later, however, he was back in Italy in still greater strength, and at the Diet of Roncaglia left the northern Italian cities in no doubt as to his own concept of imperial sovereignty as four celebrated jurists from Bologna—a university to which he had always shown particular favor—demolished all their cherished ideals of municipal independence as pipe dreams, totally devoid of legal foundation. Henceforth every city would be subjected, through a foreign governor or *podestà*, to complete imperial control. He then turned his attention to the Papacy. The death of Pope Adrian in 1159 gave him his opportunity. Recognizing—rightly—that the next Pope if freely elected would be sure to continue along the lines set by his predecessor, he now deliberately engineered a schism within the Curia—a schism that gave rise to one of the most purely ridiculous incidents in all of papal history—another that, though for rather different reasons, one would dearly love to have witnessed.

Just as Cardinal Roland of Siena—who as Adrian's chancellor had been the principal architect of his foreign policy—was being enthroned in Saint Peter's as Pope Alexander III, his colleague Cardinal Octavian of S. Cecilia suddenly seized the papal mantle and tried to put it on himself. Alexander's supporters snatched it back; but Octavian had taken the precaution of bringing another, into which he somehow managed to struggle— getting it on back-to-front in the process. He then made a dash for the throne, sat on it, and proclaimed himself Pope Victor IV, and the imperial ambassadors in Rome immediately recognized him as the rightful pontiff. Virtually all the rest of Western Europe gave its allegiance to Alexander, but the damage was done, and the chaotic Italian political scene was further bedeviled for the next eighteen years by a disputed Papacy.

Throughout Lombardy, the effect of the Diet of Roncaglia had been electric, and the cities of northern Italy had sprung to arms. The emperor, however, had come prepared for trouble. In 1159 at Crema, he tied fifty hostages (including children) to his siege engines to prevent the defenders from counterattacking; in 1162, he finally brought the Milanese to their knees and razed their city flat, so that for the next five years it lay deserted and in ruins. But this only stiffened the resistance. Past rivalries long forgotten, the cities formed the great Lombard League to defend their liberties. Venice joined, Sicily and the new Pope Alexander III lent their active support, and soon Frederick began to feel, for the first time, the full weight of the Italian opposition.

Soon, too, his luck began to turn. In 1167 a march on Rome was brought to nothing when plague broke out in the imperial ranks; the emperor was obliged to retreat, almost defenseless, through hostile Lombardy and barely managed to drag what was left of his exhausted army back over the Alps. In 1174 he returned, but the momentum had gone: on May 29, 1176, his German knights were routed at Legnano by the forces of the League. It was the most crushing defeat of Frederick's career, a defeat in which he lost most of his army and narrowly escaped with his own life; and, it marked the end of his ambitions in Lombardy. At last he had been brought to his senses. After four long Italian campaigns, he was finally persuaded that the Lombard cities were determined as ever to resist him and, since the formation of their League, were well able to do so. For him to persist any longer in the policy on which he had already wasted the best years of his life would make him the laughingstock of Europe.

And so indeed would a continued refusal to recognize the Pope. Frederick's puppet anti-Pope Victor had been a disaster.

He had failed altogether to establish himself in Rome and in 1164 had died miserably in Lucca, where for a number of years he had eked out a precarious living on the proceeds of not very successful brigandage, and where the local authorities would not even allow him burial within the walls. An attempt to install a successor had also failed; by now, even throughout the empire itself, Pope Alexander was universally accepted. There was nothing for it: Imperial ambassadors were sent off to Anagni, there to discuss with him the terms of the reconciliation. Essentially, they were simple enough. The emperor would recognize Alexander, make restitution of certain Church possessions, and conclude peace treaties with Byzantium, Sicily, and the Lombard League. The Pope in return would confirm Frederick's wife Beatrice of Burgundy as empress, his son Henry as king of the Romans, and several prelates as the rightful bishops in sees that they had originally owed to anti-Popes.

As to the place of the projected meeting, there were obvious problems with any of the Lombard cities. Venice was the obvious choice. Though a founder member of the League, recent differences with Byzantium had prevented the city from playing a very active part in the East's affairs; at one moment, beneath the walls of Ancona, Venetians had even found themselves fighting side by side with forces of the Western Empire. Venice possessed a record of independence longer than that of any other northern Italian city and had the space to accommodate, in the style to which they were accustomed, all the European notables—princes, bishops, ambassadors, and representatives from the Lombard cities and towns—who were expected to be present.

Venice had always been a law unto itself. For one thing, it was a relatively new arrival on the European scene. In the days of classical antiquity it did not even exist; who, after all, would dream of establishing a village, let alone the most sumptuous of cities, in a desolate waste of sandbanks and shoals in the middle of a malarial and probably malodorous lagoon? It was only in the fifth and sixth centuries, when the barbarians swept down from Central Europe into the Italian peninsula, leaving a trail of devastation behind them, that the inhabitants of the mainland towns fled for their lives to the only refuge available to them. Shallow water affords far better protection than deep—any captain unfamiliar with the area would have been certain to run his ship aground—so there they settled and there they remained. On the Italian mainland they simply turned their backs—they were not Italians, they were Venetians—keeping their eyes resolutely fixed on the East. At the time of the first settlement they had been part of the Byzantine Empire, and although they had now been politically independent for over four hundred years, it was still from Constantinople that they drew their artistic and cultural inspiration. More important still, at least for most Venetians, was the fact that the East was the source of almost all their commercial wealth, with their markets extending well beyond the Bosphorus—to the Black Sea, to Persia, to the Indies, even to far Cathay. It was no coincidence that Marco Polo was a Venetian; he could not have been anything else.

In its early years, Venice had suffered from one major embarrassment: no classical past. In consequence the city tended to be patronized, both by her mainland neighbors and by the emerging nations of Western Europe. This problem Venice had largely solved when, in 828, two young Venetian merchants quietly removed the body of Saint Mark from its tomb in Alexandria and brought it to Venice. As the shrine of one of the evangelists, it now enjoyed all the respect its people could have hoped for, and by the middle of the eleventh century it was clear nonetheless that the ceremony now proposed could only add further to the city's reputation. It welcomed the papal and imperial ambassadors with enthusiasm and began to make preparations.

Pope Alexander had made one condition only: that he should enter the city first, and that Frederick should not be admitted until he had given his consent. He arrived with his Curia on May 10, 1177. Waiting to receive him were the doge, Sebastiano Ziani, and the patriarchs of Grado and Aquileia, who ceremoniously led him to Saint Mark's for high mass. Only then did he board the state barge and travel up the Grand Canal to the patriarchal palace at S. Silvestro, which was put at his disposal for as long as he chose to remain in the city. It was there that the second round of peace negotiations began, attended not only by representatives of the emperor, but also by those of the League and of Sicily. Meanwhile Frederick, displaying what was for him an unusual degree of restraint in a situation he must have found deeply humiliating, waited at Ravenna. The negotiations dragged on for nearly two months. By the beginning of July, however, agreement was in sight, and the Pope allowed Frederick to approach Chioggia at the edge of the Venetian lagoon, where he could keep in touch with developments. By this time the emperor's patience was wearing thin, and at one moment he came perilously near to defying the papal veto, bursting into the city, and forcing Alexander and the Lombards into granting him more favorable terms. Had he done so, all the careful diplomacy of the past year would have been in vain; fortunately, he thought better of the idea, and on July 23 agreement was complete. On that same day a Venetian flotilla brought him to the Lido, where a delegation of four cardinals was waiting to receive him. In their presence he solemnly acknowledged Alexander as pontiff, and they in turn lifted his sentence of excommunication. Now at last he could be admitted to Venice. Early the next morning the doge himself arrived at S. Nicolò di Lido whence, with an impressive retinue of nobles and clergy, he personally escorted the emperor to the steps of the Piazzetta.

The Venetians' love of pomp and pageantry was already well established. This was one of the greatest days in their history, and they were determined to do it justice. Could we only have been there ourselves, we should have seen the whole city *en fête*, with flags flying and carpets hung at every balcony. Alas, we have to rely on the eyewitness accounts of others, the most vivid of which is the so-called *De Pace Veneta Relatio*. Its author is unknown, but he seems to have been a German churchman of some importance.

At daybreak the attendants of the Lord Pope hastened to the church of Saint Mark the Evangelist and closed the great portal of the church, and thither they brought much timber and deal planks and ladders, and so raised up a lofty and splendid throne. And they also erected two masts of pinewood of wonderous height on each side of the quay, from which hung the standards of Saint Mark, magnificently embroidered and so large that they touched the ground. The Pope arrived before the first hour of the day (6:00 A.M.) and, having heard mass, soon afterward ascended to the higher part of his throne to await the arrival of the emperor. There he sat, with his patriarchs, cardinals, archbishops, and bishops innumerable; on his right was the patriarch of Venice and on his left that of Aquileia.

And now there came a quarrel between the Archbishop of Milan and the Archbishop of Ravenna as to which should be seen to take precedence, as each strove to sit himself in the third place from that of the Pope, on his right side. But the Pope determined to put an end to their contention and, leaving his own exalted seat, descended the steps and placed himself below them. Thus was there no third place to sit in, and neither one could sit on his right. Then at about the third hour there arrived the doge's barge, in which was the emperor, with the doge and the cardinals who had been sent to him on the previous day;

and he was led by seven archbishops and canons of the Church in solemn procession to the papal throne. When he reached it, he threw off the red cloak he was wearing and prostrated himself before the Pope, and kissed first his feet and then his knees. But the Pope rose and, taking the head of the emperor in both his hands, he embraced him and kissed him, and made him sit at his right hand, and at last spoke the words "Son of the Church, be welcome." Then he took him by the hand and led him into the Basilica. And the bells rang, and the "Te Deum Laudamus" was sung. When the ceremony was done, they both left the church together. The Pope mounted his horse, and the emperor held his stirrup and then retired to the doge's palace. And all this happened on Sunday, the Eve of Saint James.

And on the same day, the Pope sent the emperor many gold and silver jars filled with food of various kinds. And he sent also a fatted calf, with the words "It is meet that we should make merry and be glad, for my son was dead, and is alive again; and was lost, and is found."

For Pope Alexander, the Treaty of Venice marked at once the climax and the culmination of his pontificate. He had to endure eighteen years of schism and ten of exile from Rome, to say nothing of the implacable hostility of one of the most formidable men ever to wear the crown of the Western Empire; and he had to wait until he was well into his seventies before receiving his reward. Now, however, that reward had come—nor was it limited to Frederick's recognition of his legitimacy. The emperor had also admitted all the temporal rights of the Papacy over the city of Rome, and the six-year truce that he had concluded with the Lombard League was clearly only a preliminary to his acknowledgment of the independence of the individual Lombard cities. It was the most signal victory ever to have been won by a pope over imperial pretensions, and it had been due

A crowd of church officials and Venetian locals gathers at the Piazza San Marco as the German Emperor Frederick Barbarossa pays public homage to Pope Alexander III. The dramatic gesture of submission was recaptured by sixteenth-century painter Francesco Salviati (and pupils) in a fresco for the Sala Regia at the Vatican Palace.

above all to the wisdom and patience with which Alexander had steered his Church through one of the most troubled periods in its history.

And those qualities remained with him. Never during the emperor's stay in Venice did the Pope show the slightest inclination to crow over his former enemy. One or two subsequent historians of Venice have perpetuated the legend of his placing his foot on Frederick's neck, of the emperor muttering under his breath, "Not to you, but to Saint Peter," and of Alexander replying sharply, "To me *and* to Saint Peter." But this story is confirmed by no contemporary writer and is utterly inconsistent with all the firsthand evidence that has come down to us. Frederick, too, seems to have behaved impeccably. Indeed, on the day following the great reconciliation, he tried to carry courtesy even further: Having again held the papal stirrup on leaving the Basilica, he would have led Alexander's horse all the way to the point of embarkation if the Pope had not gently restrained him.

Venice too reaped its rewards. The emperor was the city's guest for eight full weeks, leaving only on September 18. Pope Alexander remained until mid-October, after a total stay of well over five months. For much of that time Venice was crowded as never before, its floating foreign population of travelers and merchants now swollen to many times its normal size by all the greatest princes and prelates of Europe, each bent on outshining his rivals in the splendor of his retinue. One, the Archbishop of Cologne, brought with him a suite of no less than 400 secretaries, chaplains, and attendants; the patriarch of Aquileia boasted 300, as did the archbishops of Mainz and Magdeburg. Count Roger of Andria, second envoy of the King of Sicily, had 330; Duke Leopold of Austria, with a train of only 160, must have cut a sorry figure indeed.

Politically too there were benefits. From Frederick Barbarossa the Venetians obtained free passage, safe conduct, and full exemption from imperial tolls in all parts of the empire. Pope Alexander for his part granted indulgences to most of the principal churches in the city and brought about a final settlement of the age-old struggle between the patriarchs of Venice and Aquileia that had created so much bitterness over the centuries to Venetian ecclesiastical affairs. But Venice's greatest gain was in prestige. Throughout that memorable summer, it had been the focus of attention of all Europe—the capital, in a very real sense, of Christendom. The city's doge was playing host to the two leaders of the Western world, the city specifically chosen by both the papal and the imperial negotiators because—to quote once more from the *Relatio*—she was "subject to God alone . . . a place where the courage and authority of the citizens could preserve peace between the partisans of each side and ensure that no discord or sedition, deliberate or involuntary, should arise." Admittedly, the city only just succeeded, but succeed it did, and in doing so it assumed a new status as a great metropolis and European power. That July day in Venice was, in its way, a summation of all medieval history. If only we could have been there. . . .

Further Reading

Mary McCarthy, *Venice Observed* (London, 1956).

James Morris, *Venice* (London, 1960).

J. J. Norwich, *Venice: The Rise to Empire* (London and New York, 1977).

KATHERINE FISCHER DREW

Magna Carta and the King's Men

Katherine Fischer Drew is the Lynette S. Autrey Professor of History Emeritus at her alma mater, Rice University, where she taught European History from 1950 to 1998. On her retirement, she received the Meritorious Service Award of the Rice Alumni. A member of Phi Beta Kappa and a Fellow of the Medieval Academy of America, she held a number of prestigious fellowships over the course of a distinguished career, including a Guggenheim Fellowship, a Fulbright grant, and a Senior Fellowship awarded by the National Endowment for the Humanities. Her chief interest has been in the social and legal history of the Middle Ages, and her books include studies of the effects of the barbarian invasions and a number of monographs on laws, law codes, and their social effects. Her most recent publication is *Magna Carta* (2004).

It is to this last subject that she draws our attention here, as she explains the origins and composition of one of the most famous documents of Western history.

Magna Carta and the King's Men

Everyone knows that sometime in June 1215, King John of England faced rebellion by a number of the king's barons who had been joined by the city of London. Attempts to work out a compromise had failed and now John felt compelled to sign the document placed before him in the meadow along the Thames River known as Runnymede. John was confident that his new ally, Pope Innocent III, would agree to his request to be released from his sworn oath to uphold the document now named Magna Carta on the canon-law ground that a forced oath is not binding. Pope Innocent did release John from his oath, but that did nothing to pacify the rebellious barons, who continued their revolt against a John who took the field against them. And John's campaign was waged so fiercely that the barons in revolt felt compelled to seek an ally from abroad, namely the Dauphin Louis of France, heir to the king, Philip II Augustus.

The civil war continued for more than a year without decisive success on either side. King John was holding his own, but the strain of the war on his physical and psychic stamina led the king to undertake an unwise shortcut across the upper part of the deep inlet of the Wash between Lincolnshire and the county of Norfolk, a crossing during which, according to some of the chroniclers, he lost his baggage and became so upset that he fell ill and died in October 1216 (Innocent III had died several months before).

The death of John effectively ended the civil war. The barons who had remained loyal to John immediately recognized John's nine-year-old son as King Henry III and issued a somewhat revised Magna Carta (1216). The rebels were pardoned without loss of property and the civil war was over. Magna Carta was issued again in 1217 with further revisions, accompanied by a Charter of the Forest containing an expanded version of those articles in the original Magna Carta that dealt with the law as applied to the royal forests. A final version of Magna Carta and the Charter of the Forest was issued in 1225, and that was the form in which they were issued thereafter whenever baronial unrest threatened to boil over, and it was in that form that Edward I reissued the documents in 1297 to become the first of the Statutes of the Realm (the collected laws of England).

This outline of the early history of Magna Carta seems pretty well established. But where did Magna Carta come from? Who was responsible for bringing together such a coherent statement of many of the legal customs of England?

In the past it has been suggested that the members of the king's "inner circle" likely to have exerted the most influence in shaping Magna Carta were Stephen Langton and/or William Marshal. There is no doubt that either or both of these men were individuals of great prestige and influence in the king's court, and both worked very hard to find a compromise that would avoid civil war. But neither of these men was sufficiently familiar with the intricacies of what had become the English common law to be able to produce the sixty-five articles of Magna Carta. Only if someone had actually attended those sessions in which the baronial demands were incorporated into the form of a formal charter would that person likely be able to solve the question of decisive influence. But if one wishes to have been there and pretends to have been there, it may be possible to advance some more likely answer.

Before turning to what may actually have happened, it is desirable to consider why Stephen Langton and William Marshal were unlikely to have had the knowledge to personally influence the actual composition of Magna Carta.

The original Magna Carta, the "Great Charter of Liberties," signed by King John of England in 1215, has been lost (although four copies survive). This is the version issued in 1225 by Henry III, which is preserved in the UK's National Archives.

Stephen Langton was Archbishop of Canterbury at the time Magna Carta was signed. Although born in England, he had been educated at the newly forming university of Paris and then became a teacher of theology at Paris: later he was invited by the recently elected (1198) Innocent III to join the papal Curia in Rome. In England there had been a disputed election to the archbishopric of Canterbury following the death of the incumbent Hubert Walter in 1205, and both sides appealed to Rome. This gave Innocent III an opportunity to quash both elections, and to name and consecrate Stephen Langton as archbishop. But John refused to allow Langton to enter England from 1207 to 1213. During this time England was first placed under an interdict and, when this did not compel John's submission, the king himself was excommunicated. The interdict does not seem to have aroused any great protest on the part of the people of England, as only a minority of the English clergy went into exile to avoid the ban on most church services, but excommunication of the king was another matter since the Pope gave his approval to a plan proposed by the French king Philip II to invade England to force compliance with the papal agenda. John was not prepared to fight, so he accepted Innocent's demands and more: He agreed to receive Stephen Langton as Archbishop of Canterbury, he agreed to accept back the exiled clergy and restore what he had gained by treating their holdings as feudal vacancies, and he further surrendered England and Ireland to the Papacy and received them back as fiefs of the Papacy. In return, Innocent lifted the interdict and excommunication, and received John as a vassal of the Church.

Stephen Langton proceeded to England to assume his place as Archbishop of Canterbury and one of the great magnates of the kingdom. In both roles he was a very busy man because much of the property and income of the archbishopric had been compromised during the time the archbishopric was vacant and under the control of the king's men. His duties at court were also heavy because the Archbishop of Canterbury headed the list of the great barons of the realm who formed the king's council and were in frequent attendance on the king.

Stephen Langton attended meetings of the rebellious barons in order to understand the grievances of these men and encourage compromise. By this time the Coronation Charter of Henry I issued in 1100 was known to the rebels. In this charter Henry had promised to reject those overbearing practices followed by his father, William I the Conqueror, and by his brother William II–practices such as forcing heirs to pay unusually large reliefs in order to inherit from their fathers, selling offices, abusing the right to control female heiresses' marriages, and holding fiefs and taking their income during the minority of the heirs. Langton knew about this document and had some knowledge of English legal customs through his attendance at the king's inner council, which sat frequently as a court of law. So Stephen Langton was coming to have personal experience with English law, but he could not possibly have learned enough in a few short months to propose solutions to the many complaints against John's justice and the difficulties of getting a plea heard.

If Langton was not the voice behind Magna Carta, then could it have been William Marshal?

William Marshal, an elder statesman in John's court, had been in royal service since 1168, serving almost all that time in France. When he was about thirteen, he had been sent to live in the household of a relative in Normandy, where he seems to have learned little of "letters" but much of the knightly activities of fighting, hawking, and tournaments. Marshal was released from the Normandy household in 1168 and entered the service of his uncle, the Earl of Salisbury, who was providing a military escort to accompany the queen (Eleanor of Aquitaine) and her son Richard on the way to Poitou to establish a court there (Poitou was part of Aquitaine, Eleanor's inheritance). The party was ambushed, the Earl of Salisbury was killed, and William Marshal was captured and held for ransom. Eleanor paid the ransom and took Marshal into her service. In 1170, Henry II of England detached Marshal from Eleanor's court and attached him to the household of his eldest son (the fourteen-year-old Henry, who had just been crowned king to assure the succession). The young king, Marshal with him, took up residence in France to remain there until his death in 1183. Marshal was then given permission by Henry II to undertake the crusade on which the young king had vowed to go. Three years later Marshal returned and entered the service of Henry II, who was now more or less constantly at war with Philip II of France in alliance with Henry's rebellious sons Richard and John. When Henry II lay dying of his wounds in 1189, Marshal was by his side; neither of the sons was.

William Marshal was immediately accepted into the household of the new king, Richard I, and went to England with him for his coronation. Richard remained in England for only a few months to plan a regency government for England and raise funds so that he could go on a vowed crusade to the Holy Land (the Third Crusade). Marshal was attached to the English government as one of a number of justiciars, presumably because of his military reputation (which was high), since he had no administrative or judicial experience. He remained in that position until Richard's return in 1194. Again Richard was in England for only a few months to reorganize the government and raise money before returning to France to recover territories seized by the French king Philip II during his absence. Marshal returned to France with Richard and remained there until Richard's death in battle in 1199. By this time, Marshal's reputation was such that he was in on the negotiations that resulted in John's coronation as king of England (John was the youngest son of Henry II and Eleanor). These were significant negotiations since there was another candidate for the throne, a candidate backed by the king of France, the twelve-year-old Arthur, posthumous son of Henry II's third son Geoffrey, married to Constance of Brittany.

William Marshal now entered John's service. In 1204, John lost Normandy and the rest of the Angevin holdings in France except part of Poitou and all of Gascony (Poitou and Gascony were the northern and southern parts of Aquitaine). So in 1204, John returned to England and ceased to be an absentee ruler; Marshal returned with him.

With gifts given to him by Richard and John, William Marshal had become one of the great magnates of the realm, holding the earldom of Pembroke in the March of Wales and the lordship of Leinster in Ireland in addition to an estate in Normandy and numerous smaller grants. Marshal stayed at court, participating in the financial, judicial, and other administrative duties of the magnates who were closely associated with the royal government in its many activities, remaining there until 1205, when he was dismissed by John for disloyalty: He refused to fight against the king of France because he had done homage to Philip II as the liege lord of Marshal's holdings in Normandy. Marshal retired to his estates and lived primarily in Ireland until John, fearful of the real disloyalty of some of the other barons, recalled Marshal to court in 1210 to resume his role as a counselor of the king. The judicial activity of the king's court had been increased by John's decision in 1209 to dissolve the court that heard nonroyal pleas (coming to be known as the court of common pleas), which had settled at Westminster. Such cases would now have to go to the king's court, which followed the king wherever he happened to be. Finding the king's court and securing a hearing there was a long, time-consuming process, and only the wealthiest and most determined could have a case heard there. In addition to the difficulty of getting one's suit before the king's court, there was some doubt that one could find justice there. The problem was that John frequently sat with the court. It was not that John was unfamiliar with English legal customs, but that he knew them so well that he could manipulate them to royal advantage. John's legal training had been very good. He was placed for a time in the household of Ranulf Glanville, then chief justiciar of England—equivalent to an apprenticeship in the common law—and later he lived at the court of Henry II and became familiar with the judicial activity of the king's court. But this training did not prevent conflicts of interest in his decisions, and these are reflected in Magna Carta in the many provisions to regulate legal procedures and the court system.

By 1210, John was aware of serious baronial discontent in the north and elsewhere, hence his recall of Marshal. Tension between king and barons became more serious in 1212 when a plot against the king's life was discovered and a number of high-ranking barons were outlawed (i.e., exiled). Discontent against John and his petty (and some not-so-petty) revenges, and his exorbitant demands for fines and reliefs for grants, and sales of wardships, and marriages had surfaced in the form of protests among the younger barons.

Further, John was always planning to recover his lost French provinces, and by 1214 he was demanding knight service in person or the payment of scutage (a money payment in lieu of actual service). The disaffected barons argued that their assessed knight service did not cover military action overseas, and if they did not owe knight service for the coming action overseas, they did not owe scutage in lieu of that service. John used pressure, and where he was strong enough took hostages to ensure military service. The reluctant service of such men with the army did not help morale, although the mercenaries (the bulk of the army) were reliable enough. John's mistrust, however, dominated and contributed to his refusal to challenge the Dauphin's army in the west of France and thus was immediately responsible for the defeat of his German ally at the Battle of Bouvines in eastern France in 1214. John returned home with a disgruntled army.

By the fall of 1214 the meetings of the discontented barons were becoming more frequent and better attended. Stephen Langton and William Marshal often met with them; they continued to represent the king but worked for a compromise solution that would gain both baronial and royal support. These meetings had become acquainted with the Coronation Charter of Henry I (1100), called a charter of "liberties." Henry I's charter claimed to rectify some of the same grievances against Henry I's brother (William II) and father (William I the Conqueror)—financial exactions, arbitrary policies, lack of justice—that were much like the baronial complaints against John. By spring 1215 the rebels were demanding that John accept Henry's charter as a starting point for discussion; John refused. The more radical barons denounced their allegiance to John and began war against him (the feudal defiance of a tyrant). When the city of London joined the rebels, John had at least to listen to their demands.

During the spring of 1215, while dissentient barons and defiant king failed to come to any kind of agreement, a number of the king's close advisers were working behind the scenes for a compromise, Stephen Langton and William Marshal among them. But neither of these two men knew the subtleties of current English customs because Anglo-Saxon and Norman law had merged to create an essentially distinct hybrid law that was peculiar to England (the English common law). Stephen Langton had had a very good education but no experience with English law, except what he had picked up in a few months attending the king's court (which did not meet while John was out of the country on campaign) and through his meetings with the rebellious barons. William Marshal had had no formal education to speak of (he was literate in courtly French), but he had become familiar with the personnel and activities of the king's court. He had obtained much experience as a justiciar during Richard I's absence from England for more than three years on the Third Crusade, followed by his captivity in Germany, but he was not chief justiciar and was diverted in the later part of this period in trying to outmaneuver John, who was trying with the help of the French king Philip II to replace his brother Richard on the throne of England. After Richard's return, John capitulated and served Richard as he attempted to recover the lost territories in France. Marshal was there in France also, but his role depended more on his military experience than on his administrative experience. So there does not seem to be any way that either Stephen Langton or William Marshal could have produced Magna Carta: a statement of the "liberties" of Henry I's charter, brought up to date with current legal customs and expanded to incorporate modifications that would reflect specific grievances expressed by the barons and citizens of London. The miracle of Magna Carta is that it covered the complaints and aspirations of three significant groups: the Church (represented by the spiritual barons, i.e., the higher clergy), the barons (including both spiritual and temporal lords), and the towns (represented by the city of London). The claims of the Church and barons to share in the work of government predated the Norman conquest; the inclusion of the towns in 1215 was something new.

If the expertise to accomplish this miracle of consolidation cannot be credited to Stephen Langton or William Marshal, how was it accomplished?

We need to look more closely at the king's court, not as simply a judicial court dealing with royal pleas (i.e., suits involving the king), but as a court dealing with every possible activity of royal participation or decision making. Who are the king's men?

The English king, like any other medieval monarch, did not govern in isolation; in fact, the actual presence of the king was not necessary for good government. Note, for example, that such a very effective king as Henry II (1154–89) spent more of his time on the Continent in his French territories than he did in England. Or note the case of Richard I, who spent all of his ten-year reign out of England except for a few months in 1189 and 1194. And yet the English government functioned very well without them. How do we explain this?

The answer lies in the king's court, a very large body of men and a few women. When the king went abroad, his closest advisers went with him. A few of these men came from the magnates (greater barons) of the realm, but there were more men chosen from the knights (lesser barons), and even on occasion men were chosen from the burgesses (townsmen). All were either well educated or well trained and could be assigned to any task for which the king needed somebody to represent him. None of these were salaried men. The magnates could expect their reward when some major escheat (land without an heir) came into the royal possession and might be granted to one of them. The lesser men lived in court at the king's expense, including livery. After years of good service they could expect good gifts themselves, a church benefice (if they were in orders), or the wardship of a minor heir and his estate, or the managing of an heiress for whom he would arrange a marriage. All of these could provide a significant income and did not require the presence of the holder. (Salaries began to appear later in the thirteenth century, but royal gift-giving did not disappear, nor did payments for using one's influence at court.) In addition to these important men of the king's court, there were a number of household officials and their staffs to oversee certain activities: a chamberlain was responsible for receiving and disbursing the king's money (kept in the king's chamber), a chancellor managed the chapel and the writing office (for correspondence, preparing charters, issuing writs, etc.), and an officer was in charge of the large mounted escort that accompanied the royal retinue on the move. In addition to all these, the king had a large household to handle living and travel arrangements.

Nonetheless, although the king abroad was accompanied by a large retinue, the major players in the government of England remained behind. Government service was still generalized, and the same individual might be utilized in a number of different activities. However, a definite trend toward specialization was under way by the end of the twelfth century, when the chief justiciar was a man with long service in dispensing royal justice (the common law), the treasury was headed by a number of barons of the exchequer, and the chancellor headed an increasingly large office to handle correspondence, issue writs for use of the royal courts, issue charters, and keep records for the other branches of government (written records were rapidly replacing oral testimony in the law courts). These men were well educated, some in the new universities, but more in cathedral schools, with private tutors, or in households where apprentice-like conditions prevailed. They were all king's men who spent part of their time in Westminster, a suburb of London where the courts were found, and part of their time traveling through the shires. By their presence, they brought the king's authority to county (shire) and hundred (a smaller unit) courts.

So Henry II and his sons Richard and John had at their disposal a well-developed bureaucracy. Where did it come from?

In the early Anglo-Saxon period there were in England a number of small kingdoms, each with its own government. The creation of a single kingdom of England was the product of a series of events that began in 797 with Viking raiders (mostly Danes) sacking the monastery of Lindisfarne in Northumbria. Destructive raids continued in the early ninth century, raids that by midcentury had turned to conquest and settlement. All of the Anglo-Saxon kingdoms fell to the Danes except Wessex in the southwest and part of Mercia just to the north of Wessex. Beginning with King Alfred at the end of the ninth century and continuing through the reigns of the next two kings, the Danelaw (the area settled by Danes) was reconquered, and a single kingdom of England was created for the first time.

During the course of the tenth century, England became the best-organized state in Western Europe, with a nascent bureaucracy centering in the king's court. Law codes in the vernacular predate Alfred, but beginning with Alfred we have a rapidly expanding body of laws written in Anglo-Saxon and translated into Latin. That the English king of the eleventh century already had a competent corps of workers is demonstrated by the machinery of government inherited by the Norman William I the Conqueror in 1066.

When William defeated King Harold and the English army in 1066, he claimed the throne of England as heir to Edward the Confessor, who had died early that year, the last of the rulers of the house of Wessex. Since the English army was demoralized by the defeat at Hastings and the death of their leader Harold, William was accepted by the king's council (witan) and crowned king. William claimed the land of anyone who had fought against him and distributed it among his personal followers as well as among the adventurers who had joined his army of invasion for adventure or for profit. Sporadic resistance to the Norman conquest continued for some years, especially in the northern part of the kingdom. Each time resistance appeared, William put it down harshly and confiscated the property of all involved on the grounds that they were traitors. Over the years much property came to be in dispute since there were the claims of the dispossessed as well as the claims that arose from William's tendency to bestow the same land on two or more different persons.

By 1085 it was clear that the king needed a record of all landholdings in England, and at his Christmas court in that year, William announced plans to conduct a survey of the entire kingdom of England. This resulted in the production of what is known as the Domesday Book, a survey in such depth and detail as to be almost unbelievable. It could have been accomplished only by a large corps of men already trained in making written records: the king's men.

This emerging bureaucracy continued slowly to evolve under the strong hands of William I, William II, and Henry I (1066–1135). The death of Henry I brought a disputed succession and civil war during which the machinery of government broke down and some parts of England became simply ungovernable. A negotiated settlement allowed Henry II (son of a daughter of Henry I) to succeed in 1154 on the death of King Stephen.

Henry II's main goal was to restore the strong royal government of his grandfather. Henry II's legal and administrative reforms produced the government that John inherited in 1199. It was a government in which the royal power was very strong, and that power was exercised by the king and his men. It was a formula that worked well if the king selected his men carefully and both parties respected one another. But it broke down under John because John distrusted everyone and treated them arbitrarily, even those who remained loyal. As a result, his men were convinced that many of the complaints of the rebellious barons were justified.

In the end they were more loyal to the government they served than to the king. It is in the ranks of the mostly nameless bureaucrats that the creators of Magna Carta will be found.

Only among the king's men would be found such a knowledge of legal custom as it had evolved between the tenth and early thirteenth centuries. These were the men who, under the leadership of William Marshal and the papal nuncio (not Stephen Langton, who had been recalled to Rome for failure to obey the papal demand that he excommunicate the rebellious barons), restored peace to the land and set in motion a return to that good government as outlined in Magna Carta. I wish I had been there to see these professionals in action; I wish that they could have known the future of their charter.

Further Reading

Katherine Fischer Drew, *Magna Carta* (Westport, CT, 2004).

V. H. Galbraith, *The Making of Domesday Book* (Oxford, 1961).

J. C. Holt, *Magna Carta*, 2d ed. (Cambridge, 1992).

Ralph Turner, *Judges, Administrators, and the Common Law in Angevin England* (London, 1994).

BARBARA A. HANAWALT

Rebel Leader Confronts King at Smithfield in 1381

Barbara A. Hanawalt is the King George III Professor of British History at Ohio State University. She earned her PhD at the University of Michigan, and she has published *Crime and Conflict in English Communities, 1300–1348*, *The Ties That Bound: Medieval English Peasant Families*, *Growing Up in Medieval London: The Experience of Childhood in History*, and *"Of Good and Ill Repute": Gender and Social Control in Medieval England*. Her latest book is *The Wealth of Wives: Women, Law, and Economy in Late Medieval London*. In addition, Professor Hanawalt has published a number of articles on medieval English social history and edited a number of collections of essays on the intersection of medieval history and literature. Her writings include pedagogical works as well, including six chapters in the college textbook *The Western Experience* and two books for adolescent readers.

Her subject in this essay is an unprecedented confrontation between subject and king that was a harbinger of the vast changes in political and social life that followed the end of the Middle Ages.

Rebel Leader Confronts King at Smithfield in 1381

Events happened very rapidly in London in June 1381. "The Peasant Revolt," or "the Great Revolt," as historians have called the popular rising against the royal government, became a confrontation outside London's walls on June 15 between the leader of the rebels, Wat Tyler, and the fourteen-year-old king Richard II. Each side had its supporters, and the peasants and townsmen were drawn up behind Wat Tyler. The rebels, a mixture of peasants from Kent and Essex, laborers from London, veterans and deserters of military campaigns in France, and others who joined the ranks, descended on London on the Wednesday before Corpus Christi Day, or June 13, 1381, and held the city through June 15. Their argument was not against the king. Like many peasant revolutionaries, they did not think that the king was at fault, but that his evil advisers had misled him. Their initial plea was for an abolition of serfdom; that is, they wanted to be free from obligatory labor and free to move from manors. As one of their leaders, a priest named John Ball, is said to have preached: "When Adam delved and Eve span, where then were all the gentlemen." The ideology was of one simple equality.

Discontent among laborers, peasants, artisans, and small employers of laborers arose from a number of causes that accumulated in the late thirteenth century and became more overwhelming after the outbreak of the Black Death in 1348–49. Population had increased substantially by the beginning of the fourteenth century, but heavy rainfall ruined crops in successive years and the famine killed a number of the poor. According to the chroniclers of the time, the poor died in lanes and streets. Even the better off suffered deprivations. The population recovered quickly in the second quarter of the century because those who survived had sufficient land, good harvests, and could marry and raise children. It was, therefore, a prosperous and robust population that became victims of a disease that did not spare nobility, clerics, peasants, or poor. While famine killed the poor, the plague spared no one.

The bubonic plague or Black Death came to England in 1348–49. The symptoms were swellings of the lymph nodes *(bubos)* and bleeding under the skin, which caused black blotches, giving the name "black death" to the disease. When the symptoms appeared, the victims lived only three days. Other varieties were swifter and killed within a day; the pneumonic version was carried on the breath of the infected person. London lost, by modern estimates, at least half of its population, and England as a whole lost a third to a half of its inhabitants. So many people died in some places that the few survivors could not bury the dead. The plague revisited every generation, or about every twenty years. Other diseases entered Europe as well, so that in the late fourteenth and fifteenth centuries the population of England remained lower than it had been in 1300.

Survivors of the trauma realized that the economic situation had changed. Although we now refer to Adam Smith for "the law of supply and demand," the peasants and their lords knew exactly what this meant in real terms in 1349. Peasants and town artisans had died in substantial numbers, but the survivors quickly understood that those who remained could require wages far in excess of those they had received in 1346–47. They also realized that they could move from place to place because lords needed to have their crops planted and harvested and would pay the higher wages. Lords could not keep their serfs on the manors and could not rely on the forced labor as they had once done. Many peasants abandoned manors in search of higher wages. Lords also suffered from the dearth of consumers for crops, as the population remained small. The two sides of the equation reached the same conclusion quickly. The king and his council of nobles reacted with the Ordinance of Laborers in 1349, which required peasants and artisans to work for the same wages and sell their goods at the same prices as in 1346–47, before the great depopulation from plague. In 1351 the Statute of Laborers, passed by the House of Lords and the House of Commons, ratified the control of prices and wages at the preplague level. The statute was hard to enforce, however, and when royal officials managed to do so, their efforts met with resistance from peasants, laborers, artisans, and even those few with landholdings who had to hire labor. Dissatisfaction was brewing in the land. To those in power and those with large estates, it seemed as if the world had been turned upside down and the underclass was gaining at the expense of the established order. Parliament kept reissuing the Statute of Laborers and the government kept trying to enforce it, but this move only increased the peasants' resentment as their economic expectations rose. As Adam Smith pointed out, legislating against the law of supply and demand could not be successful.

War was another factor in the outbreak of rebellion. The French and English kings had been engaged in a conflict that historians call the Hundred Years' War from the first naval battle in 1340. The English had won some pitched battles, but could not occupy France. Fighting continued and the government was forced to conscript unwilling peasant and urban recruits to the army. Many of the soldiers learned to live by plunder in France and returned to England with no intention of doing honest labor. They formed robber gangs that preyed on the local population but, since some were protected and employed by lords to subdue rebellious peasants, they were hard to control. The coastal men in the southeast, particularly in Kent, had been organized into a militia for defense against French raids, so that when these "peasants" marched on London, they were not simply armed with pitchforks, scythes, knives, and staffs. The war had spread military knowledge and discipline into the population, and these experienced militiamen knew how to follow commands and keep together in an organized attack.

The war was expensive. The crown requisitioned supplies from the English countryside including grain, horses, bows, arrows, and a number of other goods. The peasants and artisans were never paid for these goods and resented the imposition. London merchants, along with others, complained that they suffered from French piracy, and often the merchants themselves were held for ransom. The disruption to shipping was so desperate in southeast England that ports silted up and went out of use.

To cover the cost of war, the government had to impose more drastic taxation. The English had been accustomed to taxation, but it had been a tax on movable goods, and only those who possessed over ten shillings' worth were taxed, so that it was a type of graduated tax. In 1377 the Parliament, perhaps following the instruction of John of Gaunt, Duke of Lancaster, suggested a per capita tax. The duke was Edward III's son and uncle to Richard II. The new tax, which one of the chroniclers called "a hitherto unheard-of tax," proposed to collect a groat (four pence) from each person, male and female, over the age of fourteen. While past taxes had been based on the ability to pay, only beggars were omitted from this taxation. Clergy had a separate tax. Edward III died in 1377 and the Duke of Lancaster became regent to young Richard II, Edward III's grandson. The boy was only eleven and very much under the control of his mother, uncle, and his advisers. In 1379, as the French threatened to invade

England and John of Gaunt failed in his campaign against them, another poll (or head) tax was imposed. Corruption had diminished the income from taxes in 1379, and a further, more punishing, tax was imposed in 1380. The Archbishop of Canterbury, Simon Sudbury, became chancellor and required a tax of one shilling (twelve pence) of all people over the age of fifteen. As revenues fell, it was apparent that evasion was widespread. In one town the tax records show that the servants ran to the back of the town as the collectors approached, and then ran around the town to the front of it when the collectors had passed through. One of the king's sergeant-at-arms suggested commissions to ensure collection. The commissioners were effective and the crown was able to collect four-fifths of the taxes assessed, but success came at a high price. The counties that experienced the special commissions were the ones to revolt first.

Commissioners appointed in May 1381 to collect the 1380 tax ran into armed resistance in June in an Essex village. The peasants refused to pay, and when the commissioners threatened them with violence, the peasants collected the men of neighboring communities and drove the commissioners and their clerks out. When the crown sent a judicial commission to indict and arrest the perpetrators, the rebels gathered together, drove out the chief justice, and beheaded the jurors who were bringing the indictments against them. The nobility and people of money in the area either fled to London or to other counties. After spending a frightening night in the woods without food, the rebels went to an estate of Sir Robert Hales, royal treasurer and grand master of the Hospital of Saint John of Clerkenwell, broke into his well-stocked manor house, drank three casks of good wine, ate all the food, and pulled down the house.

Word of the revolt in Essex quickly spread to other parts of the kingdom. Jack Straw became the leader of the Essex men and directed them to London. In Kent a group of rebels gathered and made rudimentary plans. They agreed among themselves that the coast should be defended from possible French incursions and that those militia defending the coast should stay at their posts. In Maidstone, Kent, they broke into a jail and released the prisoners, a pattern they would follow throughout the revolt. They then selected Wat Tyler from that town as their leader. They also had with them the priest, John Ball. They marched on Canterbury and told the monks to elect a new archbishop, since they planned to kill Archbishop Sudbury. In five days they had done so. Marching through Kent, they gathered followers and converged on London on June 12, eve of the Corpus Christi celebrations. Throughout their march the Kentish rebels had demanded oaths of loyalty to Richard II, while they also required a condemnation of Archbishop Sudbury, Sir Robert Hales, and the Duke of Lancaster. They halted on the south shore of the Thames, where they requested a meeting with the king. Richard II moved to the Tower of London with the intention of doing so and took a barge down the river toward Greenwich for a meeting, even though Sudbury and Hales along with others told him it was too dangerous. Perhaps a meeting would not have been fatal for the king, but the advisers had reason to fear for their own lives.

The weather was warm and the days long as midsummer approached. Corpus Christi Day was an important holiday in the Catholic calendar (England was still adherent to the Pope at the time) and included processions through the streets following the communion wafer carried in a crystal box, plays, and an excuse for drink and feasting. Denied an interview with the king on the eve of the feast, the Kentish rebels advanced along the south side of the Thames. They attacked the archbishop's palace at Lambeth and destroyed records there, finally ruining it. They also attacked and destroyed the hated Marshalsea Prison, where political prisoners, felons, and debtors were held. On Thursday, the day of the feast, they crossed London Bridge, probably with the complicity of the reveling commoners of London and Southwark. Meanwhile, the rebels from Essex, under the leadership of Jack Straw, advanced and destroyed another manor belonging to Sir Robert Hales. The rebels now had a sizable force in London including those from Kent, Essex, London, and others who joined in. They broke into Fleet prison and released all the prisoners. They burned the houses of those who had collaborated with the justices in arresting people and burned all the houses belonging to Hales. The number of rebels is impossible to estimate, but the damage they did is well recorded, and all chroniclers agree on the main events of the revolt in London.

One of the first targets was the palace of the Duke of Lancaster, the Savoy. Lancaster was not there. Accounts vary on whether the men of London, Essex, or Kent were the leaders in the attack, but all the chroniclers agree that on Thursday, June 13, the rebels made their way up Fleet Street to Temple Church, the main church of the Knights of Saint John, and burned all the records there. They then went on to the Savoy where they broke down the gates, gathered all the torches they could find, and set fire to the fine bedding, clothing, and hangings in the house.

The palace contained many objects of gold and silver as well as precious gems, and, as the story unfolded in the various accounts, a further ideology of the revolt appeared. The rebels did not want to be labeled as looters, and it would have been fascinating to hear their discussions on how to prevent thefts. One account said that they ground the gems into powder and another says that they threw into the flames two men who were caught with stolen objects in their possession. The event became even more dramatic when some of the rebels threw kegs of gun-powder into the burning hall. Other rebels, it was said, found the wine cellar and stayed there drinking until the stones fell around them and trapped them. Death rewarded their gluttony.

On their way back to London, the rebels burned the hospital of Clerkenwell, belonging to the Knights of Saint John, and joined other rebels before the Tower, where Richard, Hales, Sudbury, the queen mother, and other nobles had taken refuge. From a window in the Tower the king could see the Savoy and Clerkenwell, along with other houses, burning. He could also see the rebels swarming through the London streets looking for targets for their violence. The king, accounts tell us, was very afraid, as were his advisers. It would have been revealing to see him decide to placate the mob by agreeing to hear their petitions. He thanked his commons for their faith in him and had a document read stating that he would pardon everyone for the felonies they had committed up until that hour. He then asked that they send their complaints in writing to him, and said that he and his council would determine each case. He put his signet to the document and had it read by a man standing on an old chair in front of the rebels. But Richard II and his council underestimated the intelligence of the commons, just as they had when they passed the Statute of Laborers. The rebels knew that putting their names to a written document would mean that they would fall prey to the judicial machinery and be hanged. They called Richard's reply a mockery and immediately ordered that all lawyers, or anyone who could write or who worked for the court system, should be beheaded. And many were, that day and thereafter. The rebels burned the house of the infamous man who had suggested that inquisitions be used to discover tax evaders. Throughout England documents were destroyed, and justices, lawyers, and jurors were killed. The king's appeal to people who had suffered so much from the ability of various courts to keep written records on them and have them arrested led to a backlash against the law and the literate.

Richard and his counselors obviously misunderstood the depth of the rebels' resentments and the specific targets of oppression that they wanted to destroy. On Friday, June 14, Richard and the others seemed to have begun to comprehend. Richard offered to meet the rebels at Mile End to hear their complaints, selecting a site that was outside the walls and gates of London. The hope was to rid the city of the rebels. Some went to meet him there, but a large contingent, perhaps including Wat Tyler, stayed at the Tower. Richard had instructed Sudbury, Hales, and others to try to save themselves by leaving at a small water gate while he diverted the mob. The rebels, however, had collusion of some of those inside the Tower. An old woman observed the attempted escape and they had to return to the Tower. Archbishop Sudbury had time to say mass and pray before the rebels gained entry into the Tower and roughly took him, Hales, and several others, including the man who had started the commissions to nab tax evaders, out to Tower Hill, where they beheaded them. They paraded the heads on poles through the streets of London to Westminster Abbey and displayed them on London Bridge, as was the common fate for convicted traitors. Meanwhile, the conference at Mile End had failed.

On Saturday, June 16, the king went to Westminster Abbey, as did many of the rebels. The rebels found the marshal of the Marshalsea, the warden of the prison that was already liberated, who was known to be a notorious tormentor of prisoners. They pulled him from the religious shrine he was clinging to, dragged him out, and beheaded him. The king, perhaps witnessing this event, came to say his prayers at the altar and spent an hour there talking with a hermit who lived at the abbey. He then proclaimed that the rebels who were in the city should meet him at Smithfield, again outside the city walls. The chief enemies of the king having been destroyed along with much of their property in London, the commons agreed to meet at Smithfield.

The rebels were in orderly ranks behind Wat Tyler. John Ball and Jack Straw apparently were also present. The king had a much smaller party including William of Walworth, who was the mayor of London, city officials, some nobility, and a number of knights. Among those present might have been the man who wrote the *Anonimalle Chronicle*. This anonymous author, probably a member of the king's household, provides the most reliable account of the revolt. The young king had Walworth summon Wat Tyler to his presence. Tyler came on horseback, a symbol of his equality of rank with the king and nobles, although the chronicler described it as a small white horse. When he arrived armed with a dagger, he dismounted and half knelt to the king. Then, breaking all protocol of a commoner to the king, he took the king by the hand and shook it vigorously—a moment that would have been the most extraordinary of the many remarkable sights of these heated days. Calling the king "brother," he offered forty thousand commoners who would be "good companions" to the king. The presumption of such physical intimacy was insulting, and the chronicle accounts of the king's forbearance shows how intimidated the royal party was. Richard again asked Tyler and the others to go to their homes, but Tyler responded that they would not disband until their demands were met. The king asked to hear them. The rebels had formed a more sophisticated ideology since the early days of June when the revolt was against taxes and in favor of a biblical social equality. Tyler now demanded that outlawry be banned in the future, that the land belonging to the nobility be divided among all men, and that no lord have lordship in the future, except the king. Church land should likewise be divided among the commons, and England should have only one bishop. Finally, he demanded that all serfs be free and that in the future everyone would be of one condition and status. These were revolutionary demands. They would eliminate serfdom, the grasp of the nobility and the clergy over people and land, and eliminate hierarchy, except for a king and archbishop. Young Richard said that he would do all within his power, but that he reserved the regality of his crown. He again urged Wat Tyler to go home— yet another moment when I wish I had been there. Tyler was not satisfied and became insulting. He called for water, because of the heat of the day, and washed his mouth out and spit it out in a "rude and villainous manner" before the king. Then he called for a jug of ale and drank this before getting on his horse.

At this point the confrontation became violent. A valet of the king came forward and Tyler called upon a follower to behead him. The mayor of London, Walworth, then moved to arrest Tyler. Tyler struck at him with his dagger, but the mayor was wearing armor and escaped injury. Walworth then inflicted wounds on Tyler and the valet thrust his sword into him. Tyler spurred his horse toward the rebels but dropped to the ground. The rebels drew their bows and began to shoot, but young Richard had the presence of mind to spur his horse toward the commoners and tell them to assemble at a field not far away. Meanwhile, the mayor of London closed the gates and managed to collect an orderly group of militia to surround the rebels. Tyler had been carried to the hospital for the poor, Saint Bartholomew's, not far away. Then the king's men carried him back to the field and beheaded him in front of his followers. The king had the head brought near him and again told the rebels to go home. They asked for forgiveness and agreed to depart if they were given charters of pardon and freedom from serfdom. Rich-

WAT TYLER-for his insolence is killed by WALWORTH and
KING RICHARD puts himself at the Head of the REBELS.

An English etching illustrates the fateful encounter between King Richard and Wat Tyler with his followers. In medieval style, the king is depicted twice— once next to the rebel leader who is about to be beheaded (left), and again on the right, addressing the commoners.

ard agreed. The king, of course, immediately revoked the charters and began the process of hunting down the rebels.

The revolt collapsed: perhaps because Wat Tyler was dead, perhaps because the chief architects of the poll tax were killed, or perhaps because harvest time was coming and the rebels had to return to their crops. Corpus Christi holiday was over and it was time to think of food for the next year. Some people were punished for their role in the revolt, but it was not a bloodbath. The clergy and the lords continued to be afraid of the commoners, and conservative writers complained about them, as did the chroniclers who recorded the events of the revolt of June 1381.

If we cited the wisdom of Adam Smith about the impossibility of enforcing the law of supply and demand, we should end with Karl Marx and the withering away of feudalism. Peasants did not need to continue the revolt. They had gained little by their violent rebellion, but gradually it became impossible to return to the old manorial system with its enforced labor and lack of mobility. England did not have an adequate population to support the old system nor a sufficiently oppressive regime to do so. New economic opportunities, such as wool production, were exploited. Serfdom and manorialism gradually did fade away in England, as Marx suggested, but the equality that the rebels had desired was not achieved in the fourteenth century.

Further Reading

R. B. Dobson, ed., *The Peasants' Revolt of 1381* (London, 1970).

Charles Oman, *The Great Revolt of 1381* (Oxford, 1906, new ed. 1969).

Steven Justice, *Writing and Rebellion: England in 1381* (Berkeley, 1994).

LAURO MARTINES

Ten Thousand Brutes in Renaissance Florence

Lauro Martines was Professor of History at UCLA from 1966 to 1992. Previously he had served for two years in the U.S. Army and taught at Reed College. He has had numerous fellowships, including residences at the Villa I Tatti in Florence and the Villa Serbelloni in Bellagio. Since retiring from UCLA he has lived in London, though he has also served as Visiting Director of Studies at the École des Hautes Études en Sciences Sociales in Paris in 1992 and 1994. Among his many books are *Power and Imagination: City-States in Renaissance Italy*, *An Italian Renaissance Sextet: Six Tales in Historical Context*, *Strong Words: Writing and Social Strain in the Italian Renaissance*, and *April Blood: Florence and the Plot Against the Medici*, which was on the bestseller list in London for two months. Professor Martines has also published a novel: *Loredana: A Venetian Tale*.

For his essay here he takes us back to days of fearsome danger in the Florence of the Renaissance.

Ten Thousand Brutes in Renaissance Florence

In the 1490s, Florence was the most literate city in Christendom, and although its population amounted to a mere fifty thousand people, a rich scatter of private palaces along its widest streets and the international renown of Florentine bankers attested to an accumulation of remarkable wealth and to the refined tastes of its financial and political oligarchy.

It was still a medieval city, with streets that were mostly narrow and darkened by shadows, while its great turreted gates and outer ring of gigantic walls were fixed reminders of the sinister dangers of war. Lacking a standing army, forced to rely on foreign mercenaries, and ranking as the weakest of Italy's five dominant states, Florence dreaded military hostilities. War wrecked business, with taxes that ate deeply into private wealth, and it released waves of soldiers who knew no law. Sweeping over Florentine lands, they would torch buildings, plunder livestock, pilfer every form of movable wealth, murder and rape at will, and then vanish, leaving swaths of death, destruction, and untold misery in their tracks.

Despite such passing furies, however, Florence's domestic palaces, convents, friaries, and parish churches housed countless works of surpassing beauty, both painted and carved. Freestanding statuary, preeminently from the hand of Donatello, had made a dramatic appearance in the fifteenth century. And an abundance of private libraries, with books often out on loan, served to satisfy the need for the pleasures of literature. The city, in short, bred outstanding spirits: men who responded to the summons for talent in the decorative arts, in letters, and even in

In November 1494, an army matching in size a fifth of Florence's population pushed through the maze of narrow streets in the densely built capital. Above is a detail from the map of Catena, a view of Florence painted in 1490.

politics and diplomacy, where modern learning and knowledge of the ancient world won favor and honors. Michelangelo, Botticelli, Machiavelli, Ficino, Guicciardini, Lorenzo the Magnificent, Pico della Mirandola, Leonardo da Vinci (on visits), and many another exceptional talents walked the streets of Florence in the 1490s. Travelers arrived from distant lands to look upon its treasures and, if possible, to converse with Florentines, who were themselves famous for their swiftness of speech and wit.

• • •

Yet this was a decade that would bring the city to the edge of a cataclysm, for in the early evening of November 17, 1494, King Charles VIII of France marched into it with ten thousand soldiers. Never before had such an army passed through those great walls. Horrors were not meant to penetrate the Florentine urban space. Even its official place of execution was situated outside the Gate of Justice, on the eastern spur of the city.

Entering at the western Gate of San Frediano, drawn sword in hand and lance on hip, the mounted Charles rode in as a conqueror. His intentions were murky; his soldiers had occupied two Florentine seaports, Pisa and Livorno, and two magnificent fortresses on the city's northwestern frontiers. And since they had also sacked the neighboring town of Fivizzano, terror coursed through Florence as the populace wondered if the invaders proposed to sack it, too.

Citizens had known of the coming occupation for weeks. On November 4 and 5, French officers had been in the city, chalking up the houses to be occupied by soldiers. An astounding penalty of five hundred gold florins awaited anyone who dared to remove the markings. Residents had promptly concealed their valuables, and as the fear of mass rape was general, all young wives and girls of good family had been put into convents. Servants and old women, a diarist reported, were the only females to be seen in the streets.

Major splits in the Florentine ruling class sharpened the fears of citizens. On November 9, Lorenzo the Magnificent's son and political heir, Piero de' Medici, had fled into exile, abruptly terminating sixty years of Medici rule. A revitalized republic took over at once, to be eyed with suspicion and fear by partisans of the old regime.

Having gone out of the city at the outset of November to meet King Charles on a self-appointed embassy, Piero de' Medici had surrendered the seaports and the fortresses of Sarzana and Pietrasanta, while also binding Florence to the payment of a colossal tribute of 200,000 gold florins. In the months leading up to this catastrophe, he had infuriated Charles by refusing to let the city accept the large aims of his Italian adventure; but now, face-to-face with him and in a panic, Piero instantly capitulated. Stunned by this cowardly behavior, a group of republican firebrands in government inspired a revolt against the Medici (November 8–9), engineered a coup d'état, and put the foremost Medicean collaborators out of political action.

Open and keen political discussion, a Florentine passion long suppressed under the Medici, now burst forth, and *fiorentini* seemed to wake to a new day. This was the argumentative Florence that sharpened minds and tongues, in literary and artistic matters, too.

• • •

Charles's quarrel was not really with Florence at all. Seeking to make good his bloodline's old Angevin claims to the kingdom of Naples, he had invaded Italy in the first days of September and was on his way down the peninsula to seize it from the kings of Aragon. At the head of a huge artillery train and a fighting force of nearly thirty thousand men, he entered Florence with only part of his army. His other forces were on the move and too far afield to have an impact on the Florentine scene.

Two urgent questions now confronted the new republic: Did the invaders plan to sack the city? And should Florence yield to the royal demand that Piero de' Medici be allowed to return home? Piero's craven concessions had spun the king around in his favor.

For the moment it seemed wise to show a conciliatory face. France, after all, was a traditional ally and a leading market for the luxury cloth and services of Florentine merchants and bankers. Accordingly, when the invaders entered Florence, the city made every effort to offer them a friendly reception with songs, decorative hangings, triumphal arches, fireworks, decked-out streets, and banners displaying the French royal arms. But behind this elaborate charade—and intermittent cries of "France!

France!"–fear gripped the hearts of the inhabitants, awed by this display of armed might. A diarist described the soldiers as brutes, barbarians, and half animals. They came "from cold places that produce animal-like men with ugly languages," and the royal guard, "taller and thicker than the ordinary," were "from Dalmatia and other strange places." Citizens gaped at the parading 7,000 Swiss infantrymen, 700 armed horsemen, 500 mounted archers and another 1,000 on foot, in addition to spearsmen, crossbowmen, artillery gunners, and men carrying halberds. That night King Charles was lodged in the Medici Palace, but six small cannons were mounted on carts outside the entrance; and a band of buildings, in a full circle around the palace, was commandeered by the army to provide protection for the king and his top brass.

In the first two or three days of the occupation, shaken by the visible might of that foreign soldiery, Florentines appeared cowed and defenseless. Michelangelo, in terror, had fled the city in October. But the twelve-year-old Guicciardini, under his father's pious influence, was often locked in prayer, while Machiavelli, already in his mid-twenties and with a colder eye, toiled to understand the springs of the unfolding events.

The French took charge of the city gates but failed to impose strict controls on bridges and did little to disarm citizens. They had the utmost faith in their own arms and skills, for if–using demographic calculations–we exclude women and children from the Florentine population, then it is clear that the city had 8,000 or 9,000 men at most, and many of these would have been old, sickly, or too frightened to fight.

The fears of people in the streets were fixed on the mass of foreign soldiers, but fears in the government palace concerned the king's demand for the rehabilitation of the Medici lord. Although Charles's ultimate intentions remained unclear, his initial talking point, broached by emissaries first, then by him face-to-face, was the return of Piero. And this is where republican leaders dug in their heels. They were prepared to negotiate over the seaports of Pisa and Livorno, and over the return of the western fortresses. Hard-nosed bargaining reduced the demanded tribute to 120,000 gold florins, payable in installments, and held off the king's desire to leave a royal vicar in the city. But the government refused under any circumstances to have Piero back. A revolution had taken place. Large numbers of anti-Medici political exiles had already been invited back to Florence; laws had been swiftly suspended; despotic councils had been pushed aside; Medici properties had been confiscated; Piero's wife and mother-in-law had been thrust into a convent; terrible accusations had been made against the Medici; the city was awash with wrath over the family's misdeeds; and the explosive revival of the republic had opened the doors to keen political ambitions, modest men, and a vision of honest and more popular government.

Ah, to have been in Florence during those November days, as there was far more going on here than meets the eye. Ever since the thirteenth century, the genius of the city had taken it against popes, princes, and neighboring warlords. A keen civic life, gathered chiefly around the promises and perils of politics, was the source of the energies that also flowed into all "higher" cultural activity, and in November 1494 that wellspring—the secret of the whole history of Florence—was briefly on show.

Republican passions produced a new and heady context of ideas for the likes of Machiavelli, Bernardo Rucellai, Jacopo Nardi, and soon the redoubtable Guicciardini. The metamorphosis in historical and political writing, as registered in the Florence of these years, beginning with the diaries of Piero Parenti, was to have no parallels in later European history.

The city's republican leaders said no to Piero, because his return could lead only to executions, exiling, and sequestration of

the houses, lands, and chattels of many distinguished families—
"rebels" such as the Nerli, Valori, Pazzi, and Corsi, and certain
branches of the Capponi, Soderini, Rucellai, Strozzi, Albizzi,
Corsini, and Gualterotti.

Resistance to the king was focused on the political will to
keep Piero de' Medici out of Florence, and this resolve sidelined
the fear of a possible brutal assault on the city. Here, in a fierce
determination, was the emotive ingredient that brought about a
change of mood and attitude in propelling the city from terror
to anger, and then to something like courage.

Anger also went with the knowledge that Piero's wife and
mother-in-law were using their refuge, the convent of Santa Lu-
cia, to work feverishly behind the scenes, pleading for Piero's
pardon with some of King Charles's chief counselors. Born into
the most powerful of all Roman clans, the Orsini, the two ladies
had no qualms about buying favor with jewels, money, and

Piero de' Medici (left), also called "the Unfortunate," didn't inherit the political brilliance and stamina of his father, Lorenzo il Magnifico. Piero was a
teenager when he hastily and needlessly surrendered his hometown, Florence,
to twenty-four-year-old King Charles VIII (right).

promises linked to their lofty connections in Rome. They claimed that Piero had been summarily exiled without even the pretense of a trial. Bring him back, they pleaded. Let there be a hearing, and if he was found guilty of tyrannical behavior, he would then go willingly into exile. But no republican was foolish enough to believe this for a second. And Machiavelli scoffed at the very idea, though he himself was torn between loyalty to the new republic and a lingering hope for the political patronage of the Medici.

One of the richest men in the city, the glamorous Lorenzo Tornabuoni, a Medici partisan and known throughout Florence as a model of grace and courtesy, had close contacts with important men in the royal entourage, including the king's uncle, Philippe de Bresse. His backroom pleas for Piero so incensed a group of young Florentine noblemen that "they threatened to set fire to his house and cut him to pieces"—such was the incandescence of passion at that moment. Yet there was also astuteness in the republican ranks, for when the exiled Piero, a clotheshorse and proud of his looks, sent in a request for his clothing and linens—he was in Bologna—the government gave its consent, allowing him to keep the needed grace and dignity of his raiment.

Two days before the king's entry into Florence, the Signoria, the city's governing council, consulted 500 prominent citizens, to find that they were united by "hatred for the past regime of tyranny" and by a fervent commitment to their "regained liberty." A day after his entry, the Signoria and 300 citizens went to Charles in the Medici Palace, where they claimed him as the liberator "of our city of Florence," but thereby underlined their rejection of pleas for Piero. On the twenty-first of November, in yet another major consultation, the Signoria heard three leading ecclesiastics, all of them learned men, rail against the Medici lord: the Bishop of Volterra (Francesco Soderini), the Bishop of

Cortona (Guglielmo Capponi), and the Bishop of Arezzo (Cosimo de' Pazzi). All came from among the city's most illustrious houses. Soderini made an impassioned speech for the freedom of the city and against the Medici. The people of Florence, he declared, should all be ready to fight and die for the republic, even if the struggle meant sacrificing their families.

Medici sympathizers attempted to provoke clashes with the king's army. They hoped that the king would then, in high dudgeon, dispatch soldiers to surround the government palace and compel Piero's return to Florence. On November 21 there was a fracas at the entrance to the palace, caused by two French soldiers raging to get into the building. Alarm swept through the city; soldiers readied their weapons; citizens on horseback took control of the bridges on the far side of the Arno River; and the troops around the king's lodgings prepared for action. The Signoria, however, kept its cool; no warning bells were rung, and the episode went no further. The commotion at the palace doors had been paid for by Lorenzo Tornabuoni.

It was only after this incident, and the Signoria's visit to the king, that Charles finally agreed to drop the topic of Piero for a period of four months.

A general shift in mood had been set in motion. As the days passed, the people of Florence began to act more boldly against the foreigners. Every night brought robberies, violent quarrels, and woundings or killings in fights between soldiers and inhabitants, and talk in the city was all about this.

On the twenty-fourth, the Borgo Ognissanti, a long, narrow street just north of the river and to the west, was the scene of the most alarming incident. Arrested in the neighboring Lunigiana Mountains, several Florentines were being led along the Borgo by their French captors, who were threatening to execute them because they were unable to pay the assessed fines. They were weeping and begging for money from passersby when, near the gracious church of Ognissanti, already jeweled with Domenico Ghirlandaio's frescoes, children began to shout for their release. Local noblemen suddenly rushed at the group and forcibly freed the captives. Florentine pride burst through the bonds of fear. The clamor now took wing and spread everywhere; men began to arm themselves, soldiers raced to the Medici Palace, and Florentines rushed to the government square. Proceeding from the great western gate, the Porta Prato, near the start of the brawl, five hundred Swiss infantrymen, their banners flying, sought to enter the narrow Borgo, lined by buildings on both sides. They were repelled by a hail of missiles from the upper windows, and a few soldiers were killed. Women took the lead in this airborne assault. One diarist noted that "chests, ashes, bedsteads, boiling water, rocks, roof tiles, and other objects were thrown down. . . . Fear was noticed among the French [*sic*]. . . . Most of them were trembling like women. The tumult was brought to a halt by the fear on both sides."

This direct assault on Swiss infantry, in a fresh mode of street fighting, marked a turning point in Florentine relations with the French. Later that day the Signoria dispatched another embassy to the king, again asking him to conclude an agreement. The parties drafted a set of provisional articles, and now at last Charles appeared to comply, only to turn, at the last moment, to vent his dissatisfaction. Whereupon, in a famous scene provoked by the "ugly words" of the attending French lords, the principal emissary, Piero di Gino Capponi, tore up the supposed agreement "into a hundred pieces" and declared, "Most Christian prince, we shall sound our bells and you your trumpets, and we will show you our armed populace." All of a sudden, claimed a contemporary, "fearing the infinite multitude of people that the city's great bell could assemble," the royal party called back the emissaries, who were on their way out. And now, throwing in playful words, the king confirmed the agreement.

Two days later, on the twenty-sixth, he swore personally to the articles of the pact "at the sacred stone of the Cathedral's high altar." On the twenty-eighth, king and army left Florence, to continue their march to Rome and then to Naples.

Just how fearful the king and his counselors were we shall never know. The previous week had seen marked changes of feeling on both sides, but the people of Florence, with a reputation for brains and craftsmanship, had finally shown a decisive pride and trust in their own inventiveness.

The king's counselors wanted him to get out of Tuscany and on with his business in Naples, the true aim of his expedition. Moreover, they surmised that to sack Florence would end in a bloodbath for its citizens, but it was clear, too, that hundreds and possibly thousands of soldiers, including French officers and noblemen, would also perish. The king's very life might be in danger. His captains contemplated and then drew back from the universal horror that a sack of Florence would inspire. A generation later, the infamous sack of Rome (1527) would occur at a time when much of the European and Italian moral climate had been transformed.

Kings, officers, and soldiers had seen Florentines with their backs to the wall, particularly in their stance regarding Piero de' Medici. They had also noted the courage of Florentines in local clashes, leading up to the explosion in the Borgo Ognissanti. With the covert encouragement of the Signoria, citizens were meeting in secret and making plans to defend themselves.

The muted background included other activities as well, the details of which were very likely leaked to the French. On the twenty-first of November, the priors of the Signoria began to stock their palace, a massive fortress, with arms and provisions. They sent agents into the countryside to raise a force of thirty thousand men, to be led to the walls of the city. Peasants from the hinterland had not been barred from coming into Florence;

the government urged rich citizens to retain armed men in their houses; and all would be ready to rush to the Piazza della Signoria at the hammering sound of the tocsin.

Significantly, too, the king had canceled a scheduled lunch with the priors on the twenty-fourth, despite the fact that they had vowed to appear without arms of any sort. On the insistence of the royal party, their weapons were removed from the palace, but they had then been smuggled back into the building through the windows of the customs office (Dogana) in the northeastern wing of their great palace. If King Charles did not trust the priors, neither did they trust him.

Is it possible, then, that in their caution the commanders of that army of ten thousand soldiers had come to fear the Florentine people, while these, in return, had lost part of their fear of the invaders?

Something like this seems to have happened. Knowing the streets of the city perfectly, and expecting to be favored by the fact that most of them were narrow enough to turn falling objects into deadly missiles, or to hold crossing chains to trip up horses, Florentines had started to tilt toward the belief that they might be able to withstand a French assault. They hoped that any such encounter would end in a truce around the government palace, always provided, of course, that they could keep the king's artillery from bringing down its great walls—though there too the foreign besiegers would have met a cascade of missiles from the palace's battlements far above the piazza. When the audacity of citizens was combined with the mixed feelings and troubled conscience of the great lords in King Charles's train—men such as Galeazzo Sanseverino, Philippe de Bresse, and the Cardinal Giuliano della Rovere (later Pope Julius II)— the people of Florence had a moral advantage that would cut through any armed clash between the two sides. The city's magnificent churches, its palaces and palace interiors, the wonders of local craftsmanship, and the ranks of learned Florentines had not failed to move and mollify the chiefs of the French invasion.

Florence's fury with the Medici, after decades of their political sleaze and theft of public moneys, collided with fear of the foreigners, especially when the king championed Piero de' Medici's cause, and this heady anger served to scale down raw fears.

There was another compelling element at work, as yet unmentioned. I refer to the impact of the religious emotion that was linked to the force and fire of the Dominican preacher Girolamo Savonarola.

Already renowned in Florence, this charismatic personality, hailing from Ferrara, had been catapulted to the forefront of public life in the days leading up to the November crisis. Having preached in the Cathedral and elsewhere in the city over the previous three years, he had a vast following of supporters, and many already saw him as a prophet in the Old Testament mold, a bearer of God's voice. Known especially for his attacks on the corrupt Church and pleasure-loving clergy, and on the greed and cruelty of the rich and mighty, he was easily associated with the new tide of feeling against the Medici. And the city's intelligentsia, along with masses of craftsmen, including artists such as Botticelli and Filippino Lippi, rallied to his side.

Early in November, with Piero de' Medici out in the field on his ill-fated embassy, the Signoria had selected Savonarola and five prominent citizens to go to King Charles to negotiate a treaty with him. Charles was so impressed by the Dominican friar that he made a point of dealing with him; and later on, in the course of negotiations with the Signoria, he was to show the same esteem for him in Florence as well. The news that he was intrigued by the friar became common knowledge in the city. In visits to the king, particularly in the Medici Palace, Savonarola's pitch was that he, Charles, had been elected by God to punish Italians and the Italian Church for their terrible sins. He was, in effect, a divine scourge; but he must spare Florence, a God-fearing city, and march on south, without delay, to his appointed task.

When Charles and his army finally left Florence on November 28, a great multitude of Florentines from the middle and upper classes, including men in public office, believed that Savonarola had rescued the city from a brutal sacking. In the days before the French departure, their faith in the friar had led them to feel that Florence would not be assaulted, that they would somehow be saved, despite their sins, and that they could use their newfound religion as a shield. Into the melee of emotions that had been stirred up by the presence of ten thousand "brutes," the fiery Dominican had injected the galvanizing tonic of religious sentiment, and this too had inspired the citizens of Florence in their confrontations with a terrifying soldiery. The city's verve, spirit, and genius had been fused with piety.

Further Reading

Luca Landucci, *A Florentine Diary from 1450 to 1516*, trans. Alice de Rosen Jervis (London and New York, 1927).

Lauro Martines, *Fire in the City: Savonarola and the Struggle for Renaissance Florence* (New York, 2006).

Pasquale Villari, *Life and Times of Girolamo Savonarola*, 2 vols., trans. Linda Villari (New York, 1890).

GEOFFREY PARKER

August 9, 1588: The Spanish Armada (almost) Surrenders

Geoffrey Parker is Andreas Dorpalen Professor of History at Ohio State University. His books include *Philip II*, now in its fourth edition; *The Grand Strategy of Philip II*, winner of the Samuel Eliot Morison Prize from the Society of Military History; *The Dutch Revolt*; *The Military Revolution: Military Innovation and the Rise of the West, 1500–1800*, now in its third edition; and *The Spanish Armada* (with Colin Martin). In 1992 the King of Spain made Professor Parker a Knight of the Order of the Grand Cross of Isabella the Catholic in recognition of his work in Spanish history.

In this essay the author sits in on a council of war on the Spanish warship *San Martín de Portugal*, flagship of the Spanish Armada. The date is August 9, 1588, and the Armada has been soundly defeated in the previous day's battle.

August 9, 1588: The Spanish Armada (almost) Surrenders

To everyone's surprise, on the afternoon of August 9, 1588, the flagship of the Spanish Armada *San Martín de Portugal* took in sail and hoisted a signal flag to summon a council of war.* The squadron commanders soon arrived from their vessels and made their way to the high afterdeck, where a short, heavily built, bearded man of thirty-eight, simply attired, stood awaiting them. Around his neck hung the insignia of the Golden Fleece, Spain's most exclusive order of chivalry. Six months earlier, Don Alonso Pérez de Guzmán, "el Bueno" (the Good), seventh duke of Medina Sidonia, had reluctantly accepted the commission to serve as Captain-General of the Ocean Sea for Philip II, ruler of the first global empire in history. The duke now commanded the 130 ships and 30,000 men laboriously assembled over the previous three years. Relatively little of the Armada was Spanish. Many ships were merchantmen from the Mediterranean and Baltic, arrested by Philip's agents when they docked in Spanish ports and equipped with additional guns and munitions. In most cases, their original crews remained and grudgingly shared the limited shipboard space with the king's soldiers.

The duke greeted each of his squadron commanders in turn. Miguel de Oquendo, in charge of the Guipúzcoan Squadron; Martín de Bertendona, commander of the Levant Squadron; Juan Gómez de Medina of the supply ships; and Agustín de

---

*All dates follow the Gregorian Calendar, used in most of Europe. England in 1588 retained the Julian Calendar, in which all dates fell ten days earlier. According to the "English style," Medina convened his council on the afternoon of July 31.

Ojeda of the communications squadron; Don Diego Enríquez, who had taken charge of the Andalusian Squadron after the ignominious surrender of its flagship and its commander to Sir Francis Drake; and Peruchio Morán, who had assumed command of the Squadron of galleasses after the English had captured the flag galleass and killed its commander the previous day. As each member of the council came to the afterdeck, he faced not only the duke but also Diego Flores de Valdés, chief adviser on naval matters, and Don Francisco de Bobadilla, commander of all the soldiers aboard the fleet. These two men served aboard the *San Martín* on the direct orders of the king—perhaps, some speculated, to make sure that the reluctant captain-general obeyed his orders to the letter.

Oquendo and his brother officers found that the mood aboard the flagship had changed dramatically since their last council meeting there just ten days earlier, when the Armada was entering the English Channel. Spirits then had been high, with everyone confident that they could either outmaneuver or defeat their English adversaries. On that occasion, Medina Sidonia had reminded his subordinates of the king's express orders to proceed up the Channel until they reached the coast of Flanders, where thirty thousand veterans assembled by the Duke of Parma, Philip II's governor in the Netherlands, would be waiting. As soon as the Armada arrived, Parma's troops would embark on the fleet of barges he had prepared, and the fleet would escort the expeditionary force to the coast of Kent where, like the Romans and the Saxons before them, the troops would storm ashore, march on London, and replace the government of Elizabeth Tudor with a Catholic regime. Accordingly, with every deck cleared for action, the fleet had advanced in battle formation: a half moon that measured three miles from one tip to the other. Repeated attempts by Elizabeth's navy to break its formation had failed, and on August 6 the Armada dropped anchor off Calais, twenty-five miles from the ports that contained Parma's barges. They remained there for thirty-six hours before the English launched eight fireships against them.

Although the fireships inflicted no direct damage, they forced all the Armada's ships to slip their moorings in order to escape; but then the tide and wind drove them helter-skelter past the Flanders coast, where Parma was waiting, and into the North Sea. With the Armada's battle order broken, on August 8 the English warships closed in to engage the Spaniards. Their flagship absorbed "107 direct hits on the hull, masts and sails by cannon shot, which would suffice to destroy a rock." As they came aboard the *San Martín* the following day, the members of the council noted the sails riddled with shot, the splintered bulwarks, and the spars and rigging still lying on the deck. They also noted splatters of blood everywhere, and some seriously wounded men receiving last rites from the duke's chaplains. But most of all they noted the absence of their two senior colleagues.

Juan Martínez de Recalde, Medina Sidonia's deputy, commander of the Biscayan Squadron, who in the battles in the Channel had commanded the rear guard, the place of greatest honor, was nowhere to be seen. The other absentee was Don Alonso Martínez de Leiva, who, although he commanded no squadron, had taken charge of the entire vanguard.

At first the absence of his two senior commanders puzzled the duke. Had they been summoned, he wondered? An orderly confirmed that he had taken the duke's own felucca—one of eight Venetian rowing barges used to carry messages among the fleet's commanders—to convey the order but, the man added awkwardly, Recalde had told him that because "his opinion in some other meetings had counted for nothing," he intended to stay put and supervise the urgent repair work required to keep his damaged ship seaworthy. Leiva had said much the same thing. The duke angrily dispatched his felucca with a second summons for Recalde and Leiva to attend the council. While awaiting the arrival of his lieutenants, he decided to open the debate on what the Armada should do next.

The senior officers who now filled the *San Martín*'s great cabin boasted a wealth of collective experience. Flores had commanded the annual trading fleets that sailed between Spain and America (sometimes larger than the Armada itself); Bertendona and Oquendo had also commanded flotillas sailing from Spain into the North Sea and back. They, like almost all the other members of the council, had also taken part in Spain's swift conquest of Portugal in 1580 and of the Azores in 1582–83. Bobadilla, the senior general, had campaigned for twenty years in the Netherlands, Portugal, and Italy.

Yet despite all their achievements, not a single officer had confronted a situation similar to the one that faced them on August 9, 1588. To begin with, the English had repeatedly demonstrated their tactical superiority at sea. According to one senior Spanish officer, the English had been "able to tack four or five times in the time it took us to go about once," while, according to another, in comparison with some of their English adversaries, even the swiftest ship in the Armada "appeared to be standing still." Not a single Armada ship had managed to close with an adversary so that its soldiers could get on board and gain control. Instead, the English had forced the surrender of four galleons and bombarded at least one other ship so severely that she sank with almost all hands. Many other ships emerged from the battle severely damaged. Oquendo reported to the council that his own flagship "lay open through incoming shot, so that the pump was working night and day." Juan Gómez de

Medina worried that his flagship was so "damaged by the artillery with which the English Armada had bombarded him, as
well as by the recoil of the guns he had fired against them," that
she could no longer keep up with the fleet. Yet a third galleon
was "a thing of pity to see, riddled with shot like a sieve," while
the English had assailed a fourth "so heavily with their guns that
they completely shattered her." According to her captain, she
had received "damage from the many shots which the ship had
received below and aloft and from the prow to the stern, and below the waterline in places difficult to repair."

The duke listened grimly to these and other demoralizing
after-action reports. He then reported that the fleet "had no ammunition left, not even two roundshot with which to withstand
the enemy." Nevertheless, that morning he had tried a desperate gamble. The English fleet continued to follow the Armada,
in battle array, about four miles astern. Hoping to provoke the
melee that had eluded him thus far, the duke ordered the Armada to turn and face its pursuers. To everyone's surprise, the
English halted and kept their distance. Puzzled, the duke now
hoisted the signal flag to summon his council and get their advice on what to do next.

• • •

It is here that we encounter a "node of uncertainty": a point at
which historians would give almost anything to know how and
why a critical decision was taken, but lack the necessary evidence. No minutes survive for the meeting of the council of war
on August 9, 1588, and although five subsequent accounts of
the Armada campaign mention the discussion, only three came
from participants. Medina Sidonia included the council's final
decision in his *Campaign Journal*, but did not record the preceding discussion. The other two reports came from Recalde and

Leiva, present for most (but not all) of the council's discussion. Leiva gave the most explicit account of what had happened in a letter written to Recalde a week afterward:

> *They did not tell us about anything until after it had been decided; neither did they call us to the council except when they discussed starting talks about surrendering to the enemy. You and I were of the opinion that we should return to the Channel and that there we should complete and execute what our king commanded. They told us that they had neither powder nor cannonballs nor supplies, and in those circumstances we bowed to their judgment, with which, sir, I shall console myself no matter what happens later.*

What more did "they" say? If I had been there at the council meeting, among the staff officers who looked on as the Armada's senior officers debated their fate, what might I have heard?*

> *The Duke:* . . . so that, gentlemen, is our current situation. What are we to do now?
>
> *Juan Gómez:* Your Grace, my ship, built in Rostock and thus meant to sail these seas, sustained such heavy damage that it can barely sail or steer and, as you just informed us, she is not alone. I have to tell you now that, just before I left to come here, I heard some of the crew murmuring that if we did not surrender, we should all drown.
>
> *Bobadilla:* I always said the crews on those German merchantmen were totally unreliable! We

---

*Wherever possible in the dialog that follows, I have used words and phrases used about the Armada by the participants themselves, albeit in subsequent letters rather than at the council. Other quotations come from the surviving sources.

should have replaced them all with Spaniards before we left.

Bertendona: Just a minute. Perhaps the pusillanimous Germans have an idea we can use. Father *[he turns toward Medina Sidonia's chaplain, standing behind the duke]*, we Catholics believe that it is not necessary to keep faith with heretics: Am I right?

Chaplain: Right, Sir!

Bertendona: And is it not true, Don Francisco, that if we could only get our ships alongside the English warships, our troops and crews are in every case far more numerous than theirs?

Bobadilla: Yes. So far as I can see, the English ships carry no troops whatever, just sailors. It seems that they rely entirely on their artillery. If we could ever get alongside them and board, they seem to have no second line of defense.

Bertendona: Well then *[he smiles slowly]*, why don't we offer to surrender and then, when their ships draw close to take over, we board them? We would not have to capture them all, just enough to deter the rest from opposing us. Then we could sail back to Flanders, pick up the Duke of Parma and his troops, and carry out the invasion. What do you think about that, Chaplain?

Chaplain: I see no theological obstacle, Sir. They are all heretics, enemies of God. And God will not allow them to prevail.

Oquendo: No theological obstacle, perhaps, but here's a practical one. How do you propose to deliver this surrender?

Ojeda: I'm ashamed to say that most of the ships in my squadron, which normally handle communications, have still not rejoined the fleet after the battle.

The Duke: And I just sent my barge away to collect Recalde and . . .

[At this point the door of the great cabin opens and in stalks Recalde followed by Leiva. The duke brings them up to date on the council's discussion, which leaves both men stunned. Before they can speak, Bobadilla hastily interjects.]

Bobadilla: Well, perhaps it is not yet time to discuss surrender. Let us first discuss other possible strategies.

Leiva: We haven't got many. We all knew that entering the Narrow Seas was a mistake. I opposed as much as I could the decision to anchor off Calais, but nobody listened.

Recalde: Yes, once we entered the North Sea the enterprise was doomed, and so . . .

The Duke: Gentlemen, the urgent question before us now is not how we got here, but how we get out.

[There is an awkward pause, after which Leiva clears his throat.]

Leiva: Well, since Your Grace asks for our advice, I will be frank. The king entrusted us with the most important mission in the world, with the whole world looking on. Eventually we shall all have to explain what we expected, and what we did, to His Majesty. How will we—how will you *[he looks straight at the duke]*—explain to him our failure to carry out his plan? I see only one possibility. Return to the coast of Flanders so that we can complete and execute what His Majesty commanded: Escort the Duke of Parma and his men to the coast of England, and support their landing in every way we can.

Recalde: I second that motion.

Diego Flores [sarcastically]: Had you come to the council when the duke called you, gentlemen, you would have heard him say that our leading ships have all sustained serious structural damage and they also lack sufficient ammunition to engage the English fleet which, as you may have noticed, lies in full battle order only four miles to windward.

Recalde: Funnily enough, Señor Flores, I did catch sight of the English fleet as I came here this afternoon! But I noticed something else about it. This morning, when His Grace turned his ship to face the enemies, what happened?

Bertendona: The English took in sail and refused to close with us, as usual! Do you think that was significant?

Recalde: Yes. Admittedly they also hung back as we sailed up the Channel. We took it for cowardice at the time, but we now know they are no cowards. I believe they were already running short of ammunition and were trying to conserve it until they were sure about our strategy. Only then did they attack in full strength. But now, knowing our plan, they still hang back. Why?

Leiva: Aha, because they are short of ammunition just like us! Yesterday they must have fired off thousands of rounds.

Bertendona: They can only carry so many rounds. Their ships are smaller than ours and yet some of them must have fired five hundred times yesterday. They must be running low on ammunition; some of them may be out, just like us. *[Aside to Recalde, but overheard by Flores]* I wish I knew how they manage to fire so fast. . . .

Diego Flores: That's precisely the problem, gentlemen. We *don't* know how they can fire so fast, nor do we know how many rounds they carry. It would be insanity to risk our ships in their current state in another engagement when we have no idea—I repeat, *no* idea—whether or not we would receive another bombardment like yesterday's. Our ships could not survive a second day of that. We might as well surrender our ships and save our men as try a death charge that will kill us all.

The Duke [suddenly animated]: Absolutely not! I will hear no more talk of surrender. A knight should be prepared to fight to the death, and I am prepared to go down fighting. We *will* make another attempt to join forces with the Duke of Parma.

Diego Flores: Your Grace's words remind us all of our duty, and yet I perceive a major obstacle: The wind is against us. We could not go back just now even if we wanted to.

Leiva [sneering]: But you heard His Grace, Señor Flores: We *do* want to. And what alternative do we have? Shall we follow the example of Columbus and Magellan and make a voyage into the unknown? If we do not sail back the way we came, there is only one other route to Spain, and that is to sail northward around Scotland and then westward around Ireland. By the time we get into the North Atlantic it will be September, and the terrible storms we have all heard about could drive our entire fleet aground and wreck it. Better to die fighting than to drown!

Recalde: And even if we did get round Ireland, I might add, we would probably find the English fleet lying in wait for us. And here's one more problem if we sail around Scotland and Ireland. Although I've seen many seas, I have never sailed that route. Neither, I suspect, has anyone else here. Señor Flores, the king placed you in charge of navigation for the fleet. Did you perhaps bring maps or charts for the route you now propose so we can steer a safe course?

Flores: Of course I didn't! No one ever thought we would need them. We have already sailed beyond the area covered by the charts we brought from Spain . . .

Recalde: Oh.

Flores: . . . but I do have charts that cover the south and southwest of Ireland and, if memory serves, Señor Recalde personally sailed those coasts about ten years ago.

Recalde [smiling at Flores for the first time]: You are correct, thank you. I navigated an area called Blasket Sound in 1579. Unfortunately, however, we are now, what?—a thousand miles? fifteen hundred?—away from there. How do you propose to guide all our damaged ships in safety back into the seas covered by the charts you *did* bring?

[There is an awkward silence.]

Bobadilla: Perhaps there is another way. What about steering for some port in Norway and spending the winter there, refitting and rearming. Then we could come back again next year and carry out His Majesty's plan.

Juan Gómez: Your Grace, with respect, I see two obstacles to Don Francisco's plan. First, some of those German sailors whom Don Francisco so despises have told me that Norway is the most barren land they have ever seen, just small fishing villages and only a couple of small towns. We have thirty thousand men aboard this fleet—correction: We *had* thirty thousand men aboard this fleet *[the duke winces]*—which is larger than most towns in Spain. Part of the food we brought with us is rotten, and the edible items are already running low. How could a barren area ever feed all our men over the entire winter? Second, just suppose that the English are, like us, currently short of ammunition. Won't they use the winter to repair and rearm from their dockyards? We, however, have no idea where—or if—we can find gunpowder, cannonballs, rigging, and all the other artifacts this fleet needs. So when we leave Norway and meet the English again next spring, the odds will be even more against us.

Leiva: Much as I like the idea of occupying the land of the Goths and taking our revenge for their occupation of Spain all those centuries

ago, your Germans are right. Better to go down
fighting than to starve!
Recalde: Why are we discussing these distant and
dangerous destinations when, only fifty miles
away, the Duke of Parma is waiting for us with
his men and his barges. Only yesterday we
could see the Flanders coast. Parma will have
heard our guns; he will assume we will return
and therefore keep his troops embarked. I say
we should take the risk and return. The king has
given us strict orders. He will expect strict execution.

*[A long pause follows as each member of the council
ponders how Philip II might react if they fail to follow
his instructions. Gradually, all eyes turn to Medina
Sidonia, who will be the first to suffer the king's wrath
if he makes the wrong choice. . . .]*

The historical record now resumes, because the Medina Sidonia's *Campaign Journal* states that the council reached the unan-
imous decision that, if at all possible, the Armada should turn
about and return to the Channel for a second attempt to pick
up Parma and invade England. Only if the wind proved contrary would the fleet attempt the long north-about return to
Spain. The members of the council returned to their ships, leaving the duke—once again advised only by Diego Flores and
Bobadilla—to wait for the wind to change. He did not wait long.
According to Recalde's *Campaign Journal*, the next day,

*Wednesday, the 10th of August, the decision to return to
Spain [by the northern route] was notified to the whole fleet
and the duke gave orders that all ships should reduce the rations to a half pound of biscuit, a half pint of wine and a*

pint of water to each person per day, so that supplies should
not run out because of the long voyage.

This was indeed, as Recalde boldly informed the duke, a "dreadful decision." Apart from all the hazards related to the council, even if all the food aboard the fleet had been edible (and it soon became clear that much of it was not), the reduced rations rep-

CHART OF THE ARMADA'S COURSE.
Pine's Engraving, 1739, of Tapestry then in House of Lords.

An English engraving of 1739 replicates "A Chart shewing several Places of Action between the English and Spanish Fleets with the Places where several of the Spanish Ships were destroyed in their return to Spain, North about the British Islands." The original, a tapestry commissioned by Admiral Howard, the commander of the English Navy, was woven in the 1590s. The council meeting on August 9 took place just where the fleets are shown off "Yarmouth."

resented a daily intake of less than a thousand calories: not enough to sustain life, let alone health, for any extended period.

Two days later, as the two fleets drew level with the Firth of Forth, the English fell back. Recalde and Leiva had guessed correctly: The English shot lockers were almost empty, and their strategy had become (as their commander put it) to "put on a brag countenance" in order to fool the Armada. The English were also short of provisions, and some ships had developed plague. They therefore returned to port instead of lying in wait for the Armada off Ireland; but, as Juan Gómez had predicted, the English refitted and rearmed their vessels over the winter, and in 1589 an English counterarmada sailed to Spain and sacked the port of Corunna. Juan Gómez was also correct about the inadequate resources of Norway: In the event, when three damaged Armada ships put ashore there, their crews almost starved.

Juan Gómez's ship ran aground, on Fair Isle, because of the severe damage sustained in battle, and he was lucky to escape first to Scotland and then to Spain. Some other members of the council perished when either autumn storms or the urgent need for food and water led to the wreck of over twenty Armada ships on the coast of Ireland. Don Diego Enríquez drowned when storms drove his ship onto Streedagh Strand on Ireland's western coast; Don Alonso de Leiva also drowned amid storms off northern Ireland. Miguel de Oquendo guided a few ships back to his native San Sebastián, but died there a week later. Although Juan Martínez de Recalde's superb seamanship (and his experience in 1579) enabled him to pilot his ship into Blasket Sound to take on fresh water, he returned to Spain a broken man, telling a minister as he came ashore that he was "inconsolable at seeing how such a glorious victory slipped through our fingers." He died two weeks later.

Neither he nor Leiva therefore survived to give a personal account to Philip II, as they intended, of how exactly the Armada had failed to achieve its objectives and whom they held responsible. So although Diego Flores was imprisoned and never again held a position of command, he gained his freedom after only a year. Don Francisco de Bobadilla went on to command an army, and Martín de Bertendona became commander of the fleet. The Duke of Medina Sidonia partially recovered his reputation by conducting a spirited defense of Cádiz when attacked by an Anglo-Dutch fleet in 1596, and continued to serve his king in Andalusia until he died in 1615. These men were doubly lucky: At least half of those who set sail on the Armada in July 1588 did not celebrate the following Christmas with their families. Perhaps five thousand ended the year in an enemy prison; probably twice as many perished in action, in a shipwreck, or when they sought refuge on a hostile shore. Almost half of the ships also failed to return. A few commandeered merchantmen seem to have secretly returned to their home port, and the English captured two large vessels; but the rest perished either on the voyage or soon after their return.

It could have been worse. The fate of the Armada, in the words of one Spaniard of the day, may have been "the greatest disaster to strike Spain in over six hundred years" (that is, since the Moorish conquest), but at least Medina Sidonia had brought back half the fleet and half the men. If he had heeded the advice of those who advocated surrendering the whole fleet on August 9, 1588, it is hard to see how Spain could have defended itself against the counterarmada that was launched the following year, let alone maintained her dominant position in European affairs for another half century.

Further Reading

Colin Martin and Geoffrey Parker, *The Spanish Armada,* 2d ed. (Manchester, 1999).

Garrett Mattingly, *The Armada* (Boston, 1959).

Peter O. Pierson, *Commander of the Armada: The Seventh Duke of Medina Sidonia* (New Haven, CT, and London, 1989).

Geoffrey Parker, "Anatomy of Defeat: The Testimony of Juan Martínez de Recalde and Don Alonso Martínez de Leyva on the Failure of the Spanish Armada in 1588," *Mariner's Mirror* 90 (2004): 314–47.

KATHERINE DUNCAN-JONES

The Globe Theatre, February 7, 1601

Katherine Duncan-Jones, formerly Professor of English Language and Literature at the University of Oxford, is a Senior Research Fellow of Somerville College, Oxford, and an Honorary Senior Research Fellow of University College, London. Apart from a single year in Cambridge, she has spent her adult life in Oxford, where her research and teaching have focused on Elizabethan and Jacobean literature. Among her books are *Sir Philip Sidney: Courtier Poet* and *Ungentle Shakespeare: Scenes from His Life*. She has also prepared two volumes in the Arden edition of Shakespeare's works: *Shakespeare's Sonnets* and, with Professor Henry Woudhuysen, Shakespeare's *Narrative and Other Poems*. Professor Duncan-Jones has published numerous articles on Elizabethan and Jacobean literature as well as many theater reviews, mostly of productions of plays by Shakespeare and his contemporaries, in the *(London) Times Literary Supplement*. She is currently working on a book-length study of Shakespeare's reputation within his own lifetime.

Her contribution to this book brings to life what was probably the most fraught performance ever of a Shakespearean play.

The Globe Theatre, February 7, 1601

Early February was hardly the best time of year for an outdoor performance. The days were still gray and short, with long frosty nights. Crisp quilts of snow trimmed the complex traceries of London's rooftops, spires, and chimneys. But ever since construction of the Globe Theatre in Southwark in August 1599, the close friends of Robert Devereux, Second Earl of Essex, had been addicted to theatregoing. These lively young courtiers found afternoons at the Bankside theatres much more to their taste than the complex intrigues and stiff protocols of Elizabeth I's court in Westminster. As Rowland Whyte reported to Robert Sidney in October 1599, "My Lord Southampton and Lord Rutland come not to the court; the one doth very seldom; they pass away the time in London merely in going to plays every day."

London—which here includes the Bankside, south of the Thames—was a political and geographical entity wholly distinct from the court, which was generally based in Westminster during the winter months. What at first may have looked like a natural cultural gap between the habitual recreations of an elderly female monarch and those of noblemen young enough to be her grandsons soon emerged as a far more dangerous division—one that seemed to point sinisterly toward the possibility of her deposition or even assassination.

Orphaned at the age of ten, the Earl of Essex (born 1565) had grown up as one of the queen's own wards. In the summer of 1587 he became her special favorite and close companion, spending long relaxed evenings with her in private. One of his servants observed that "my lord [Essex] is at cards or one game or other with her, that he cometh not to his own chamber till the birds sing in the morning."

In the next few years he received major promotions and rewards from Elizabeth. But he soon displayed a moody and headstrong temperament. In 1589 he joined an expedition to Portugal without the queen's permission. Though sent by her on an expedition to northern France in 1591, he did not fully obey his instructions, a pattern that was to continue. Both abroad and at home Essex showed an independence of spirit and of political allegiance that was bound, sooner or later, to pose a threat to the authority of the queen who had given him so much. His last and most responsible military appointment came in 1598–99. He was appointed as general to the large expeditionary force sent over to Ireland to quell a long-standing rebellion against English rule led by Hugh O'Neill, Earl of Tyrone. Here Essex immediately spent too much money, bestowed knighthoods on large numbers of his followers, and entirely failed to adhere to previously agreed plans of campaign. Rather than achieving military victory over Tyrone and his forces, he chose to have a private "parley" with him. For half an hour the two noblemen spoke to each other, both mounted on horseback, on opposite sides of a shallow river. They appeared to be very friendly with each other, and Essex claimed to have secured a truce. News that Elizabeth was severely displeased with this deal prompted him to hurry back to England to talk to her himself, contrary to explicit instructions that he was to stay at his post in Ireland until recalled. Still sweaty and caked with Irish mud, he entered her bedchamber at Nonsuch Palace on the morning of September 24, 1599, where he immediately knelt and kissed her bony hands and shriveled breasts. Elizabeth was still in her nightgown, her long gray hair loose about her shoulders. He hoped to regain her love by a combination of self-pity and macho charm, as he had so often done in the past. Later that day, however, after the astonished Elizabeth had had time to reflect and consult her counselors, Essex was taken prisoner pending the preparation of various charges against him.

Elizabeth and Essex never saw each other after that day. In June 1600 he was deprived of all his offices (and the fees attached to them) and sentenced to house arrest "during the queen's pleasure." By the beginning of February 1601, Essex had been a prisoner for sixteen months. For a young man who had had so much, and only a couple of years earlier had been widely viewed as the greatest man in England, this was a terribly crushing situation. Though Essex scribbled letters to Elizabeth expressing abject repentance and endless adoration, it would not be surprising if, in truth, he longed for her death as his only sure release.

Meanwhile, Elizabeth had other favorites who were less

A nineteenth-century caricature by Richard Doyle shows an enraged Queen Elizabeth shaking her fist at the defiant Robert Devereux. He endures the scolding with stoic pride while petrified court members stare in disbelief.

volatile. Her long-term friend and adviser Lord Burghley had died full of years in August 1598, despite being lovingly fed and nursed by the queen herself. These days she seemed perhaps even more intimately devoted to his son, Robert Cecil, who had inherited his father's wisdom in statecraft along with his mother's bookishness and high intelligence. Cecil also displayed the special tenacity and determination often found in those who live with a physical disability. He endured his bent spine, and the malicious taunts that it provoked, with dignity and stoicism. It required even more stoicism for him to accept the fact that both of his children—motherless since 1597—were affected by similar problems. Cecil wrote to his son while he was at Cambridge urging him to "grow taller," while his daughter, more seriously afflicted, was kept away from the merciless gaze of courtiers. Though just under forty in 1601, Robert Cecil already looked like a little old man, white-haired and stooping. As Elizabeth's devoted "beagle"—technically her first secretary, the equivalent of a modern British prime minister—he was almost always in attendance either holding papers at her elbow or else kneeling in doglike submission at her feet. Others close to the queen, such as her "little black husband" Archbishop Whitgift, and the Lord Admiral Charles Howard, hero of the 1588 defeat of the Spanish Armada, were genuinely elderly, one seventy, the other sixty-five.

In contrast to these Privy Councillors, Essex and his friends were fine physical specimens, excellent horsemen, and energetic sportsmen. They were especially skilled in swordsmanship. Among the many books recently dedicated to Essex was a groundbreaking practical treatise on swordsmanship, George Silver's *Paradoxes of Defence*, which he and his friends found of immediate use. In 1600 the Privy Council took measures to prevent a duel between the young Lord Grey (born 1575) and the Earl of Southampton (born 1573), dedicatee of William Shakespeare's *Venus and Adonis* (1593). Formerly an associate of Essex, Grey now allied himself strongly with Cecil and with the court. On January 9, 1601, these two fiery noblemen encountered each other on horseback in the Strand. In the ensuing scuffle, Southampton's boy page had a hand lopped off by one of Lord Grey's much more numerous retinue. Though Grey was punished with imprisonment, to Essex's increasingly paranoid circle his assault on Southampton in the Strand looked like a direct, physical threat from the court faction, and an injury that required to be revenged sooner rather than later. Grey's release from prison on February 2 was among several triggers for Essex's attempted coup a week later. It seemed that the queen and her advisers were not willing to protect Essex and his friends from their murderous enemies. When Essex was summoned to appear before the Privy Council on February 7, he didn't go, having convinced himself that the court party wanted him dead.

The play that the Essex party asked the Lord Chamberlain's Men to perform at the Globe that day was one that opened, very aptly, with a violent dispute between two leading courtiers who are promised, and then suddenly denied, an opportunity to settle their differences by means of public combat. Richard II's refusal to permit the nobility to settle their disputes in such a time-honored manner was one of many striking parallels between himself and Elizabeth I. It was a risky policy, for the suppression of such combats was liable to provoke furious resentment among feuding nobles, who might now divert their rage toward the monarch who had frustrated both of them. In the case of Richard II, the aggrieved Henry Hereford, Earl of Bolingbroke, returned from banishment in France to cultivate popular support and take possession of the throne, on which he had some claim through descent. In 1399, Richard was deposed and soon afterward murdered, or else, as some chroniclers said, he died of starvation. Bolingbroke became King Henry IV. Further unhappy parallels linked Elizabeth with Richard. Both monarchs lacked heirs. Richard's first marriage was childless. His second, to a girl of seven, was probably never consummated. Elizabeth was unmarried, and by this late stage of her reign had fully convinced her subjects that she intended to remain so. Nor could even the most enraptured of her loyal subjects hope that, in her late sixties, she could conceive a bodily heir. Both Richard and Elizabeth were accused of surrounding themselves with flatterers. In the later years of Elizabeth's reign, court toadies were popularly known as "Richard II's men." Both monarchs experienced severe difficulties with neighboring Ireland. Both, in later years, presided over an England whose economy was in serious decline. Richard raised money by leasing out, or "farming," crown lands; Elizabeth raised it by bestowing "monopolies," a form of privatized taxation, on her favored courtiers. Elizabeth's recent refusal to renew Essex's "farm of sweet wines"— a license to receive taxes on imports of such wines—had left him almost ruined.

Always superstitious, a nervous Elizabeth survived the extremely inauspicious two-century anniversary of Richard's deposition and death in 1399. However, she could never feel herself to be out of danger, for she continued to be acutely sensitive to further parallels between Richard's reign and her own. Whereas Henry Bolingbroke had been banished to faraway France, her former favorite the Earl of Essex had been banished from court by barely two miles. While he was under house arrest, he and his many friends and supporters composed a kind of alternative, dissident court in the City of London. His powerful Welsh steward Sir Gilly Meyrick was allowed to keep open house not just for Essex's fellow noblemen, but also for radical Puritan preachers, Catholic recusants, and disaffected intellectuals led by the Oxford scholar Henry Cuffe. Among such company, players, too, came and went freely. Many earlier performances of *Rich-*

ard II took place in or near Essex House, conveniently located in the Strand close to the Middle Temple.

On a chilly winter day it might have seemed more practical to have *Richard II* once again performed indoors, in the great hall of Essex's own large house. The decision to commission a performance by the Lord Chamberlain's Men at the Globe suggests a deliberate intention to include the ordinary citizens of London in the favorite recreations of Essex and his conspiratorial circle. The player Augustine Phillips, whom Meyrick approached, claimed to have been reluctant to agree to his request because he believed "that play of King Richard to be so old and so long out of use as that they should have small or no company at it." Yet in practice the company probably had the usual playbills printed and posted up around the city to publicize the performance, and rumors that it had been specially called for by Essex's noble friends would ensure a good crowd despite the poor weather.

The play insisted on by Essex's friends is alluded to in some documents as "Henry IV," thus linking it with the *Life of Henry IV* by the historian John Hayward, dedicated to Essex in 1599. This bestselling work was quickly suppressed, and Hayward spent the rest of Elizabeth's reign as a prisoner. However, though Hayward's prose history had been called in to be burned, Shakespeare's richly poetic play of *Richard II* was still in the public domain. Editions of it had been printed in 1597 and (twice) in 1598. At this time the play may have been described as *Henry IV*, to indicate that it covered the same events as Hayward's censured book. Though the 1623 first folio separates *Richard II* from *1* and *2 Henry IV*, during the closing years of Elizabeth's reign the three plays may have been known as the first, second, and third parts of *Henry IV*.

Augustine Phillips and his colleagues must have been aware that they were being drawn into dangerous territory. They hoped, however, that the patronage of the lord chamberlain, George Carey, Lord Hunsdon, a much-loved close cousin of the queen, would protect them from serious consequences should the queen herself survive any impending debacle. And should she be displaced, even perhaps assassinated, they could hope for generous treatment from the new regime. In fact, so excellent was this playing company that they couldn't really lose. Any party in power was likely to wish to employ them. This proved to be the case when the King of Scots came to the throne in 1603 and immediately took the Chamberlain's Men under his own personal patronage and protection.

At midday on February 7, Sir Gilly Meyrick and others took dinner at "one Gunter's house" near the Temple Gate. Gunter is a Welsh name (Gwendwr), and their host probably belonged to Meyrick's extensive network of Welsh connections. Among the other dozen diners were Lord Mounteagle, Sir Charles Percy, Sir Christopher Blount, and the Master of the Ordnance Sir John Davies (not to be confused with either of the poets of the same name). From the Temple Gate it was a short stroll down to the Temple Stairs, where they hired barges to take them across the Thames to Southwark. Sir Charles Percy had been a prime mover in persuading the Chamberlain's Men to stage *Richard II* that afternoon. He was one of seven younger brothers of the Earl of Northumberland. As a younger brother with no realistic chance of getting a major inheritance, he was more or less bound to be something of a malcontent, rich in lineage and in the silk doublets permitted only to the nobility but distinctly poor in prospects. Sir Charles could also lay claim to an honorably rebellious descent, for his forebear Henry Percy (sometimes called Harry), nicknamed Hotspur, had offered a serious challenge to the kingship of Henry IV. Perhaps it was because of the arrogance natural to one of his rank that Sir Charles Percy, unlike his companions, was late in arriving at the theatre that afternoon (plays normally began at two o'clock). Perhaps it also took him some time to settle Master Gunter's bill for dinner, or else to persuade him to put it on the slate. In any case, his celebrated ancestor, Harry Hotspur, would not make an appearance in the play until the end of act 3.

All the noble spectators knew the play extremely well already. The most exciting scene, the one in which Richard reluctantly and ditheringly hands over the golden crown to Bolingbroke, occurred late on. Meanwhile, there was time for the illustrious company to amuse themselves in the Globe Theatre's Lords' Room, a large and well-fitted balcony on the stage right where they themselves contributed much to the spectacle enjoyed by groundlings and holders of twopenny "rooms." While more humble audience members pulled their cloaks tightly around them and warmed their hands on roasted chestnuts, the young lords enjoyed the comfort provided by braziers of hot coals and an ample supply of sweet wines—the purchase of which, alas, no longer enriched their absent leader the Earl of Essex. Still confined to his house, Essex spent that Saturday afternoon lying on his bed after an exhausting bout of tennis. Neither the game of tennis nor his ensuing siesta sweating it off allayed his intense agitation and furious paranoia. He was supposed to appear before the Privy Council that very day, but had decided not to do so. Something had to give, quite soon.

I wish I'd been in the Globe Theatre that afternoon, not just to see the swashbuckling young blades carousing in the Lords' Room, but to observe their interaction both with the players and with the rest of the audience. Was it William Shakespeare, the player best qualified to memorize all of the king's long and richly poetic speeches, who performed the part of Richard, opposite his colleague Richard Burbage as Bolingbroke? The close friendship of these two brilliant men, both onstage and off, lent wonderful assurance to the manner in which they played "off" each other. Shakespeare, the poet-player, as the narcissistic, posturing Richard, finds his verbose poetical fancies punctured by Bolingbroke's laconic common sense. Burbage was a practical man, skilled in carpentry and painting. He was also known as a bit of a bruiser, whereas there is no evidence that Shakespeare was ever violent. Though the two kings played by Shakespeare and Burbage are mortal opposites, there is a marvelous moment when their minds and imaginations suddenly chime in unexpected sympathy. Richard sends for a mirror so that he can examine the evidence of his sufferings reflected in his ravaged face. But finding this inadequate, he impulsively smashes the glass:

> As brittle as the glory is the face . . .
> Mark, silent king, the moral of this sport,
> How soon my sorrow hath destroyed my face.

To this the new king, not quite so "silent" after all, responds in a line that can be read as prose, unusual in this all-verse play:

> The shadow of your sorrow hath destroyed the shadow of your face.

Richard is surprised, and impulsively grateful to Bolingbroke for this insight:

> Say that again!
> The shadow of my sorrow. Ha, let's see.
> 'Tis very true, my grief lies all within.

But by act 5, the man whose favorite emblem as King Richard was a golden sun in glory is a king no longer, but a solitary prisoner who knows that he will not have long to live. This change of regime, as enacted on February 7, was aptly mirrored in the sinking of the winter sun, with the Globe Theatre's stage now lit patchily by torches. Richard passes by on his way to the Tower of London, which Essex, in "real time," was considering seizing by force. Essex's indecision about whether to lead his followers eastward to the Tower or westward to Whitehall Palace was one of the reasons why his violent uprising on Sunday, February 8, came to so little. Meanwhile, at the Globe, Charles Percy's forebear, the Earl of Northumberland, tells the captured Richard, "You must to Pomfret, not unto the Tower." In faraway Pontefract Castle, near Wakefield, in Yorkshire, Richard is shown meeting his end bravely at the hand of one of Bolingbroke's followers, Piers of Exton. Exton immediately repents of the bloody deed. And, rather than rewarding the assassin to whom he had given encouragement, albeit ambiguously, the new king condemns him and vows to spend the rest of his life and reign mourning for Richard's death and striving to expiate his own guilt. Though the play showed an unpopular and childless monarch being forced to abdicate, and soon after, being assassinated, it offered no assurance that such a sequence of events was likely to lead to any better or more stable form of government.

The playwright, like the players, and like the Essex conspirators, left all options open. That is what made the piece so endlessly fascinating. Like Elizabeth, Richard was an anointed monarch, seen by many as divinely appointed and blessed with a semidivine charisma. Like Elizabeth, he had become remote and unpopular. Like Elizabeth, he surrounded himself with counselors who could be relied upon not to question his policies. Bolingbroke, in contrast, was a popular, accessible figure, much loved by the people, as Essex had been until the collapse of his Irish campaign in the autumn of 1599. Shakespeare's play can be read—and performed—as a celebration of the tragic brilliance of a divinely appointed king who is brutally, even sacrilegiously, murdered at the command of a prosaic "modern" ruler or secular opportunist. Yet it can equally well be received as an exemplary warning against the remote solipsism of Richard's style of monarchy, a style that determines the inevitability of its collapse. From moment to moment, almost from second to second, an audience will waver between fascination with Richard's aesthetic, quasi-divine charisma and respect for Bolingbroke's more straightforward grasp of political realities. That still applies to the play as performed today, but must have applied with a special intensity on February 7, 1601. I wish I could have seen Shakespeare and Burbage alternately—or perhaps even simultaneously—winning audience sympathy, and doing so in the presence of audience members for whom the play's historical subject matter had an absolutely immediate relevance.

After it was all over—after Essex had led his violent but ill-thought-out "rising" in the City of London, had faced trial in Westminster Hall, and been executed in the Tower of London—the ghost of King Richard II, together with that of Robert Devereux, still haunted the queen. She had survived the most immediately threatening conspiracy and uprising of her whole long reign—a conspiracy that was the more horrible because it was led by a young man whom she had once adored and on whom she had bestowed massive favors. Essex's name was not to be mentioned in her presence. Yet she could make it quite clear that she was still thinking about him, and about his treachery. The very same parallels that Essex and his supporters had invoked to legitimate their uprising were used quite differently by Elizabeth. She drew considerable comfort from considering the ways in which her own sufferings mirrored those of a much-wronged royal forebear.

Just six months after Essex's ill-fated rising, on August 4, 1601, Elizabeth received an elderly visitor in her privy chamber at Greenwich Palace. The constitutional lawyer and antiquary

William Lambard had been entrusted with the archive of ancient rolls and records housed in the Tower of London. He had reduced their contents to a collection of digests, or summaries, for the benefit of the queen, who insisted on seeing him in person. She took the book into her hands "cheerfully," saying, "You intended to present this book unto me by the Countess of Warwick, but I will none of that, for if any subject of mine do me a service, I will thankfully accept it from his own hands."

She read rapidly through the work in Lambard's presence and asked him to elucidate various legal terms, saying that "she would be a scholar in her [old] age." She then "fell upon" the account of Richard II's reign, saying, "I am Richard II, know ye not that?" Though Elizabeth did not mention Essex, Lambard knew exactly what she meant, commenting that "such a wicked imagination was determined by a most unkind gentleman, the most adorned creature that ever your Majesty made"—to which she replied, quick as a flash, "He that will forget God will also forget his benefactors; this tragedy was played forty times in open streets and houses."

"Forty" should not be taken too literally—it was the stock biblical figure for "a large number." Elizabeth was fully aware that Essex and his followers had been obsessed with the deposition of Richard II, and that after the suppression of Hayward's historical account, they turned instead to repeated theatrical enactments of "this tragedy." She then read further in Lambard's book and asked more questions about its Latin terminology. Then, returning to Richard II, she demanded "whether I had seen any true picture, or lively representation of his countenance and person?"

Lambard admitted that he had seen only "such as be in common hands."

As a final reward to him for his labors on her behalf, Elizabeth promised Lambard that as he made his way out of the palace he should be shown her own especially fine and authentic portrait of Richard II, a gift to her from Lord Lumley, "a lover of antiquities." Lambard died only two weeks after his memorable audience with the queen. She herself survived, still nervous about plots and treachery, until March 1603. Unlike Shakespeare's Richard, she was not assassinated. But she did refuse all food and drink in her final days. As a close student of the chronicles, she was aware that some described Richard, too, as dying of voluntary starvation.

Elizabeth was wise enough not to blame her Lord Chamberlain's Men for their performance of *Richard II* the day before Essex's attempted coup. She made this abundantly clear by having them perform a play at court on the very day on which she signed Essex's death warrant. This was Shrove Tuesday, a traditional time for partying. The play was most likely a comedy, and probably one of Shakespeare's. I would like to have seen that play, too. But most of all I would like to have seen Shakespeare's *Richard II* at the Globe Theatre on the afternoon of February 7.

Further Reading

Robert Lacey, *Robert, Earl of Essex: An Elizabethan Icarus* (London, 1971).

G. P. V. Akrigg, *Shakespeare and the Earl of Southampton* (London, 1968).

William Shakespeare, *King Richard II*, ed. Andrew Gurr (Cambridge, 1986).

JOHN H. ELLIOTT

With the Prince of Wales in Madrid, 1623

John H. Elliott was Regius Professor of Modern History at the University of Oxford until his retirement in 1997. Previously a lecturer in history at Cambridge University and Professor of History at King's College London, he was from 1973 to 1990 Professor of History at the Institute for Advanced Study in Princeton. He has specialized in the history of Spain, Spanish America, and Early Modern Europe. His books include *Imperial Spain, 1469–1716*, *The Old World and the New, 1492–1650*, *The Count-Duke of Olivares*, *Empires of the Atlantic World: Britain and Spain in America, 1492–1830*, and (with Jonathan Brown) *A Palace for a King* and *The Sale of the Century*, the catalog of an exhibition at the Prado Museum on the visit of Charles, Prince of Wales, to Madrid in 1623 and the eventual fate of Charles's art collection. Among Sir John's many awards have been the Balzan Prize, the Wolfson Prize, and the Parkman Prize, given by the Society of American Historians.

In this essay, he has us join the heir to the throne during an episode that must rank among the most unusual in the history of the English royal family.

With the Prince of Wales in Madrid, 1623

As darkness descended over Madrid on the evening of Friday, March 17, 1623, a travel-stained figure knocked on the door of the House of the Seven Chimneys, the residence of John Digby, Earl of Bristol, England's ambassador to Spain. The man, who gave his name as Mr. Thomas Smith and carried a portmanteau under his arm, insisted that he must speak to the ambassador in person. Outside the house, on the farther side of the street, another figure stood waiting in the shadows before being asked to enter. I should have loved to have seen the look of astonishment on Bristol's face as he found himself face-to-face not only with the Marquis of Buckingham, Lord Admiral of England and the favorite of King James I, but also with the king's only son and heir, Charles, Princes of Wales.

The journey of the two men had started on February 27 (or February 17 in England, which had failed to adopt the new Gregorian Calendar now in use through much of Continental Europe), when they slipped away from Buckingham's house in Essex and set out for the port of Dover. They had assumed for the journey the innocuous-sounding names of John and Thomas Smith and disguised themselves by putting on false beards.

In spite of, or perhaps because of, the disguise, they were briefly detained in Dover, but managed to talk their way out of the embarrassment and embarked for France. After sightseeing in Paris, where they lodged above a post-house, they and their two traveling companions, Francis Cottington, a diplomat who had served as chargé d'affaires in the Madrid embassy, and Endymion Porter, an Englishman whose Spanish family connections gave him a good knowledge of the language, made the ten-day journey to the Spanish border. From here the prince and the marquis, accompanied by a single servant, pressed on ahead to reach the Spanish capital five days later.

Travel in seventeenth-century Europe was generally uncomfortable and all too often dangerous: Roads were poor or nonexistent; roadside inns were dirty and infrequent; and wayfarers might at any moment be set upon by robbers or bandit gangs and relieved of their possessions, or their lives. For the heir to the throne of a major European state to travel in disguise and ride virtually unaccompanied across half the continent was an unprecedented event. Not surprisingly, as news of the Prince of Wales's extraordinary journey spread, it set all Europe talking.

What had induced the son of the King of England to embark on such a perilous undertaking? And what had induced his father to authorize such a harebrained project? The story went back nineteen years, to the Anglo-Spanish peace settlement of 1604, which brought to an end two decades of war between the England of Queen Elizabeth and the Spain of Philip II. Both monarchs were now dead. Philip II had been succeeded on the Spanish throne by his young son, Philip III, and Elizabeth on the English throne by an already experienced ruler, James VI of Scotland. The two countries were divided by religion and by national antipathies exacerbated by the long years of war. James VI and I, now the ruler of a united Great Britain, nurtured hopes of enhancing the prestige of the Scottish House of Stuart by marrying his children into the leading dynasties of Continental Europe. He also saw himself as the arbiter of Christendom, who would reconcile the warring faiths of Catholic and Protestant, and bring the blessings of peace to a war-torn continent. Spain, for its part, was anxious to see the heretical English return to obedience to Rome, or, at the very least, to alleviate the lot of the minority community of English Catholics, the so-called "recusants," who had been penalized for adhering to their faith during the long reign of Elizabeth.

It is not therefore surprising that the idea of an Anglo-Spanish marriage should have been floated during the course of the peace negotiations. The first talk was of a marriage between the Infanta Ana, the daughter of Philip III, and Prince Henry,

A 1624 painting by royal portraitist Daniel Mytens shows Charles I as the Prince of Wales. The soon-to-be king wears decorations from England's ancient order of chivalry, the Order of the Garter, including a pendant depicting Saint George slaying the dragon.

the elder of James I's two sons. But the Spaniards were adamant that the infanta could not marry a heretic, and that Henry should be brought up as a Catholic at the Spanish court. Since these conditions were unacceptable, the talk came to nothing. In 1612, Prince Henry died unexpectedly, and his sickly twelve-year-old brother Charles replaced him as heir to the British throne. Three years later the Infanta Ana was married to Louis XIII of France. The prospects for an Anglo-Spanish marriage hardly looked encouraging.

In 1613, however, a new Spanish ambassador, Don Diego Sarmiento de Acuña, was appointed to London, "the ablest minister by many degrees that hath been employed unto you from this State," Digby reported to James I from Madrid. Don Diego, who four years later was to become the Count of Gondomar, arrived in England with high hopes of drawing the country into the Spanish Habsburg web. Deploying his sharp wit and formidable diplomatic skills, the new ambassador struck up a close personal relationship with the king and broached again the idea of a dynastic union between the two royal houses. This time it was to be a marriage between Prince Charles and the Infanta Ana's younger sister, María, born in 1606.

By 1615 a draft marriage treaty had been prepared, and in Madrid a junta of theologians gravely discussed the issues involved in marrying the sister of the King of Spain to a heretic. James, for his part, needed the Spanish money that would come as a dowry, and was prepared to agree that for the first years of their life any children of the marriage should be brought up as Catholics, but he knew that it was politically impossible for him to accede to another condition, that he should allow his Catholic subjects liberty of worship. As conditions were batted to and fro between London and Madrid, the international situation began to deteriorate. James's son-in-law Frederick, the Elector Palatine, rashly accepted the crown of Bohemia, which had come out in rebellion against the Austrian Habsburgs, and not only lost his new kingdom but also most of his German lands, which were occupied in 1620 by Spanish forces moving down from Flanders. The English Parliament, strongly Protestant, clamored for military intervention on the Continent in support of Frederick and his wife, the princess Elizabeth. James I himself, while deeply concerned about the fate of his son-in-law and daughter, was anxious to avoid Continental entanglements and looking with increasing desperation for a diplomatic solution to the problem. Spain, for its part, was anxious that England should not come to the help of the Continental Protestants at a moment when Europe was descending into the conflagration that would later be known as the Thirty Years' War. The bait of a marriage might help keep England neutral.

At this moment a new regime came to power in Spain. Philip III died on March 31, 1621, at the age of forty-two. He was succeeded on the throne by his sixteen-year-old son, now Philip IV of Spain. The new monarch's favorite, the domineering Don Gaspar de Guzmán, Count of Olivares, at once began gathering the reins of power into his own hands. Olivares's objective, like that of his predecessors, was to avoid open hostilities between England and Spain, but he was in no hurry to conclude a problematic marriage alliance if he could achieve his objective by other means. He and his ministerial colleagues therefore sought to play for time, and in this they were helped by the fact that a papal dispensation would be needed for the marriage of the new king's sister to a heretic. Since Rome, like Madrid, was determined to wrest every possible concession from the King of England, time was indeed on his side.

As the months passed, the Prince of Wales grew increasingly impatient. A shy, reserved youth with a pronounced stammer, who had lived in the long shadow cast in life and death by his gifted elder brother Henry, Charles was anxious to make his own mark on the world. In this he was encouraged by George Villiers, Marquis of Buckingham, "the handsomest-bodied man of England," whose grace and charm had captivated the king and won him royal favor and high office. But James was now aging, and Buckingham had to look to his future. The prince was of an age when he was in love with the idea of falling in love, and Buckingham was all too happy to aid and abet him in his hopes and dreams. So, too, was Gondomar, who worked hard to promote the project for a marriage.

Exasperated by the failure of the diplomats to bring the marriage negotiations to a satisfactory conclusion, Charles and Buckingham decided to take matters into their own hands. In the spring of 1622 the prince approached Gondomar, who was on the point of returning to Madrid, and offered to travel to Spain in person and incognito, if that would persuade Philip IV to give him his sister's hand in marriage and let her return with him to England. An astonished Gondomar jumped to the obvious conclusion. The Prince of Wales would hardly make such an amazing offer and place himself so unreservedly in the hands of the King of Spain unless he were planning to convert to Rome.

It remained for the prince and the royal favorite to persuade the king that the best hope of breaking the diplomatic impasse was for the prince to travel to Spain to woo and win his bride. James was distraught, but after much slobbering and weeping finally gave his assent. "Baby" and "Steenie," as he called Charles and Buckingham, were to go like "two venturous knights" for "the daughter of Spain." So it was that, a few weeks later, two mud-stained travelers were ushered into the presence of the English ambassador in Madrid.

It would be good to know what was said in the conversation between the three men on that Friday evening in March 1623. No doubt Bristol was all obsequiousness and flattery, but inwardly he was seething. All his patient diplomacy, which seemed to him to be gradually edging the two parties toward an agreement, now threatened to be undone. The heir to the British throne, by disregarding all protocol and turning up uninvited in Madrid, had in effect made himself a hostage to the Spanish crown. Bristol's first task was to get a message through to Philip and his ministers, and this he did by way of Gondomar, now back in Madrid. If we do not know what the prince said to Bristol and Bristol to the prince, we know exactly what Olivares said to Gondomar and Gondomar to Olivares when an excited Gondomar went round to Olivares's apartments in the royal palace of the Alcázar early the next morning. "What brings your worship here at this hour and in such a cheerful mood?" asked the count. "Anyone would think the King of England is in Madrid." To which Gondomar replied, "Well, if not the king, at least the prince is here."

Olivares, who suspected nothing, was, not unnaturally, taken aback. On the one hand he was delighted, since he assumed, like Gondomar, that the prince could only have come to Madrid because he was on the point of converting to Catholicism. On the other, he was deeply concerned at the possible consequences of this unforeseen event, which might force his own hand and that of the king and drive them into approving a marriage they did not want unless James now agreed to conditions that he had hitherto found unacceptable. He at once went to see the king, who, in front of a crucifix at the head of his bed, took an oath that he would not give way on any point of religion that had not previously been conceded by the Pope. Turning to Olivares, he then promised to observe all the obligations of hospitality imposed upon him by the arrival of the prince. Returning to his apartments, Olivares settled down to prepare suitable arrangements for the formal reception and accommodation of the prince and his party. That afternoon he sent his coach round to fetch Buckingham, and the two royal favorites along with Gondomar, Bristol, and Cottington spent an hour together conversing in the coach before Olivares led Buckingham by a back entry into the royal apartments for a private audience with Philip. Olivares then accompanied Buckingham back to the House of the Seven Chimneys, where he greeted the prince in the name of the king.

The Spanish court was the most rigid of European courts, and it was necessary to conform to the strictest protocol. This meant that the prince's presence in Madrid, although now generally known and the subject of enormous speculation and excitement, could not be officially acknowledged until he had made his formal entry into the capital.

Etiquette was paramount, but the situation was so unprecedented that on the Sunday morning it was agreed that the prince should get his first glimpse of his intended bride when the king and queen and the infanta would ride in the park in their carriages, while Charles would surreptitiously observe them from Bristol's coach. The sight of the infanta, who was distinguished by a blue ribbon on her arm, duly persuaded Charles that he was more in love than ever. That evening, in the palace gardens after dark, Philip and Charles met for the first time. Preparations still had to be completed for the prince's state entry, but by Sunday, March 26, everything was ready, and the prince made his official entry into the capital amidst great public celebrations and took up residence in the suite of rooms hastily prepared for him in the royal palace.

Buckingham and the prince along with a growing entourage, as more and more courtiers came to join him from England, were to spend over five increasingly frustrating months in Madrid before leaving the capital on September 9 for the journey home. During that time they were entertained with endless rounds of festivities including tournaments, bullfights, theatrical performances, and fireworks displays. But on the principal point, the prince's request that he should be allowed to take the Infanta María home as his wife, the Spanish endlessly prevaricated. It became increasingly clear to them with every passing week that the prince had no intention of changing his religion. As a result, the more ardent he became in pursuit of the prize, the more obstacles they erected to ensure that it remained beyond his grasp.

• • •

It would have been fascinating to be in Madrid during those months and watch the drama move toward its dénouement of mutual disillusionment. All the principal actors were subsequently to play leading roles on the European stage. There was the Prince of Wales himself, starstruck by the sight of the infanta and overwhelmed by the grandeur and decorum of the Spanish court. Two years later, he would succeed his father as Charles I of England. There was his opposite number, Philip IV, youth-

This painting by a court artist depicts the fiesta held in the Plaza Mayor of Madrid on August 21, 1623, to entertain the Prince of Wales. From the central balcony the Infanta María, separated from the prince only by a balustrade, watches competing teams of eight horsemen engage in a mock battle hurling bulrush darts.

fully impressed by the culture and the aesthetic interests of a prince five years older than himself, and embarking on a long reign that would end in the loss of Spain's European hegemony to its old rival, France. There was Olivares, who for twenty years would dominate the European political scene until, under the pressures of war, Spain broke apart in his hands. There was Buckingham, who would return home to avenge the humiliations he had received at the hands of Olivares by declaring war on Spain, and would become the principal minister of Charles I, only to be struck down by an assassin's knife in 1628. And there was the fair-complexioned girl at the heart of it all—an infanta—who abhorred the idea of being married to a heretic and was saved from a fate worse than death when, after the collapse of the English marriage project, she married her Austrian cousin, who in due course succeeded his father as Holy Roman Emperor.

A handful of moments stand out among the many during those five months when one would have liked to be present as an eyewitness, while remaining as invisible as the prince when he lurked in the shadows outside the House of the Seven Chimneys. It would have been exciting to follow Charles and Philip as they toured the palace together, inspecting, with the eyes of budding connoisseurs, the Titians and other great Italian masters in the superb royal collection. It would have been enjoyable, if ultimately tedious, to drop in on some of the innumerable festivities laid on for the prince's benefit and watch him gaze at the infanta for half an hour on end, "as a cat does a mouse" in Olivares's words. There came a moment, too, when he was permitted to approach the infanta and kiss her hand, with the infanta replying in a few formal words. This was scarcely sufficient for a man who had cast himself in the role of a lovelorn knight-errant from the books of chivalry. Who would not have wished to be in the orchard garden of the Casa del

Campo six weeks later, when the infanta was taking a morning walk and, in one of the most bizarre episodes of the entire visit, looked up in horror to see the Prince of Wales spring down and run toward her from the top of the high garden wall after finding the gate inconveniently bolted? The infanta gave a shriek and ran back. Her elderly guardian fell on his knees before the prince and begged him to retire, unlocking the gate to enable him to do so.

There were other dramatic moments, too, including stormy confrontations between Olivares and Buckingham, and an extraordinary moment in July when Charles amazed his hosts by declaring that he was ready to accept the Spanish conditions on the understanding that the marriage would take place by Christmas. He may have been hoping to call the Spanish bluff, but if so he failed. Olivares rightly suspected that he would not, and could not, deliver on his promises, and the prince and Buckingham, for their part, had come to realize that the game was up. Every day it became more apparent that Charles would not be returning home before Christmas with the infanta as his wife, since Olivares insisted that she could not leave Spain until the spring, following the receipt of the Pope's formal consent to the marriage. More and more the prince was coming to look like a hostage of the King of Spain, as Bristol had feared.

The best that both parties could now hope for was an honorable exit from a dishonorable affair. The Spaniards were anxious to see the last of their awkward guest, and Philip showered him with presents, including twenty-four Arab horses and one of the jewels of the royal collection, Titian's magnificent portrait of the king's great-grandfather, the Emperor Charles V. On September 9, accompanied by Philip and a large retinue of Spanish noblemen, the prince left Madrid for the monastery-palace of the Escorial, whose wonders the two men explored together before going hunting in the woods. On the thirteenth, a few miles along the road leading north from the Escorial, the king and the prince had a final conversation. It would have been good to eavesdrop on the last courteous exchanges between them. Was each pretending to himself and the other that the marriage would still take place?

Yet, if forced to choose one moment when, more than any other, I would have wished to be present, it would have been either at court or a few days earlier in the Escorial, when the prince's portrait was sketched by a young artist who a few weeks later would officially be appointed painter to the king. The sketch has long since disappeared, but what would one not have given to see Diego de Velázquez at work on the portrait of the disappointed knight-errant who was destined for the kingship of England and death on the scaffold?

Further Reading

Jonathan Brown and John Elliott, eds., *The Sale of the Century: Artistic Relations between Spain and Great Britain, 1604–1655* (New Haven, CT, 2002).

Glyn Redworth, *The Prince and the Infanta* (New Haven, CT, 2003).

Alexander Samson, ed., *The Spanish Match: Prince Charles's Journey to Madrid, 1623* (London, 2006).

MORDECHAI FEINGOLD

By Fits and Starts: The Making of Isaac Newton's Principia

Mordechai Feingold is Professor of History at the California Institute of Technology. He is the author or editor of ten books, including *The Mathematicians' Apprenticeship: Science, Universities and Society in England, 1560–1640*, *Jesuit Science and the Republic of Letters*, and *The Newtonian Moment: Isaac Newton and the Making of Modern Culture*. *The Newtonian Moment* is the companion book to the exhibition that took place at the New York Public Library from October 2004 to February 2005 and at the Huntington Library in Pasadena, California, from March 2005 to December 2005. Professor Feingold was Curator of the exhibition.

In this essay Feingold begins his trip to late-seventeenth-century England with a visit to Trinity College, Cambridge, in August 1684. There he joins a cheerful twenty-seven-year-old scholar as he interviews the dour and formidable Lucasian Professor of Mathematics.

By Fits and Starts: The Making of Isaac Newton's Principia

Sometime in August 1684, a stranger called on Isaac Newton at Trinity College, Cambridge. The visitor was the twenty-seven-year-old Edmond Halley, a scholar-adventurer with an appetite for gaiety and irreverence who had spent the greater part of the previous eight years gallivanting around the globe in order to observe the heavens and meet the leading astronomers of the day. His host at Trinity was the forty-two-year-old Lucasian Professor of Mathematics, a somber, intensely private, and devout don who rarely left Cambridge and never ventured beyond the seventy-mile triangle of his native Lincolnshire, Cambridge University, and London. Halley had purposely traveled to Cambridge to pose to Newton a single question: Assuming that the sun exerts an attractive force that diminishes as the square of the distance, what would the shape of a planetary orbit be?

The topic had preoccupied English (and Continental) mathematicians and natural philosophers ever since the German astronomer Johannes Kepler posited between 1609 and 1618 three "rules" of planetary motion, purporting to explain *what* holds the five known planets and their (five known) satellites in place: 1) the heavenly bodies move in elliptical, not circular, orbits, with the sun at one focus of the ellipse; 2) planets traverse equal areas of space in equal time intervals—and hence move faster the closer they come to the sun; 3) there exists a precise ratio between the average distances of all planets from the sun and their annual revolutions around it—or more precisely, the cubes of the mean distances of the planets from the sun are proportional to the squares of their periodic times.

Looking back from the vantage point of his own momentous discoveries, Newton argued that Kepler had simply "guessed" his rules of planetary motion–empirically deducing them from the exquisite trove of astronomical observations bequeathed to him by the Danish astronomer Tycho Brahe. And this conclusion would take hold. Voltaire, for example, disseminated the view that Kepler had merely uncovered the effects of which Newton would discover the cause. Albeit somewhat unfair to Kepler, history nevertheless confirms that much of Newton's great accomplishment was the generalization, and mathematical demonstration, of Kepler's three rules.

Newton embarked on the route to his great discovery while still an undergraduate. Following the closure of Cambridge University in the summer of 1665 when the plague struck, Newton returned to Lincolnshire, and the next two years came to be known as his *anni mirabiles,* wonder years. As he would reflect in old age, during this period he had been "in the prime of [his] age for invention," applying himself to mathematics and philosophy "more than at any time since." Such singular application resulted in his discovery of the method of fluxions–the Newtonian form of infinitesimal calculus–as well as of his theory of light and colors. The climax of this exceptionally fertile period was Newton's successful formulation of the theory of universal gravitation, according to which an attractive force extends throughout empty space, governing the motion of celestial and terrestrial bodies alike, proportionally to their respective masses and inversely proportional to the square of their distances.

As the famous story about the genesis of Newton's discovery of universal gravitation goes, sitting in the garden one evening, the sight of a falling apple triggered in his mind a momentous train of thought: Was the power of gravity limited to short distances from the earth? Could such a power extend as far as the moon and "perhaps retain her in her orbit"? It would have been wonderful to have been there to witness the moment of discovery, though there was to be an even more important moment, as we shall see, years later. As it is, the story of the apple is apocryphal, and Newton already knew the principle of inertia, for he had read about it in René Descartes' *Principles of Philosophy*, according to which a body will remain in a state of rest or of uniform rectilinear motion unless acted upon by an external force. He was also well versed in Galileo Galilei's contributions to mechanics. All this information was essential to his discovery that uniform circular motion is the result of a continued deviation of a body moving from a straight line into a circular path due to a constant force (which would be called gravity) that is proportional to the circle's radius and divided by the square of the period. The properties of such a force—already discovered, though not published, by the Dutch physicist Christiaan Huygens, who called it centrifugal force, that is, the tendency of a body to flee from a center—when considered in conjunction with Kepler's third rule, enabled Newton to determine that in the context of uniform circular motion the force (i.e., gravity) is inversely proportional to the square of the distance. Emboldened by this breakthrough, Newton wanted to subject his revolutionary theoretical insights to a test. He calculated the rate of the force that keeps the moon in orbit and compared it with the force of gravity on the earth's surface. Unfortunately, Newton's estimate of the size of the earth was too low, and hence his estimate of the distance between the earth and the moon was insufficient as well. As might be expected, the calculations conformed only approximately to his expectation, and therefore Newton, despondently concluding that the sun's vortex, and not just gravity, affects the shape of the lunar orbit, abandoned the topic for nearly two decades.

However, it was more than an inadequate estimate that had defeated Newton. Notwithstanding his remarkable results, in

1666 Newton still considered the crucial force to be an attempt to recede from the center, and circular motion to be a state of equilibrium between two equal and opposing forces: centrifugal force away from the center versus the center's gravitational pull. Only in the 1680s did Newton abandon this notion of perfect balance and develop his concept of centripetal force—a force impelling a body to seek a center, not recede from it—and only in the 1680s did he recognize the significance of Kepler's second rule, which enabled him to generalize his previous insights into noncircular motion.

Quite likely what inspired Newton to consider the effect of gravity on the moon was his reading of Robert Hooke's *Micrographia*. The optical portion of the book played for Newton a role analogous to that of Descartes' *Principles of Philosophy*; that is, it represented an abundant and challenging resource that Newton set out to destroy, or at least to transform. Hooke's theory of colors, in particular, with all its deficiencies, provided the most comprehensive mechanist account to date of the various forms of generating colors, and he had raised the bar by stipulating that a true theory of colors must encompass all of them. Having successfully confronted that challenge, Newton appears to have turned his attention to a similar challenge proffered by Hooke in the final chapter of *Micrographia*. There, after briefly commenting that the moon and the earth shared not only physical features, but a principle of gravitation, Hooke called for a search after a universal principle of gravitational attraction, one that would account for the orbits of both the planets and their satellites.

Though Newton had abandoned the search for universal gravitation after his moon test failed to conform precisely to theory, Hooke became consumed with the problem. By 1666 he began lecturing on planetary motion at Gresham College, London, and eight years later he published a précis of his ideas as the conclusion to a short pamphlet, *An Attempt to Prove the Motion of the Earth,* in which he announced the discovery of several new types of motion "not dreamt of before." He further promised to reveal a new system of the world, "differing in many particulars from any yet known," after he had carried out additional experiments. This system would be grounded on the following principles: All celestial bodies are endowed with a gravitational power toward their own centers, which attracts other celestial bodies as well as acts on their respective surfaces; all moving bodies retain their rectilinear motion until deflected by an attractive force into orbit; and all such attractive forces vary in strength depending on their distances. Hooke conceded that hitherto he had failed to discover this ratio, but remained confident that this final step was well within his grasp.

Hooke's intuitiveness and experimental acumen were truly astonishing and, on the face of things, he appears to have been on the verge of unraveling the precise nature of planetary motion. Still, Hooke himself recognized that more was needed, especially as a far better mathematician, his close friend Sir Christopher Wren, cautioned him often about the insufficiency of intuition and qualitative reasoning. Thus Hooke continued to press on with his researches until his taking charge of the Royal Society's correspondence in 1679 presented him with the opportunity to approach Newton as part of his efforts to revitalize the proceedings of the Society. On November 24, Hooke requested Newton to renew his epistolary exchange with the Royal Society, and to appraise Hooke's hypothesis of celestial motion as the product of two compounded motions: a tangential motion and an attractive force toward a center that deflects uniform motion along a straight line into an orbit.

This correspondence was the first substantive contact between Hooke and Newton since the establishment of a fragile truce between the two in February 1676. They had been at odds since

1672, when Hooke had criticized a paper Newton submitted to the Royal Society about the properties of light. The sensitive Newton, who reacted badly to criticism, had had his dislike of the critic fed by Henry Oldenburg, Secretary of the Royal Society, who served as the conduit of letters to and from Cambridge. Oldenburg was an enemy of Hooke and portrayed him as a recalcitrant detractor of Newton. Unaware of such shenanigans, Newton credited Oldenburg's innuendos and consequently singled out Hooke for particular abuse when defending his theory of light and colors. Eventually, Hooke caught on and in January 1676 approached Newton directly to apprise him of Oldenburg's misrepresentations and propose that they commence a private exchange of letters, as befitted those intent on the "discovery of truth." Newton responded with civility laced with sarcasm, the crux of which appeared to be an acknowledgment of Hooke's contribution to optics—and Newton's building on it—but which in fact inflicted a cruel backhanded compliment on the deformed Hooke: "If I have seen further it is by standing on the shoulders of Giants." Hooke chose not to respond.

Hooke's 1679 letter to Newton made an oblique reference to Oldenburg's former machinations before proceeding to address planetary motion. It would have been fascinating to see and hear Newton's reaction to reading Hooke's letter, for the topic certainly pricked Newton's curiosity. Eventually, though, he replied that he had bid farewell to philosophy some years earlier and claimed ignorance of Hooke's theory of compounded motions. His other studies, Newton claimed, prevented him from corresponding with the Royal Society. Nonetheless, as if to make amends, he included an extended "fansy" of his own about the diurnal motion of the earth: a thought experiment concerning the descent of heavy bodies. Hooke interpreted Newton's guarded response as a positive nibble and, like an expert angler, attempted to ensnare the elusive Cambridge professor by extending the line. He exposed an error that Newton had committed in his thought experiment, before intimating—intriguingly—that he could amplify his analysis with other considerations that were "consonant" with his theory of "Circular motions compounded by a Direct motion and an attractive one to a Center."

Hooke miscalculated. Newton was no ordinary catch, and his indignation grew in direct proportion to his curiosity—not least because he resented being shown wrong, especially by Hooke. Yet he wrote back, accepting Hooke's correction of his thought experiment and elaborating on his conception of orbital motion, before concluding, just as intriguingly as the Secretary of the Royal Society had done, that since Hooke's "acute" letter had prompted him to consider "the species of this curve," he could have added a demonstration, but it was a matter "of no great moment." Hooke, who had hitherto been somewhat guarded in the information he had passed on to the Cambridge professor, now realized that Newton was indeed capable of providing what he lacked—a realization that incited a flurry of activity. Hooke performed several trials to test Newton's suggestions, reexamined his own ideas, and noted triumphantly in his diary on January 4, 1680, that he had "perfected" his "Theory of Heavens." He was now ready to engage in a more open and pointed discussion with Newton. On January 6 he dispatched a long and important letter that articulated in full his physical theory of planetary motion.

Newton did not respond. He appears to have swiftly demonstrated—not an answer to Hooke's question about the shape of a planetary orbit given a force, but to its converse: What force is required in order to keep a planet in an elliptical orbit? Yet he was loath to transmit the demonstration to Hooke. Doing so, he realized, would cause him to forfeit his own earlier work, not to mention hand over to his antagonist a magnificent discovery. Newton persisted in his silence even after Hooke wrote again ten days later. This final letter undoubtedly peeved Newton even more. Hooke rather tactlessly insinuated that now that he, Hooke, had unraveled the mystery of planetary motion, all that remained to be done was for Newton to apply his "excellent method" of calculation to demonstrate the veracity of such a law of nature. The insult rankled. Six years later, in his fury over Hooke's seeming claim to priority, Newton thundered that Hooke had done nothing, yet pretended to have "hinted all," save for what was necessary to be determined "by the drudgery of calculations and observations." Nor did Newton pursue the matter further. In old age he recalled that he had let it drop because he was intent on other studies, namely alchemy. Even the spurt of activity awakened by the appearance of the comet of 1680–81—a comet destined to play a crucial role in the *Principia*—did not persist for long. Newton still needed another stimulus, one that only Edmond Halley managed to provide.

Halley himself had become interested in the question about a year before paying Newton a visit. He conjectured from Kepler's third rule of planetary motion, that a centripetal force decreases inversely to the square of the distance, but he found himself unable to demonstrate this mathematically. In January 1684, Halley shared his thoughts on the matter with his two polymath friends: the architect Sir Christopher Wren and Robert Hooke. In response, Hooke claimed that he himself had proved such a principle, to which Wren responded with skepticism. To settle the matter, Wren challenged both Hooke and Halley to produce within two months a proper demonstration, promising a forty-shilling book prize to the winner. Hooke demurred. For the time being he would rather conceal his demonstration so that those who would fail in the task might better

Astronomer Edmond Halley (1656–1742) persuaded Newton to write the *Principia*, which Halley published at his own expense and then enthusiastically promoted at home and abroad.

appreciate his demonstration when he chose to make it public. That January meeting led to several others, which proved as inconclusive as the first, and it is my contention that the ensuing impasse induced Hooke to suggest that Halley travel to Cambridge in the hope that he might prove more successful in extracting the coveted demonstration from the reluctant Lucasian

Professor. Certainly, the question that Halley put to Newton was identical to the question posed by Hooke in 1679.

I wish I could have been privy not just to the conversation between these two strikingly dissimilar individuals who shared an ardent passion for science, but also to Newton's thought processes as he listened to Halley. This was the decisive moment in the long, drawn-out story of the creation of the *Principia,* the occasion when the fits and starts at last gave way to a decisive momentum. According to the sole account of the meeting—reported by a close friend of Halley, Abraham de Moivre, nearly half a century after the event—after some pleasantries, Halley popped the question: "What [Newton] thought the curve would be that would be described by the Planets supposing the force of attraction toward the Sun to be reciprocal to the square of their distance from it"? Without hesitating, Newton replied, "An ellipsis." Halley was "struck with joy and amazement": How did Newton know? "Why," responded his host, "I have calculated it." Halley asked to see the demonstration, but Newton was unable to find it among his papers and promised to redo the calculation and send it on.

This account raises many intriguing questions that only a witness would have been able to answer. Did Halley inform Newton of his January meeting with Hooke and Wren? If so, was Newton's failure to locate the desired demonstration feigned? Quite reasonably, he might have wished to keep Halley at bay, not simply because he was unwilling to part with the solution, but because he did not yet have a demonstration for Halley's direct question. Other considerations may have been at play as well. Some two months earlier Newton had been made aware that a professor of mathematics at Edinburgh University, David Gregory, was working on the mathematics of what we know as calculus. Two years earlier the German Gottfried Wilhelm Leibniz had published on the subject, and Newton was determined

Isaacus Newton Eq. Aur.

Impelled by Halley to publish his work on calculus and the laws of motion, Newton became a recluse for eighteen months working at a feverish pace on a book that took shape in the process of composition. The *Principia* was published in 1687.

to establish his own priority vis-à-vis both Gregory and Leibniz by publishing a comprehensive account of his early mathematical works.

Halley arrived just as this project was shifting into high gear.

One may well imagine the moment when Newton realized that he might be scooped again, this time by the increasing number of talented individuals who appeared determined to crack the mystery of orbital motion. Halley's visible excitement upon learning that Newton had the coveted demonstration of the inverse square law sufficed, it seems, to convince Newton to focus on the bigger prize—and thus abandon the projected treatise on mathematics. The decision may not have been reached on the day of Halley's visit, however. De Moivre's memorandum relates that, initially, Newton failed to retrace his steps and was forced to resort to a less elegant demonstration. He then discovered that a faulty diagram had led him astray, and once corrected, "he made both his calculations agree together." At this point Newton decided to go far beyond his original promise to Halley. In November 1684 he dispatched a brief but dense tract to London, *De motu corporum in gyrum* ("On the Motion of Bodies in an Orbit"), which demonstrated both that an elliptical orbit entails an inverse-square force, and that an inverse-square law necessarily produces a conic orbit—an ellipse under certain conditions—and more besides. *De motu* served as a book proposal. For all intents and purposes Newton committed himself to publication. And if the mere promise of a demonstration had sufficed to fill Halley with "joy and amazement," one may well imagine his reaction upon receiving the nine-page précis Newton sent him. Halley rushed back to Cambridge to ensure that Newton would turn the précis into a book.

In old age Edmond Halley fancied himself as having been the Ulysses who had produced Achilles—Newton. In retrospect, it is clear that, without Halley, the *Principia* might have never been published. Halley's enthusiasm, from the start, proved contagious, and he cajoled Newton in the broadest sense of the word: offering technical advice, correcting proofs, even bearing the cost of printing. Equally important, he soothed Newton's ire—

and threat to forgo publication—upon hearing of Hooke's demand that Newton acknowledge the assistance received from him. But if Halley's commitment to Newton's cause was unwavering, so was his friendship with Hooke. And hand in hand with assuaging Newton he defended Hooke's honor, assuring Newton that Hooke had been represented to him "in worse colors than it ought." Hooke neither claimed that Newton had taken it all from him nor had he demanded that the Royal Society do him justice. Newton appeared mollified. Nevertheless, he obliterated all references to Hooke that he had intended to include in the *Principia*. Newton also subtly revenged himself on Hooke by announcing in the preface to Book III of the *Principia*, on the "System of the World," that he had originally composed the book in a popular form to increase readership, but in order to avoid disputes *with those incapable of grasping the mathematical principles upon which the system was grounded*, he translated the earlier version into mathematical propositions. Years later, he further sniped that he deliberately made the *Principia* difficult in order to avoid "being baited by little Smatterers in Mathematicks."

Obviously, Hooke was the smatterer in question. Newton said as much to Hooke face-to-face when the two met at Halley's house in mid-February 1689. Affronted by Hooke's protest that he'd been wronged, Newton bluntly retorted, *"A posse ad esse non valet consequentia."* Hooke's alleged ignorance of mathematics became with time the universal grounds for dismissing his contribution to Newton's *opus magnum*. Today we know better. Though hardly Newton's equal, Hooke was capable of handling the mathematics of orbital motion. Indeed, it was his grasp of the magnitude of Newton's achievement that fueled his bitterness about the prize that had eluded him.

As for Newton, in private he was willing to admit Hooke's contribution to the development of his ideas on the dynamics of orbital motion, but never to his aiding him in any sense when it came to the inverse square law, ellipses, or universal gravitation. Nevertheless, the vehemence with which Newton dismissed Hooke's claims indicates the depth of Newton's fear that a reader of Hooke's 1679–80 letters to him might well decide otherwise.

Newton did not discover universal gravitation in a flash, shortly after celebrating his twenty-third birthday. His supreme effort to unify celestial and terrestrial motion under a single law was twenty years in the making, and he was indebted to the direct and indirect provocations of Robert Hooke as much as to the careful midwifery of Edmond Halley. Ultimately, however, the *Principia* is rightfully Newton's masterpiece, and one would have been present at a moment that shaped the modern world had one been able to hear the conversation with Halley that set the book's publication in motion.

Further Reading

Mordechai Feingold, *The Newtonian Moment: Isaac Newton and the Making of Modern Culture* (New York, 2004).

Isaac Newton, *The Principia: Mathematical Principles of Natural Philosophy*, trans. I. Bernard Cohen and Ann Whitman (Berkeley, 1999).

Richard S. Westfall, *Never at Rest: A Biography of Isaac Newton* (New York, 1980).

ELLEN T. HARRIS

Handel Is Fired

Ellen T. Harris, the Class of 1949 Professor at the Massachusetts Institute of Technology, is a musicologist whose research has focused primarily on the areas of Baroque opera and vocal performance practice. Her most recent book, *Handel as Orpheus: Voice and Desire in the Chamber Cantatas* (Harvard University Press, 2001), won the 2002 Otto Kindeldey Award from the American Musicological Society and the 2002–3 Louis Gottschalk Prize from the Society for Eighteenth-Century Studies. Her article "Handel the Investor," published in *Music & Letters*, received the 2004 Westrup Prize. In 2005 she won the Gyorgy Kepes Prize for her contributions to the arts at MIT. Professor Harris also performs as a soprano soloist; her appearances include singing the National Anthem at Fenway Park in 1991 and, in 1997, her Boston Pops debut in Symphony Hall with John Williams conducting.

By focusing on an intriguing story about Handel, she is able in this essay to show the connections between music and more general history.

Handel Is Fired

History is full of stories, some so delightful that they pass into the realm of legend and become difficult to dislodge even when evidence proves them false. Such is the case with the employment in 1710 of composer George Frederick Handel by Georg Ludwig, Elector of Hanover. As the story goes, Handel asked for permission to travel to London for extended visits not once but twice, and the second time so overstayed his leave that in 1714 he found himself in an awkward situation when the employer he had deserted became George I of England. His reconciliation with the king then came about only as the result of a stratagem arranged by the baron Kielmansegg: Handel would compose music to be played anonymously before His Majesty during one of his water parties on the Thames. This worked so well that when the king was informed of the identity of the composer, he not only forgave Handel, but awarded him an annual pension of two hundred pounds. It's a great story, and as it originates in the biography of Handel by John Mainwaring, published a year after the composer's death in 1759—with content that could only have derived from Handel himself—it has an equally great pedigree. But its validity cannot be sustained.

First of all, Handel's music is some of the first George I heard after his arrival in England on September 18, 1714, directly contradicting Mainwaring's statement that "Handel, conscious how ill he had deserved at the hands of his gracious patron . . . did not dare to shew himself at court." That the composer was not out of favor with the king is also clear from payments from the royal treasury. Further, Handel's *Water Music,* the only music he is known to have written for a water party, was apparently not performed until 1717, when on Wednesday, July 17, "the King took Water at Whitehall" and heard "the finest Symphonies, compos'd express for this Occasion, by Mr. Handel" (the *Daily Courant,* July 19, 1717). Finally, the only known disruption in Handel's employment under George as elector occurred not because the composer overstayed a leave from Hanover, but because in 1713 he agreed to compose a *Te Deum* as part of a national celebration in honor of the Peace of Utrecht, which Queen Anne had made unilaterally with France to bring an end to Britain's part in the War of Spanish Succession. The elector, who had strongly opposed Anne's peace, chose to separate himself politically from the celebrations in the strongest terms and dismissed Handel from his service.

The whole context of Handel's employment by the Elector of Hanover, and the simultaneous favor he was shown by Queen Anne, needs rethinking. Even so, the story Mainwaring presents still deserves our attention, especially if, as seems likely, it derives from Handel himself. The history of these turbulent years in the composer's life, from his acceptance of a court position in Hanover in 1710, to his dismissal in 1713, to the accession of George I in 1714, and finally to the performance of the *Water Music* in 1717, is more complex than the old legend and full of intrigue. How I wish I could have been present in London court circles to have witnessed the political maneuverings and watched Handel's reaction. So many questions remain. Why was the composer paid by Hanover for the time he spent away from that court in London? What was the young composer's reaction to English society? How did Handel and the elector arrive at an accommodation after Handel was fired? And, in particular, what was the audience response as Handel's splendid *Utrecht Te Deum* and *Jubilate* reverberated through the arches of St. Paul's Cathedral? Though we cannot know with certainty how all the pieces of the puzzle fit together, we can go back to the beginning and, by placing ourselves in the picture, try to tell the story again and bridge some of the gaps.

• • •

Early in 1710, after spending about four years in Italy, Handel traveled north. He sought employment and carried with him a letter of introduction from Prince Ferdinand de' Medici of Florence to the court of Innsbruck. On his way to or from a visit to his family in Halle, he stopped in Hanover, having received encouragement from Baron Kielmansegg in Italy and perhaps having met Ernst August, the elector's brother, in Venice. He was quickly welcomed. George's mother, the dowager electress Sophie, reports in June that the electoral prince and princess, later George II and Queen Caroline, took special pleasure in Handel's playing. On June 15 she writes that the prince and princess were "delighted that the elector has kept him."

The terms of Handel's employment have to be reconstructed. Though Mainwaring writes that Handel negotiated an immediate leave to satisfy both a previous commitment to travel to Düsseldorf and a desire to visit London, this provides a rather one-sided and improbable account of the agreement. Handel's determination to travel to London offered the elector a special opportunity, and he must have eyed the young composer closely to gauge his potential to serve the Hanoverian court abroad. As heir to the throne, George had a strong interest in obtaining news from the English court and also in controlling information coming out of Hanover, yet Queen Anne adamantly opposed the presence of any of the Hanoverian family in England. George, therefore, depended on the presence of representatives in London, and he maintained as tight control over them as possible. In 1707, one James Scott, a former employee of the dowager electress, made an unofficial trip to London to try to negotiate an invitation for Sophie, who stood

George Frederick Handel, shown here in a contemporary portrait by Philip Mercier, resourcefully navigated his role as court composer and diplomat through the political turmoil in the years of the War of Spanish Succession. While formally having entered the service of the British crown, he continued relations with his former Hanoverian employer, George I, who would become Queen Anne's successor.

before her son in the line of succession, to visit London. The elector wrote personally to Scott of his displeasure, chastising Scott for having "meddled in such delicate affairs" and emphasizing that he had "a minister at London with whom I am satisfied, who is instructed in my intentions." It is unlikely that George would have permitted Handel to travel to London as an open member of his court (Handel was regularly identified, for example, as "the famous Mr. *Hendel,* a Retainer to the Court of *Hanover,* in the Quality of Director of his Electoral Highness's Chapple"), without providing explicit direction.

It is particularly intriguing, therefore, that the letter of recommendation Prince Ferdinand de' Medici wrote for Handel describes him more in terms of diplomatic service than as a composer, as a man of "honest sentiments, civility of manners, and full command of several languages, and a talent more than mediocre in music." Handel's predecessor at Hanover, the composer Agostino Steffani, had assumed diplomatic obligations since 1696, and composers fell not infrequently into this role: They typically had extensive linguistic ability (Handel already had German, French and Italian as well as a solid grounding in Latin), and their musical skill permitted them access to the private chambers of court forbidden to more formal representatives. George witnessed firsthand Handel's ability to merge musical aspirations with courtly manners, since at Hanover the composer immediately ingratiated himself with the princess Caroline. As recorded by the dowager electress in one of her letters, the electoral princess "is very well at the moment and no longer confined to bed. She is entertained by the music of a Saxon [Handel]."

The specific conditions of Handel's employment were probably laid out by Baron Kielmansegg on behalf of the elector. I would like to have been a silent witness to this interview to know in what way Handel was asked to serve the elector while he was in London. It seems likely that he was charged explicitly with penetrating the inner circles of Anne's court, and, if so, his immediate success is clear. By the beginning of the new year, he had already supplanted the Master of the Queen's Music in the composition of a birthday ode for the queen, performed on February 6, 1711, his first known performance in England, and when he left London in midsummer of 1711 the queen intimated "her desire to see him again." Back in Hanover, Handel was rewarded for his services; he was paid his full salary for the previous year without having composed anything for the Hanoverian court.

Over the next year Handel studied English, clearly with the plan of returning to England. In midsummer 1712, after again receiving his annual salary, he set out once more for London. He quickly became embroiled in the tug-of-war between queen and elector—the monarch and heir—when the queen made known her express desire that Handel compose a *Te Deum* and *Jubilate* for the service at St. Paul's Cathedral that would take place on a national day of Thanksgiving. This was undoubtedly as much (or more) a political as musical decision. Far from Mainwaring's implicit statement that "not only the august house of Hanover, but most of the protestant Princes" had supported Britain's efforts to end the war, Hanover and the other allies had opposed Anne's unilateral peacemaking. On December 5, 1711, shortly after the first peace articles had been signed, the *Daily Courant* had printed George's strong objections:

> *Nothing but a perfect Union between the Allies while the general Peace shall be treating, and the mutual Guarantie they shall give each other upon what shall therein be concluded, can secure them for the future. . . . 'Tis not doubted therefore, that her Britannick Majesty proposes to act in this whole Affair joyntly and in Concert with her Allies, conformably to the Assurances which she has given them. But to banish all Distrust, it would be necessary that there should be no secret Negociation, which might give Ground for Suspicion that one or other of the allies might make their own Treaty. . . . And*

this way [of working in Concert] appears to his Electoral
Highness to be more sure for procuring this End [of peace],
and for preserving such Advantages, than if Great Britain
should endeavor it, without the concurrence of the Allies, by a
separate Negociation.

Anne nevertheless continued to pursue a separate peace. The elector must, therefore, have been indignant to receive a letter from his London envoy, Thomas Grote, dated January 13, 1713, reporting that he had extended Handel's leave to allow him to compose a major work to be "sung in St Paul's Cathedral when peace is proclaimed."

My lord Bolingbroke told me in the name of the queen that
Her Majesty had commissioned Your Highness's Kapellmeis-
ter, Handel, to compose a piece of music for her. Because she
would like him to remain here until this is done but has
found out that Your Highness's permission for him to remain
here has come to an end, I would like to inform Your High-
ness in confidence that Her Majesty wishes Handel to remain
here for a while. I have promised that with pleasure and here-
with report, as I didn't doubt that Your Highness would be
pleased that one of your servants would have the honour of
serving Her Majesty in some way. This music is, I under-
stand, a Te Deum, which shall be sung in St Paul's Cathedral
when peace is proclaimed, and more than a hundred musi-
cians are going to be employed for this.

George had repeatedly gone on record against Anne's policy, but now her shrewd maneuver of commissioning celebratory music from his own Master of Music implied his compliance. His only recourse was to release Handel from service. As Christoph Kreyenberg, the Hanoverian resident in London, wrote on 5/16 June: "A few days ago I wrote to you on the subject of Mr Handel, that since His Highness was determined to dismiss him, Mr Handel submitted to that wish. . . ."

The elector's anger must have been communicated to Handel in the missive he received from the baron Kielmansegg, which notified him of his dismissal with the curt statement "that he could go wherever he pleased." Handel found the communication "particularly mortifying" and has to have been shocked at being so summarily released. He had been a close observer of international diplomacy and war alliances ever since settling in Italy in 1706, and he surely knew the elector's position. That he believed his close association with the English court was what the elector desired cannot, therefore, be attributed to naïveté. Even George's own diplomatic envoy, Thomas Grote, had made the assumption that the commission from the queen would be welcomed at the Hanoverian court. I wish I could have seen Handel's immediate response on receiving his dismissal, but I imagine that one of his first actions was to attend the Hanoverian resident Kreyenberg to demand an explanation.

It would be fascinating to know how Kreyenberg succeeded in calming the composer, whose quick temper is well documented. He himself had no objection to the dismissal ("I will admit to you frankly," he writes, "that Mr. Handel is nothing to me"), but he knew Handel's diplomatic value. From his London vantage point, he also understood the complexities of the situation better than the impatient onlookers in Hanover. Working on two fronts, he clearly tried to broker a rapprochement. On the one hand, he counseled Handel how to "write to M. Kielmansegg to extricate himself gracefully" and, on the other, gently reminded the elector of Handel's service in providing stories of the Hanoverian court to the English ("you understand the stories to which I am referring") and in gathering information, especially on the queen's health.

After a number of delays, the national service of Thanksgiving finally took place on July 7, 1713. It had become a carefully staged event with the purpose of portraying unity, for not only did Hanover and the other allies oppose the peace, but Anne also faced strong opposition at home from the Whig Party. This theatrical side of the celebration was wryly noted by Lady Cowper in her diary: "This Day, the Church Opera, after many Rehearsals was finish'd at the Cathedral of St. Paul." As it turned out, the Whigs of both houses of Parliament stayed away, which was "not much to be wonder'd at; since it would have been preposterous, if not a mocking of Religion, for Men to return Almighty God Thanks for a Peace, which they had endeavoured to prevent, and still disapproved." Further, a memorandum written from Hanover to Kreyenberg on July 4 reiterated the elector's commitment "to continue the war against France," pointing out that by engaging the French army he was protecting England from a French invasion to put "the pretender" on the throne. It urged the British nation to "exert itself, for the Elector cannot save them against their will."

Despite political opposition to the peace, the performance of Handel's *Utrecht Te Deum* and *Jubilate* at the Thanksgiving service was his compositional epiphany in England. He had previously achieved great success with operas in Hamburg and Venice, and his opera *Rinaldo* had been a hit in London during his first year there. But whereas opera attracted a relatively small section of the population, the Thanksgiving service was planned to capture the entire body politic within the cathedral: the monarch, lords spiritual, lords temporal, and commons. This was Handel's first public work in English, and he had never performed before so large a crowd. Although he would not have displaced the Chapel Royal organist for the whole of the service, he surely took over the keyboard for his own composition, as was his norm. The choir consisted of the men and boys of the Chapel Royal, and the combined forces of voices, strings, bassoon, and trumpets amounted to about fifty, a large performing group, but only half the number the elector's envoy had predicted. They all would have crowded around the organ in the gallery, maintaining close aural connection with one another and visual contact with the composer. At least three public rehearsals of the piece both in St. Paul's and the Banqueting House undoubtedly gave everyone more security in their parts than would often have been the case in an era when much music was performed within days of the completion of the composition.

The sound in St. Paul's, as in most cathedrals, is very reverberant, and Handel seems to have accounted for it from the very opening of the *Te Deum* with its loud, separated chords for all strings and woodwinds followed by a soft, descending echo in the strings. The long sustained notes on "we acknowledge thee" against the fabric of more active sound must have resonated throughout the cathedral, as would the punctuated full-choral repetitions of "all" in "all the earth doth worship thee," the reverberation emphasizing the meaning. In the softer sections for soloists, the contrapuntal intertwining would have wafted more gently to envelop the listeners, as in the opening of "Vouchsafe, O Lord, to keep us this day without sin." In the final movement of the *Te Deum*, the block, choral repetitions of the word "never" in "let me never be confounded" resound with absolute conviction, the music emphatically supporting Queen Anne's peace. Could one sustain doubts after hearing this music? I would like to have been there to hear and see the effect, but I cannot imagine that it was anything but overwhelming. The queen herself was not able to attend the service at the last minute because of her gout, but even if she also missed all of the public rehearsals, she surely heard of the music's powerful

Queen Anne (1665–1714) reigned for twelve years over England and Scotland (which were united as Kingdom of Great Britain in 1707) as well as over Ireland. She was the last monarch of the House of Stuart as she left no heir. Anne had lost all of her eighteen children either during pregnancy or at birth or shortly after (only one son survived until the age of eleven). Furthermore, the queen suffered from a painful and disfiguring disease that forced her increasingly to shift power from the crown to the ministry (a style of ruling that was to continue with her successor).

effect. The *Utrecht Te Deum* established Handel as an English composer, and his work became a pattern-book for English settings of the *Te Deum* to follow.

Handel's participation in the Thanksgiving service was recognized by Queen Anne at the end of the year with the grant of two hundred pounds, to be paid annually. Mainwaring states, "This act of the royal bounty was the more extraordinary as his foreign engagements were not unknown." But by the end of 1713, Handel no longer had any "foreign engagements," as he had been dismissed six months earlier from his Hanoverian service—or was he? He was formally fired, certainly, but just as certainly he was retained in some capacity. Kreyenberg's final letter to the elector on this subject, dated 3/14 July 1713, makes this explicit—its final phrases, given below in italic, written in numeric code:

> *I am pleased that you have written to me about Mr Handel. I had not expected that he would remain in His Highness's service, nor was I considering that but merely the manner of his dismissal; I have done it in such a way that he is quite content, giving him to understand that he is by no means in disgrace with His Highness, and dropping a few words to the effect that he will be quite all right* when the elector comes here. He will continue to tell me all he knows.

• • •

Whatever pleasure the queen took in stealing Handel away from the service of the elector would have been muted had she known that he had agreed to continue serving the Hanoverian court. We will never know the extent of Handel's diplomatic service to George or, for that matter, to Anne. Kreyenberg's letter makes it clear that Handel passed stories both ways, but implies that what was passed on to the English court merely served the purpose of emphasizing the religious commitment of the Hanoverians to Protestantism. Here is another moment when I wish I could have been present—to be privy to these communications and know precisely what information was exchanged. All that can be said is that when George I arrived in London only a little more than a year after these events, Handel was, as Kreyenberg had arranged, "quite all right." According to the London newspapers, when the King and the Prince of Wales attended services at the Chapel Royal in St. James's on their first Sunday in London (September 26), "a *Te Deum* was sung, compos'd by Mr. Hendel" (the *Evening Post*, 25–8 September 1714). After the arrival in October of Caroline, now princess of Wales, the Chapel Royal service on October 17 included both a *Te Deum* and an anthem by Handel. Clearly the composer had survived the growing tension between Queen Anne and her successor, and it is impossible to judge who used whom most effectively.

Nevertheless, if Handel breathed a sigh of relief on the accession of the elector, it was premature. Any notion that he would be taken up by the new king as the primary composer at court was quickly squashed. In Anne's court he had supplanted the Master of the Queen's Musick and Composer to the Chapel Royal at least in part for political reasons. Now George I had to consider political circumstances as well. Whereas Anne had found it expedient to use the composer of the Hanoverian court, George I, as a foreign ruler, found it necessary to limit the number of Germans in his service and turned away from Handel to William Croft, the English composer to the Chapel Royal. Although Handel's pension continued, he was not asked after the initial welcoming services to compose again for the Chapel Royal for eight years.

As we know from the dowager electress Sophie's letters from Hanover in 1710, it was the electoral prince and princess, not George, who particularly delighted in Handel's music. They were all about the same age, and Handel maintained a special relationship with the princess, later Queen Caroline. Unfortu-

Because Queen Anne died without leaving an heir she was succeeded by her second cousin, George I of the House of Hanover, who was a descendant of the Stuarts via his paternal grandmother. Shown above is his coronation as the King of Great Britain on October 31, 1714, at Westminster Abbey (where two months earlier the porphyry-ridden, absurdly swollen body of Queen Anne had been buried in a vast, almost-square coffin). George Frederick Handel was to become the new king's court composer.

nately, the kind of tension and competition that had existed between Anne and George did not subside with the Hanoverian succession, but simply passed down to the new monarch and heir. Throughout the remainder of his career, Handel navigated stormy seas caused by rivalries between the reigning King and the Prince of Wales. The first manifestations of this appeared in the spring of 1717 when a breach occurred between the king's party and the opposition headed by the prince, and the king was unable to travel to Hanover for the summer. Instead, elaborate and public events were planned to raise the king's profile with the public. One of these was the water party on the Thames on July 17 at which Handel's music was played. Given the timing, could Mainwaring's story about a reconciliation between Handel and George I relate to these events rather than the accession?

Possibly, during these years when he was not commissioned to write for the court, Handel had begun to associate closely once again with the prince and princess, leaving an impression that he had aligned himself with the opposition. Baron Kielmansegg, who repeatedly appears at critical junctures in Handel's relationship to George I, may then have helped to arrange Handel's participation in the water party so that the king could be surprised by the music and given the identity of the composer after hearing it. If such a situation did arise, and the *Water Music* was written as a means of reconciling with the king, the ruse must have worked. Newspaper reports state that the king so enjoyed the music that he asked for it to be played three times. Mainwaring connects Handel's royal pensions with the success of the water party, stating that as a result of this intercession "Handel was restored to favour. . . . As a token of it, the King was pleased to add a pension for life of 200 *l.* a year to that which Queen Anne had before given him." However, Handel had not been in disgrace with the king when he arrived, as we have seen, and the signs of royal favor bestowed on the composer bear no relationship to the performance of the *Water Music* in 1717. The pension of two hundred pounds granted him by Anne continued without a break, and in October 1715, George granted Handel six months of salary in arrears for his employment in Hanover as well. Most important, as the decade drew to a close, the king became the leading patron for the newly established Royal Academy of Music in 1719, which gave Handel his first secure base for the performance of Italian opera in London.

Toward the end of his life, when Handel came to tell stories of his early years in London to his English friends, he would certainly have avoided the details of his employment by the Hanoverian court and, particularly, of his continued assistance to that court after he formally entered the service of Queen Anne. A good story about the need for a reconciliation between himself and the king would have served to bridge that particular episode, and Handel could have manufactured a story out of whole cloth. Perhaps the account in Mainwaring derives from such deliberate obfuscation, but it also may simply descend from a confused secondhand recounting of the actual story or a mistaken conflation of two stories. Time and again Mainwaring's account, even when it has been doubted, proves accurate, or at least significantly based in fact. Perhaps, Baron Kielmansegg did assist Handel in repairing his relationship with the king through the composition of the *Water Music,* even though this event occurred in 1717 rather than in 1714. From the distance of several decades, Handel could have merged these two periods, especially as the intervening years were compositionally inactive for him at court. He may actually have thought that any residual coolness from the king related back to his composition of the *Utrecht Te Deum,* at which time, indeed, he had overstayed his leave from Hanover.

If so, the original story in Mainwaring is not so far from the mark after all. With only slight adjustments, it could be transformed into the story told here, that not one, but two of Handel's great compositions, the *Utrecht Te Deum* and *Jubilate,* and the *Water Music,* were the direct result of continuing tensions and political one-upmanship between the heir apparent and the reigning monarch of Great Britain. I only wish I could have been there to witness how the young George Frederick Handel, one of history's finest composers, successfully threaded his way through the political intrigue and court machinations while at the same time bringing to life the glorious musical works that marked the beginning of his extraordinary, fifty-year span of composing in London.

Author's Note

The dates June 5/16 and July 3/14, 1713, refer to the different calendars then in effect in England and on the continent. England was still following the Julian calendar, while the continent was on the Gregorian calendar. England did not change over to the Gregorian calendar until 1752, when the eleven-day difference was erased (literally by skipping eleven days in one blow). As a result, correspondence between England and the continent typically double-dated in order to be absolutely clear on what day and what calendar was intended. The dates as I give them are precisely how the letters I quote are dated.

The date September 25–28, 1714, is the publication date of *The Evening Post*, which was not a daily.

Further Reading

Donald Burrows, *Handel and the Chapel Royal* (Oxford, 2005).

Edward Gregg, *The Protestant Succession in International Politics, 1710–1716* (New York, 1986).

John Mainwaring, *Memoirs of the Life of the Late George Frederick Handel* (London, 1760).

WILLIAM H. MCNEILL

Frederick the Great and the Propagation of Potatoes

William H. McNeill is the Robert A. Milikan Distinguished Service Professor Emeritus of History at the University of Chicago and one of the world's most respected
historians. He is the author of many books, including *The
Rise of the West: A History of the Human Community*, which
received the National Book Award in 1964 and was recently named one of the one hundred best books of the
twentieth century by the Modern Library. Among his
other books are *A World History*; *Plagues and Peoples*; *The
Human Web: A Bird's Eye View of World History*, written in
collaboration with his son, Professor J. R. McNeill; and
The Pursuit of Truth: A Historian's Memoir. In 1996 he was
awarded the Erasmus Prize, given by the Praemium Eras-
mianum Foundation to individuals or institutions that
have made notable contributions to European society, culture, or social science.

In this essay Professor McNeill joins Prince Frederick of
Prussia, who is commanding ten thousand Prussian sol-
diers in 1734. The military mission was not successful, but
Frederick learned some interesting things along the way.

Frederick the Great
and the Propagation of Potatoes

I would like to have been an inconspicuous member of the entourage of twenty-two-year-old Prince Frederick of Prussia (later the Great) in 1734, when he was commanding ten thousand Prussian soldiers in an unsuccessful campaign aimed at compelling the French to abandon their siege of the town and fortress of Philippsburg on the Rhine.

From a military point of view, nothing much happened. Yet this was, in all probability, the time Frederick learned two things that altered the course of Prussian, German, and world history. One of the things Frederick learned was that the management of Austrian armies was more slack and clumsy than his Prussians were capable of. That emboldened him to seize the province of Silesia, defying and defeating the Austrian armies soon after he became king in 1740.

The second thing that Frederick learned, however, is what really interests me, and makes me wish to have been able to watch how and when it was that he noticed potatoes, and the way they kept the peasants around Philippsburg alive and well, despite wholesale grain requisitioning by French, Austrian, and Prussian soldiers. He probably learned much else, since this was Frederick's very first military campaign, and the subtleties of emotional and professional interaction up and down the chain of command have to be experienced before they can be understood and exploited, as he later was to do so very successfully.

His father, Frederick William I, king of Prussia, was old and ill. So was Prinz Eugen of Savoy (1663–1746), the Austrian commander in chief under whom he served. In his youth Prinz Eugen had been a daring and successful commander, driving the Turks from Hungary and restraining French expansion. But in 1734 he was more than three times Frederick's age, no longer had the full trust of the reigning Austrian Emperor, and the contingents from lesser German states, like Prussia, that joined the emperor's forces suffered from dividing loyalties. Prinz Eugen was too old and tired to overcome such obstacles, and though he got on well with Frederick and recognized the excellence of Prussian discipline, slack and clumsy management prevailed in his army as a whole.

As a result, after weeks of waiting, and consuming large quantities of grain requisitioned from the surrounding countryside, Prinz Eugen's armies withdrew ingloriously, allowing the French to capture Philippsburg. On one occasion during those long weeks of waiting, Frederick briefly exposed himself to artillery fire while riding with a party of other high officers to survey the French lines. He comported himself well simply by riding out of range without haste or panic. That was the sum total of his personal engagement with the enemy.

Young Frederick already had a long history of friction with his father, who disliked his Frenchified manners, his taste for playing the flute, and his disdain for the pious, sparing, gruff German way of life his father embraced. Their differences became so intense that in 1730, Frederick tried to run away from court, but was caught, stripped of his military rank, and charged with desertion along with his friend and accomplice, Lieutenant von Katte. They were both imprisoned, and Frederick was compelled to watch von Katte's execution. After some hesitation, his father decided on a milder punishment for his only son, whom he condemned to rural isolation in the lower Oder Valley, ordering Frederick to "learn economics from the ground up"* by supervising the management of royal estates located in what was then a frontier backwater.

This meant living under the watchful eye of one of his father's confidants while visiting fields and barnyards, listening to bailiffs and peasants, and considering how to improve farming methods so as to increase the royal income. Few European rulers ever paid attention to such grubby details, but the two years Frederick spent away from court surely must have prepared him to notice what peasants around Philippsburg were doing with potatoes in 1734 when, after a partial reconciliation with his father, he found himself serving under Prinz Eugen, in command of Prussian soldiers who had nothing much to do beyond feeding themselves by sending out foraging parties to confiscate grain from peasant barns.

Had I been on the scene in 1734 with anything resembling my present state of mind, I would have been acutely uncomfortable in Frederick's company, and cannot suppose he would have confided in me. So probably I would have learned nothing about what Frederick was thinking about potatoes or anything else. After colliding with his father so dangerously, he had learned to keep his own counsel and often deliberately deceived those around him.

Still, just hanging around and watching his comings and goings might have shown an observer sensitized to the question just when it was that Frederick first noticed what a strange, unprepossessing, and totally unfamiliar kind of food—lumpy, dirty potatoes—did for the peasants around Philippsburg. For even small garden plots of an acre or less, full of potato plants, sufficed to feed a family for months! He may have witnessed peas-

---

*David Blackbourn, *The Conquest of Nature: Landscape and the Making of Modern Germany* (New York, 2006), p. 27.

Unintentionally, Frederick Wilhelm I might have done great service to his son and history when he put the rebellious Crown Prince (above, in a painting after Antoine Pesne) under arrest in the province to study economics and agriculture. There and in Philippsburg young Frederick, king-to-be, learned about the lifesaving potential of the potato.

ants eating the ugly tubers, or wondered why Prussian requisitioning parties aroused less than the usual level of despairful resistance from the peasants whose grain they seized. He may even have quizzed some local inhabitants about the plant and its uses as he had quizzed Prussian peasants in the Oder Valley about their grain farming three years before.

As things stand, there is no known record of how Frederick learned about potatoes. Somehow he did so, and his subsequent career, as well as the fate of Germany and of northwestern Europe as a whole, depended directly on what he did with his new information. It would be nice to know just when he first glimpsed the lifesaving capability of potatoes for his future subjects, and that is why I would like, professionally but not in actuality, to have been with him around Philippsburg, where almost certainly it happened.

We do know that not long after mounting the Prussian throne in 1740, he ordered local government officials to supply Prussian peasants with seed potatoes and show them how to plant and cultivate the unfamiliar crop. Moreover, Frederick's officials did not plant potatoes in gardens but in fallow grainfields, thus enormously expanding the scale of potato raising and bringing the plant to prominence in European agriculture for the first time.

Before exploring the far-ranging consequences of that practice, let me explain how a plant native to the altiplano of Peru got to the Rhineland, and the inconspicuous—one might say underground—part it had played in European agriculture prior to Frederick's time. First of all, potatoes reached Europe when Spanish ships, returning from the Peruvian coast soon after Pizarro's conquest in 1535, found it necessary to feed their crews with native foods—potatoes and maize—because European grains were unavailable. Some of the Spanish sailors thought enough of their potato diet to carry leftover tubers ashore and try growing them in Spain. Most Spanish landscapes were much too dry for the crop to prosper; but in northwest Spain the coastal mountains intercepted Atlantic moisture, and local inhabitants were soon raising potatoes and using them as ships' stores for transatlantic fishing off Newfoundland. They, in turn, introduced potatoes to the west coast of Ireland, since they often stopped there for water and other refreshment when coming back from the Grand Banks.

A third place in Europe that potatoes took root very early was in the foothills of the Italian Alps, where moisture and temperatures were also close enough to those of the Andes altiplano for them to flourish. Spanish sailors must have introduced them to Italy in the usual unrecorded fashion. Written records allow more precision; a botanist in the Low Countries, who called himself Carolus Clusius, wrote that he first saw potatoes in a garden near Mons, Belgium, in 1588. Later, in 1601, he published a description of the plant, complete with accurate drawings. He also knew that it had come from Peru, so named it Papas Peruanorum, and remarked that it was "common" in northern Italy, but said nothing of how it reached Mons.*

When considering the spread of potatoes in Europe, one must bear in mind that people accustomed to relying on bread, derived from grain, were repelled by the appearance of the tubers. As they came from the earth, they were large and dirty, irregularly shaped, with dull brownish skins often scarred by scabs. Such an ugly, unaccustomed sort of food aroused fear and loathing. People commonly refused to taste them, and, not surprisingly, rumors of their unwholesomeness circulated widely. Indeed, in the seventeenth century, local parliaments of

---

*Carolus Clusius, *Rariorum plantarum historia* (Antwerp, 1601). This was not the earliest mention of potatoes in print, however. John Gerard, *Herball, or general historie of plantes* (London, 1597) has that honor. He was aware of the plant's novelty and made it his frontispiece, but mistakenly named it "potatoes of Virginia." Francis Drake had returned from circumnavigating the globe in 1580 with a few potatoes in his hold, and that was how potatoes reached England. But Drake's potatoes had blossoms of a different color from those the Spaniards spread on the Continent, distinguishing the two initial strains from one another.

Franche-Comté and Burgundy both outlawed potatoes on the grounds that eating them caused leprosy—an idea doubtless provoked by the leprous look of scabby potato skins. Sailors who had been compelled to eat them on transatlantic voyages were the only Europeans initially willing to accept them. Only under comparable compulsion would ordinary folk even consider doing so.

This prejudice was reinforced by the fact that once in the ground, grain grew of its own accord, whereas the necessary task of hoeing potatoes once or twice during the growing season to keep back weeds required onerous extra labor for anyone who planted them in large numbers.

Yet spread they did, and for two very good reasons. First of all, they were in fact highly nutritious, and yielded abundantly, producing two to four times as many calories per acre as any European grain could do. With such yields, extra work for extra food made sense wherever land was short and the population was dense enough to provide the extra labor that hoeing required.

But there was another, far more compelling reason to raise potatoes. From time immemorial, European armies on the march were accustomed to live by requisitioning grain stored in village barns, but at first soldiers were not interested in potatoes. By leaving them hidden in the ground, peasants could dig a meal's worth at a time and survive comfortably enough even when subjected to repeated and ruthless military requisitioning.

Wherever that elementary fact became apparent to local populations, prejudice against potatoes rapidly disappeared. Instead, peasants eagerly planted them in their gardens as an insurance against man-made famine. The region where this first happened was along the so-called Spanish Road, running from northern Italy over the Alps, then up the Rhône and down the Rhine to the Low Countries. During the Dutch wars, 1567–1648, Spanish soldiers traveled that route year after year since Dutch sailors made sea transport from Spain to the Netherlands unsafe for them. Accordingly, news of the value of potatoes as a sovereign safeguard against man-made starvation passed by word of mouth from village to village along the Spanish Road, leaving no trace of written records but making all the difference to those who planted the new crop in their gardens. Clusius tells us that by 1588, twenty-one years after the Dutch wars had begun, they had reached all the way to Mons, but no other written record exists to tell exactly when and where the new crop spread.

After 1648, when the Dutch wars ended, campaigning in the Low Countries and Rhinelands provoked by the wars of Louis XIV (reigned 1643–1715) must have had the effect of spreading potatoes farther into Germany. But no one knows just how far they may have reached since no one wrote about what grew in peasant gardens. Yet by the time Frederick showed up in Baden in 1734, peasants around Philippsburg surely knew all about potatoes and were well aware of their special value in time of war. They were, after all, located squarely astride the Spanish Road, with generations of exposure to military requisitioning behind them. Information about the value of potatoes, both in peace and war, therefore surely was readily available, and as we have seen, Frederick was unusually well prepared to take notice of such an agricultural novelty.

The question I wish I could answer, therefore, is whether Frederick already understood how effectually potatoes would keep Prussia's rural population from starving in a time of war when he put the weight of the royal administration behind the propagation of the new crop. But the fact is that the state of scholarship is such that I cannot find out and must leave my question unanswered. That is because historians have not recognized the critical role of potatoes in forestalling famine in a time of war.

Nonetheless, I have found a few cursory references to Frederick's part in establishing potatoes on Prussian soil, and two writers hint at their wartime significance. Robert Asprey, in *Frederick the Great: The Magnificent Enigma* (New York, 1986), merely says "he [Frederick] introduced the potato which won only a slow acceptance," although increased potato cultivation "more than once saved parts of his kingdom from famine." And W. D. Henderson, in *Studies in the Economic Policy of Frederick the Great* (London, 1963), comes a little closer to the point by writing: "During the Seven Years War, Frederick declared that only the foresight of Schlafendorf, who had fostered the extension of potato growing in Silesia, saved his armies from starvation."

But Henderson cites no source for that remark, and he misses its larger implication. For it was not Frederick's soldiers, but his subjects who escaped starvation by eating potatoes during the long years of war, thereby sustaining the human basis of the Prussian state and allowing Frederick to find enough new recruits to replace the heavy losses his battles inflicted on the Prussian army. Without potatoes his army could not have been maintained; the state could not have survived; and German, European, and world history would have taken a very different course from what actually resulted from the precarious Prussian victory.

Prussia's survival despite the overwhelming numerical superiority of the Austrian, French, and Russian armies has always been surprising. It depended on the death of the Russian empress Elizabeth in 1762–a personal foe–and the accession of Frederick's enthusiastic admirer, Tsar Peter III, who promptly made peace and changed sides, only to be killed after a palace coup d'état a few months later. His youthful German wife and successor, Catherine II, was at first very unsure of her hold on power and promptly withdrew Russian forces from the war. Defeated by Great Britain at sea and in both Canada and India,

France, too, made peace. Thereupon Austria, abandoned by both its allies, reluctantly decided to follow suit. To generations of historians, this dramatic cluster of political reversals, together with Frederick's numerous victories, seemed sufficient explanation of his precarious survival.

In a sense, these events *were* the reason he kept his crown and emerged from the war with enormously enhanced prestige. But Frederick's own remark, as reported by Henderson, shows that he knew another factor was also critical: to wit, the way potatoes "saved his armies from starvation" despite years of ruthless grain requisitioning by the three largest armies of the age. He must have also realized that the same was true for Prussia's civilian population as a whole. Without potatoes, that could not have happened, and potatoes would not have been in Prussian fields in sufficient number to feed the people if Frederick had not launched his deliberate effort to put them there a good twelve years before the Seven Years' War broke out.

The question remains: Did he foresee how important they would be? Did he know what he was doing in propagating them when he did? And how successful were his efforts to overcome peasant and landlord resistance before grain requisitioning by the three invading armies after 1756 convinced all concerned of their lifesaving importance? These questions remain obscure, but answers can almost certainly be discovered if and when a competent historian spends a few years searching appropriate records of Prussia's local administration and inquires into Frederick's personal efforts at agricultural oversight and management.

The multiplication of potato fields in Prussia between 1744 and 1763 had an enormous effect on Northern Europe as a whole. Invading armies soon noticed the amazing resilience of the Prussian peasantry and quickly discovered how and why they withstood loss of their stores of grain so successfully. Not surprisingly, when the war was over, the French, Austrian, and Russian governments all set out to duplicate Frederick's feat by propagating potatoes among their own rural subjects wherever cool temperatures and moist soils allowed the plants to prosper.

French efforts along this line are by far the best known thanks to the efforts of a French army doctor, Antoine Parmentier, who had spent several years as a prisoner of war in Prussia and observed the role potatoes played in Prussia's war effort. Once released, he spent the rest of his life urging his countrymen to emulate the Prussian example. His principal book, *Examen chymique des pommes de terres* (Paris, 1773), scientifically demonstrated the nutritional value of potatoes, and Louis XVI's court even lent itself to promoting the crop. For example, Marie Antoinette—famous for supposedly responding to Parisian bread riots by saying, "Let them eat cake"—once put potato blossoms in her hair at a state ball; and in 1794 the Committee of Public Safety chose to dramatize its effort to mobilize against Prussian invaders by converting the royal flower beds at the Tuileries into potato patches.

More generally, the expanded size of the French armies raised by *levée en masse* could not have been sustained without the enlarged food supply that potatoes had begun to provide in northern France and across the Germanys. During the Napoleonic Wars, armies on both sides swelled beyond earlier limits for the same reason. But, in 1812, Napoleon paid a heavy price when food supplies along his line of retreat from Moscow proved too scant to feed his soldiers, largely because Russian official efforts to propagate potatoes had lagged behind what the Germanic states had by then achieved.

Having overcome earlier prejudices and proved their food value by 1815, acreage devoted to potato growing expanded rapidly throughout climatically suitable parts of Northern Europe until 1845–47, when fungus imported inadvertently from Peru

The French army doctor Antoine Augustin Parmentier got acquainted with the politics of the potato during his time as a prisoner of war in Prussia. Back in France he became an avid promoter of the crop and introduced it to the French king, Louis XVI. The moment was significant enough to be immortalized in art, here in a nineteenth-century lithograph.

devastated European potato fields. Outright famine afflicted Ireland, and on the Continent potatoes supplemented but did not displace bread, even in the diet of the poorest classes.

Nonetheless, the "hungry forties" afflicted all of Northern Europe until warmer and drier summers made the fungus less devastating. A generation later, potato blight was reduced to insignificance when a chemical spray, discovered in 1882, proved capable of protecting the growing plants from its ravages. Then in the twentieth century, both world wars expanded the potato fields of Northern Europe even farther (sometimes even displacing grains) for the simple reason that the crop yielded so many more calories per acre than any alternative.

Even without exact and more specific information, Frederick's initiative appears to have been critical in provoking their remarkable transformation of Northern European agriculture. Before his time, landlords and rulers paid no attention to potatoes. Aside from their very earliest reception by fishermen in Spain, potatoes spread only where grain requisitioning (or in Ireland, foreign conquest) compelled peasants to resort to them. But long-established routines for cultivating grainfields left no space for the new crop, which therefore remained marginal, confined, as it was, to private gardens. Only through official intervention could potatoes become a field crop and move into the fallow grainfields of Northern Europe. That was what Frederick and his agents initiated in Prussia, giving potatoes a far larger place in European agriculture than had been possible before.

It took another century for the crop to come fully into its own and eliminate fallow fields from Northern Europe. To be sure, potatoes were not alone in achieving that transformation, for both turnips and sugar beets also became significant field crops during the nineteenth century. Hoeing, too, was eliminated by resorting to new machines for weeding root crops, using horses and then tractors. But potatoes retained preeminence among row crops, supplying an amount of human food that approximately doubled the total calorie supply coming from Northern European fields. Consequently, during the nineteenth century, as William Langer points out,* potatoes were a principal factor promoting population growth across the Northern European plain, made possible the urbanization and industrialization that transformed European society, and gave that small region of the earth a temporary preeminence in power and prestige that began

---

*William L. Langer, "Europe's Initial Population Explosion," *American Historical Review* 69 (1963); William L. Langer, "American Foods and Europe's Population Growth, 1750–1850," *Journal of Social History* 6 (winter 1973).

to fade away only in the closing decades of the twentieth century.

Without Frederick, potatoes might have spread across Northern Europe eventually, for the rewards of planting fallow fields with such a crop were so enormous that someone else in a position of power surely would have noticed the possibility sooner or later. But as things were, Frederick seems to have been the person who actually did so, vastly accelerating the spread of potatoes by royal command, benefiting spectacularly from his foresight, and reshaping Europe's agricultural as well as its military and political history in ways he could not have imagined.

Had I been with him at Philippsburg, he probably would not have discussed his new thoughts about potatoes with me or anyone else. That was not Frederick's way. But armed with my knowledge of the potato's importance for Prussia's future, it would have been interesting to discover whether he did talk to any of the local peasants, and whether their dependence on a strange new crop seemed of any particular interest to him. If I am right in guessing that it was there that he got the idea of how valuable potatoes could be, it is a moment in European history that deserves to be investigated and its far-reaching consequences more fully recognized.

Further Reading

David Fraser, *Frederick the Great: King of Prussia* (New York, 2001).

Gerhard Ritter, *Frederick the Great: A Historical Profile* (New York, 1975).

James Gaines, *Evening in the Palace of Reason: Bach Meets Frederick the Great in the Age of Enlightenment* (New York, 2005).

PAUL KENNEDY

The Battle of the Nile

Paul Kennedy is the J. Richardson Dilworth Professor of
History and Director of International Security Studies
at Yale University. He is a former Fellow of the Institute
of Advanced Studies, Princeton, and of the Alexander
von Humboldt-Stiftung, Bonn. He was made a Commander of the British Empire (CBE) in 2000 and
elected a Fellow of the British Academy in 2003. He is
the author or editor of sixteen books, including *Strategy
and Diplomacy*, *The War Plans of the Great Powers*, *The
Realities of Diplomacy*, and *The Rise and Fall of the Great
Powers*, which has been translated into over twenty languages. His most recent book is *The Parliament of Man:
The Past, Present, and Future of the United Nations*.

In this essay Professor Kennedy journeys back in time
to the Mediterranean shore of Egypt in August 1798.
There he witnesses the historic Battle of the Nile from a
unique perspective: in the company of a local fisherman, Abdullah el-Hourani.

The Battle of the Nile

Abdullah el-Hourani was a sorely puzzled man. Like his fore-fathers, brothers, and sons, he was a fisherman who lived on Egypt's Mediterranean shore. His village was a collection of mud shacks situated at the very western end of the great bay of Aboukir. Each day the Houranis would make to sea, scoop up the fish that lived off the Nile's westernmost effluents, and, if the weather was good, spend several hours on the small Aboukir Island, drying their catch. They had been doing this since the days of the pharaohs, the Phoenicians and the Greeks, the Romans, the Arabs and the Turks. Empires came and empires fell. The fishermen still fished.

But the events of late were puzzling. A short time earlier a distant cousin had come rushing into the village—the first time he had been back in fifteen years, Allah be praised!—to declare that the notorious French general Napoleon Bonaparte had landed with a mighty host to the west, advanced upon Alexandria, annihilated the detestable Mameluke army, and was now "governing" the country with strange people called philosophers, archaeologists, scientists. Why, some of those cursed French were even at Rosetta, the easternmost part of the Bay of Aboukir, and could be seen there, peering out from the battlements of the ancient watchtower. On some days they hired guides and marched off to the pyramids, where, stupidly, they made all sorts of measurements and sketches. They did not disturb the fishermen, but what were the infidels doing here at all?

Then, just a week ago—in the time of year the Christians called July, when the heat became intense—there had anchored in these very waters seventeen great and smaller warships, all bearing the flag of France. This was good news for the local traders, including (he admitted) himself. He had supplied eels, sardines, and flatfish to the thousands of Frenchmen. He had also rented out his rowboats to those who would take olives, figs, lamb's kidneys, dates, limes, and wine to the heathen warships, with their so many guns, so many crew. Why, one of them, named in the French manner *L'Orient*, was so enormous, towering a full three decks above the water, that it bore 120 cannon and housed the French admiral himself, a Monsieur Brueys. Since the admiral dined at table regularly, his needs were great, as were those of the one thousand men on board that vessel. But what did they want? They surely had not come solely to sample Abdullah's cousins' fine figs. That Corsican, Napoleon, was up to no good. But if he sought to conquer Egypt, well, he could go ahead. Better generals than he had tried and failed. Caesar himself had given up.

So there the French warships lay, swinging on their anchors across the bay, each about five hundred feet from the next. They had moved some of their guns onto Aboukir Island itself, just above where Abdullah and his brother dried their catch; and they kept lookouts to the west, day and night. What were they expecting, or fearing? Even the Bedouin, who had come out of the desert to observe the strange ships, did not know. Allah be praised!

It was midafternoon on Aboukir Island—by the Christian time it was now August 1, 1798—and, the fishing being poor, Abdullah el-Hourani was inclined to rest under the makeshift shade. But just as he stretched his legs and closed his eyes, his youngest and brightest nephew, Mohammed Abbas, jumped out of his light sailing skiff and came running up the Aboukir sands, shouting, "Uncle, uncle, look to the west! Look to the west!"

They all ran up to the top of the island from where, peering into the lowering sun, Abdullah saw what looked like a bank of clouds on the horizon. But they were not clouds; they were the white topsails and midsails of another great host of infidel warships, advancing steadily upon the anchored fleet. On the next crest, the Frenchmen manning their guns were also pointing and babbling. As it happened, Abdullah's brother was the proud possessor of a magical spyglass (for which he had bartered three full goats), and he solemnly announced that all the new vessels bore a different flag, the crossed red, white, and blue of the British navy. All the fishermen knew that flag, the Union Jack, because they had also sold their catch and other goods to the English frigates that sailed along Egypt's coastline in constant search of their nemesis, Napoleon. The English were also heathen, and blue-eyed devils at that, but they always paid in hard currency, which Abdullah thought most commendable.

The English fleet came with increasing pace, but purposefully and in perfect order, upon the anchored French. By now the sun was tumbling out of the western sky. Surely the English would not fight in the chaos of darkness, some thirty or more ships crashing into each other, unable to see their admirals' messages? They would have to heave to, anchor, and wait for the dawn. Abdullah's brothers concurred. They also decided, fervently, that they would not return to their village that night. The prospect of seeing Christians mutually slaughtering each other shortly after the sun came up tomorrow was an agreeable one.

As it happened, Admiral Brueys shared the fishermen's judgment. Although many of his sailors were still ashore to gain fresh water and thus, inevitably, fighting off the nefarious Bedouin tribesmen, the French ships were now full of bustle, the gunners assembling their powder and shot and the able seamen strewing the decks with sand (it absorbed both blood and pitch most effectively), while the crockery in the admiral's great dining room was lovingly lowered into special containers, and the ships' surgeons cleared their tables and the loblolly boys scalded the knives and scissors. But none of the French captains expected to fight tonight. Even Horatio Nelson, the most aggressive English sailor since Drake, would surely not gamble all against a strongly anchored fleet on a shallow shore in the darkness.

Brueys was wrong. Nelson had, in great frustration, crisscrossed the eastern Mediterranean in never-ending search of his foe. Now that the enemy fleet was in sight, as Captain Berry recorded in his classic *Narrative of Proceedings* of the battle, "The utmost joy seemed to animate every breast on board the squadron," and their admiral was consumed with joy. The fleet would attack without delay, Nelson ordered, increasing sail to catch every last wind of the day.

Abdullah rubbed his eyes. So the blue-eyed devils would attack after all. The advancing warships, still quiet and purposeful, were now very close to the westernmost section of the French fleet. Only a very knowledgeable observer would spot that the commander in chief's flag was flying from the mast-top of the sixth warship in line, the superb and fast seventy-four-gunned HMS *Vanguard*. Nelson had such confidence in his fellow captains that he did not need to be in the van and, besides, he could control his many craft better from a more central position. The lead ships would know what to do.

The chauvinistic British press at the time, and many a later historian, has written warmly and fondly of Nelson's fleet captains as his "band of brothers," and that language is indeed exuberant and uncritical. But the fact remains that most of those commanders, with their crews, had fought alongside the admiral again and again—or, if not with Nelson, then with the great Admiral John Jervis himself—as had of course their warships. The battle honors of both captains and ships were star-studded . . . the Saints, the Glorious First of June, Cape St. Vincent,

Tenerife, and many a smaller scrap. Nelson's second in command, Sir James Saumarez, had been in no less than four major fleet actions, including Rodney's big victory at the Battle of the Saints in 1782. What is more, these men knew that their leader had the utmost faith in them, provided they were aggressive and innovative. No captain could do wrong, to quote Nelson on a later occasion, provided he put his ship alongside that of the enemy. And that was just what they were doing.

Still, what happened then was truly astonishing, causing Abdullah and his brothers to gasp. For certain of the British warships, instead of swinging leftward to form a line parallel to the anchored French, proceeded closer and closer to the shore, clearly intent upon attacking their foe from *inside* the bay. This was pure folly! How could such large vessels—they were all two-decker seventy-fours, not frigates—not founder on the shallow sandbanks of Aboukir Bay? (One of them, indeed, the unfortunate HMS *Culloden* under Nelson's great friend Troubridge, had just run ashore on the outer sands a mile or two back.)

At first the leader of this hunting pack was Captain Samuel Hood, of the distinguished naval family. As his warship HMS *Zealous* overtook Nelson's own, the admiral shouted whether he could go clear into the inner waters despite the fact that the English ships possessed no reliable charts. Hood acknowledged and willingly went farther toward the shore—by this time Abdullah and his brothers were jumping up and down and punching the air. The ship's lead man was recording a mere four or five fathoms, so that the bottom of the heavily laden vessel must have been only a few feet from the murky shoals below. But as the *Zealous* came to the western head of the French line, it was overtaken by the fast-moving HMS *Goliath* under the command of the tough and massive Captain Thomas Foley, who had sized up the situation exactly and was running toward the inner French lines as if his ship were in completely open seas. In a later letter to his great uncle (Admiral Lord Hood), the younger man confessed that he was sure that both warships would come aground on the shoals. But they did not, and the British ships closed in on their victims. Then the next three seventy-fours, the *Orion, Theseus,* and *Audacious,* followed their example. Within a short while of the start of the battle, therefore, the Royal Navy had five quick-firing warships on the exposed inner side of Brueys's stationary fleet. Really, there had been nothing like it since Hawke's dash into Quiberon Bay in the midst of an Atlantic gale in 1759 to destroy Conflans's fleeing squadron; these folks knew how to sail.

No one can say what was in Nelson's mind at this historic juncture; pride, no doubt, in his own captains, but also, and as ever, an all-consuming desire for total victory. What was clear to him—since *Culloden* was unable to get off the Aboukir shoals, and the *Alexander* and *Swiftsure* were still racing back from a separate mission to rejoin his fleet—was that no more vessels could be risked on the inner side of his enemy's line. Nelson thus placed his own ship along the Frenchman *Spartiate* and began pummeling. It was now dark—the *Goliath* itself had started shooting just as the sun had set—and the first five ships of the French line were being fired on from both sides. Mast after mast came crashing down, French officers were swept away by the raking British fire, and their guns were steadily silenced. In retrospect, it became clear that the battle had been won by this astonishing, decapitating blow, by Hood and Foley's risky turn into the inner shoals. Can any captain in all of the world's naval history lay claim to their fame?

Still, that victory did not seem so certain at the time and especially not to the thousands of sailors on board, not to mention the many observers on shore. To watchers like Abdullah, there was no clear outcome: just gunfire, smoke, great screams, and parts of vessels drifting onshore. The French gunmen were no slouches—they were fighting for their lives, since Brueys's decision meant that they could no longer elude the Royal Navy. Moreover, the French fleet had greater firepower; *L'Orient*'s broadside alone was almost twice that of any British vessel.

Yet, as mentioned earlier, many of the French sailors were ashore (a strong reason for Brueys to remain where he was, since his diminished crews could not man the guns and man the sails at the same time). And the remaining sailors had prepared to fire their guns from the outer, starboard side. What was more, the five-hundred-foot gap between the anchored French warships meant that some of the English vessels could, if they wished, sail in between their foes, raking their vulnerable bows and sterns with full broadsides. For example, HMS *Alexander,* as if anxious to make up for lost time, simply barreled straight through the gap between the French flagship *L'Orient* and the formidable ninety-gun *Le Tonnant.* Of course the *Alexander* took a terrific battering (with her Captain Ball wounded), but this sort of maneuver meant that certain French warships were being shot at from all sides. Who could survive?

Then there was the British gunnery, perhaps the most formidable in the world. Nicholas Rodger, the great authority on the eighteenth-century Royal Navy, points out (in his classic work *The Wooden World,* 1986) that the average British warship could fire its guns at a far faster rate, and more accurately, than any equivalent French, Spanish, or Portuguese craft. Naval gunners when added to land sieges could fire three times faster than the astonished Royal Artillery. No one else, apart from some of the superheavy American frigates, came close. It was more usual for the British to fire at the enemy's decks, to decimate personnel, though here at Aboukir they seem to have concentrated on bringing down the French masts, so that flight was impossible;

then the close-in killing began. All of *Le Guerriere*'s masts were gone within an hour, which says much for the crew's shooting on board Hood's *Zealous*.

Little or nothing of this was obvious to Abdullah el-Hourani and his brothers, to the wandering Bedouin tribesmen, or to the returning detachments of French sailors. The cannon that Brueys had ordered onto Aboukir Island fired in a weak and desultory manner and then ceased. Really, there was nothing to fire at. All that could be seen were the flashes of hundreds of guns, attended by the screams of men's voices. Acrid smoke drifted toward the land, followed by floating bits of mast, sail, and rigging, empty barrels, and the occasional badly burned body. In the east, French administrators crowded onto the rooftops and battlements at Rosetta; they also knew not what was unfolding and thus which side was winning the midnight struggle.

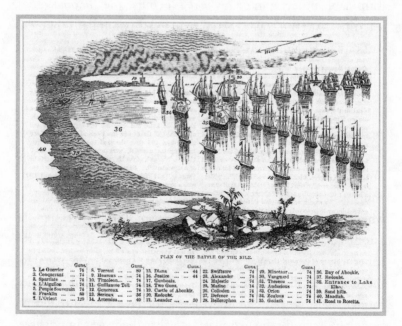

PLAN OF THE BATTLE OF THE NILE.

	Guns.		Guns.		Guns.		Guns.		Guns.	
1. Le Guerrier	... 74	8. Torrent ...	... 80	15. Diana ...	... 44	22. Swiftsure	... 74	29. Minotaur...	... 74	36. Bay of Aboukir.
2. Conquerant	... 74	9. Heureux ...	... 74	16. Justice ...	... 44	23. Alexander	... 74	30. Vanguard	... 74	37. Redoubt.
3. Spartiate ...	... 74	10. Timoleon...	... 74	17. Gunboats.		24. Majestic ...	... 74	31. Theseus ...	... 74	38. Entrance to Lake
4. L'Aigalon	... 74	11. Guillaume Tell	74	18. Two Guns.		25. Matine ...	... 14	32. Audacious	... 74	Elko.
5. Peuple Souverain	74	12. Genereux ...	... 74	19. Castle of Aboukir.		26. Colloden ...	... 74	33. Orion ...	... 74	39. Sand hills.
6. Franklin ...	... 80	13. Serieux ...	... 36	20. Redoubt.		27. Defence ...	... 74	34. Zealous ...	... 74	40. Maadlah.
7. L'Orient ...	... 120	14. Artemisa...	... 40	21. Leander ...	... 50	28. Bellerophon	... 74	35. Goliath ...	... 74	41. Road to Rosetta.

A nineteenth-century plan of the Battle of the Nile details the positions of the English and French ships in the Bay of Aboukir.

The situation of the French fleet was most unusual and dislo-
cated. The first six vessels were being battered to pieces from
both sides, slowly surrendering and being taken prize, some of
them fighting until they had no active guns left. The military
balance worsened against the French when the *Alexander, Swiftsure,* and *Leander* caught up and entered the fray, with fresh
crews and fresh guns. At this stage most of the English ships
gathered around the giant *L'Orient,* determined to seal her fate.
But the last five French battleships—*L'Heureuse* (74 guns), *Le Timoléon* (74), *Le Guillaume Tell* (80), *Le Mercure* (74), and *Le Généreux* (74), plus two 40-gun frigates, *La Diane* and *La Justice,* were
not in the battle at all and still anchored on their cables. Inex-
plicably, the senior officer of this group, Vice Admiral Villeneuve in *Le Guillaume Tell,* made no move. Thus Admiral
Brueys's flagship was left to fend for itself. Given the lack of
support from Villeneuve, the odds were terrible. But there could
be no denying the courage of the admiral, his officers, and men.
His cannon were double-shotted, and the gun crews primed for
action. Their first opponent was HMS *Bellerophon,* only half her
weight and size, but under Captain Darby one of the toughest
fighting ships in the Royal Navy. For a full hour the two ships
lay side by side, battering and counterbattering, with the
Bellerophon losing all its masts and suffering the heaviest casualties on the British side—over two hundred officers and men were
wounded, including Darby himself. When the warship drifted
off into the night, it was close to being a wreck. But the smaller
fighter had inflicted very great damage upon the French giant,
and Brueys himself had lost both legs, though he still strove to
direct the firing. It was at this stage, though, that the battle-fresh
Alexander, Swiftsure, and *Leander* had completed their encir-
clement of *L'Orient,* joining the *Majestic* in the agonizing demo-
lition job. Shortly afterward, a cannonball from the *Swiftsure* cut
Brueys in two.

By this stage the *Swiftsure* had angled itself so that it could pound the whole front starboard of *L'Orient* without itself being hit, and it was from this close-in vantage point that Captain Hallowell noticed a great fire developing on the enemy's deck, toward which the British guns now directed their shot. Before long it was clear to all that the fires would reach the flagship's magazine, and its crew, understandably, began to abandon ship and swim toward the British rescue boats (though not the heroes of Mrs. Henman's later lachrymose poem "The Boy Stood on the Burning Deck," a testimony to Commodore Casabianca, who declined to leave while his son was underneath, on the surgeon's table). Nelson himself, who had a great sliver of flesh blown off his forehead, temporarily blinding his good eye, was brought onto the deck of HMS *Vanguard* to peer at the ghastly sight. All the other ships, British and French, sought to back away, anticipating an explosion that would send blazing masts and broken ironware in all directions. The exception here was the remarkable Hallowell on the *Swiftsure,* who coolly reckoned that this naval volcano would erupt high into the sky and arch right over his own ship.

Volcano was not an exaggerated term. Abdullah and his brothers were still peering out to the gun flashes, and the teenage boys were running up from the beach to report ever more debris from the battle, including the bodies of drowned Frenchmen. Another watcher reported that a ship's boat full of exhausted and wounded French sailors had just come ashore. Things were not going well for Monsieur Bonaparte's Egyptian gamble, thought Abdullah. But nothing in his modest knowledge of how the Europeans fought battles at sea had prepared him for the sound of the blowing up of *L'Orient*. It was the most ear-splitting detonation he had ever heard in his life, and he would remember it to his dying day (Abdullah, in his old age, would have much to tell about this night to his amazed grand-children and great-grandchildren). All the shoreline observers dived to the ground, then raised their heads as they saw, for just a minute, the battle illuminated by the vast explosion, with great cannon and masts being hurled hundreds of feet into the air before the warship's back broke and it began sinking into the bay, steam and hissing replacing the flames. Then all was si-lence, on the land and on the water. The explosion had been heard as far away as Alexandria. But now all the shooting had stopped, the two great armadas overwhelmed by the experience.

The Bedouin began first to break the silence, cheering and dancing. Truly, the infidel had given them the greatest of all fire-works displays. The French observers said nothing, but looked glum. Gradually the Arab fishermen themselves joined in the cheering—Allah be praised!—and rushed down to the shore, hauling in the tar-stained masts and making fires with them. Ab-dullah himself was more quiet. Something very large had just happened out in the bay, and he did not understand it.

Then the gunfire resumed; there was still the other half of the French fleet to destroy, and Nelson's captains knew that this was what their admiral would expect. *Le Franklin*'s condition was now desperate, since it had been exposed to the full blast of *L'Orient*'s eruption, causing fires and havoc at the same time as the British warships resumed their attack. It surrendered, in mangled shape, shortly afterward, with only three lower-deck guns left from its original eighty, and two-thirds of the company killed and wounded. It is hard to believe those figures in today's much more protected world.

Interestingly, Hallowell was right: The *Swiftsure* was not badly hurt by the explosion, though it had been hit below the water-line by much enemy shot, and thus was able to pick up a fair number of *L'Orient*'s sailors—including one, totally naked save for his hat, which he claimed proved that he was a lieutenant! *Swiftsure* also participated in the surrender of *Le Tonnant* before finally pulling out of the fighting in order to stem its own serious leaks and cut away its broken masts. Hallowell and his crew had offered another extraordinary example of seamanship, gunnery, courage, and sheer professionalism.

By dawn of the next day Abdullah and his brother with the spyglass could at least make sense of what had transpired. The first six of the French warships were lying offshore, captured and battered, the dead men being buried at sea, the wounded Frenchmen being rowed to the Alexandria hospital. Then there was a gap, created by *L'Orient*'s destruction—so that was what had blown up! Allah is good! Then there lay, most unhappily, the severely damaged *Le Tonnant*. And, in the middle of the bay, the remaining British fighting vessels were again going after the French, most of which had slipped cable (to get some distance from their blazing flagship) and were now drifting. Two of them, the ironically named *L'Heureuse* and *Le Mercure*, grounded themselves on shore—Abdullah could not tell whether this was deliberate or if they had simply lost control—with their crews abandoning ship and assembling on the sands. Shortly afterward both ships went up in flames.

At this stage the remaining French admiral, Villeneuve, decided it was time to fly and fight another day. Tacking slowly eastward in *Le Guillaume Tell*, he was followed by *Le Généreux* and the two unengaged frigates. He was also joined in this escape bid by the last of the French seventy-fours, the unlucky *Le Timoléon*, which came too close to shore and struck the rocks with such force that its foremast was thrown overboard. The cheers of the Royal Navy crews echoed those of the Arabs and Bedouin on land. And, look! The captain of *Le Timoléon* had ordered his ship to be set on fire, so that it could not fall into enemy hands. Never, thought Abdullah, would he ever again see three large warships stranded on his own village beach and burning out of control.

Aboukir Bay being now free of firing, Abdullah, his brother with the spyglass, and his nephew Mohammed Abbas decided to take one of their small skiffs out upon the waters. The burning warships on the shore were now but ashes, with the Bedou still searching through the wreckage. The French soldiers and sailors who had been ashore at the time of the battle were organized enough to protect their own casualties and put them on carts for Rosetta or Alexandria; otherwise, the shipwrecked men would have been plundered and had their throats slit. Of that Abdullah had no doubt. Thank Allah that the Bedou had never learned to sail.

The last infidel ship resting in the bay was the battered but unsunken *Bellerophon*, whose mutual engagement with *L'Orient* had begun that great warship's dreadful fate. As Abdullah and his skiff drew nearer, he marveled at how this warship could still be afloat, although its crew, reinforced by assistance from other British ships, was cheerfully ramming cloth into the cannon-holes, tossing overside the broken rigging, and putting up jury-masts. And, yes, said the vessel's purser to Abdullah, they would buy eels and flounders and limes and hard biscuit and whatever else the Aboukir fishermen and merchants could bring them. But they would sail in another day, back to Malta for repairs, and then back to those cold northern waters on the other side of the world that they called home. Admiral Nelson expected them.

Abdullah's skiff turned abruptly and raced to the shore, his brother firing an ancient pistol to get the village's attention. Allah be praised! There was a lot to sell to the victorious blue-eyed devils, and it should surely be Abdullah's people and not those rotten Lebanese and Copts and Jews in Alexandria who made the profit. This idea was so salivating that he did not notice that their skiff was sailing only ten feet or so above the drowned hull of *L'Orient* itself, and that young Abbas was pointing down excitedly. Then Abdullah cried out, in understanding. It would be easy for the young divers to go right into the shattered hull, and what might they find in there! And this was the French flagship, yes? The one that had carried Napoleon himself, and the plunder of Malta? Everyone had heard of that. God was good.

When, on the following morn, Abdullah and the minifleet of Aboukir boats watched the *Bellerophon* limp away to the west, they saw only a damaged British warship and its cheering, bloodied crew. They had no idea—why should they?—that they were looking at one of the most distinguished fighting ships in all of Western history. Her first action had been at "the Glorious First of June" in 1794, where she had forced a similarly sized Frenchman, the seventy-four-gunned *Éole,* to surrender. She had then fought in many blockading actions off the French coast. The Battle of Aboukir was no doubt her greatest moment in wartime, yet she had been bruised by *L'Orient*'s many guns but never finished off. She fought later in the Channel and the West Indies, and then, marvelously, at the historic 1805 Battle of Trafalgar, where she absorbed another 132 casualties (including her captain) as she captured the French seventy-four, the *Aigle.* This great fighter—perhaps HMS *Warspite* in the first and second world wars was her equal, but which else?—was on active service in European waters until 1815. After Napoleon's defeat at Waterloo, the defeated emperor traveled to Rochefort and, destined for exile, formally surrendered in that port to Captain Frederick Maitland—and went on board HMS *Bellerophon*! The very same. Wherever I go, remarked Bonaparte, I find the Royal Navy in the way.

Abdullah was not to know all this. He was not to know that Villeneuve's escape with the four remaining French warships was successful, except that those ships never came back again. As it happened, by the morn of the battle few if any of the British vessels were in a condition to pursue the fast-disappearing French; they needed time to rebuild their masts, bury their dead, care for their wounded, and repair the captured warships so that they could be towed off as prizes. And Nelson needed time to write dispatches, an early one reporting on the amazing victory, then the later, more detailed reports. He reported his deep regrets to the commander in chief that *any* French ships had escaped, but upon receipt St. Vincent understood that, being only grateful that he had asked for Nelson to come out to the Mediterranean above many a senior-ranking officer. Besides, Villeneuve's move was just a postponement for the French vessels, not a full escape. Within two years Nelson had captured *Le Généreux*, and a cluster of his captains had taken *Le Guillaume Tell*. That was sweet.

As for Villeneuve himself, who denied charges of inaction and cowardice made by fellow officers and maintained to Napoleon (who agreed) that the battle had been lost once Foley and Hood had rounded the top of the French line, his real day of challenge lay years ahead. On October 21, 1805, Nelson and his friend Admiral Cuthbert Collingwood led their twin columns directly into a massive French-Spanish armada of thirty-three warships off the extreme southwest coast of Spain, a force under Villeneuve's command. By the end of the action, Nelson was dead but twenty of the enemy vessels were captured, destroyed, or foundered; four more surrendered a little later. Villeneuve's own flagship had been driven onto the rocks off Trafalgar, and French sea power was effectively destroyed. Villeneuve himself was captured in the middle of the battle. He had not been a lucky admiral.

Again, Abdullah knew nothing of that. He did hear, from his

distant cousin (who was now coming back much more regularly to pick up the Maria Theresa dollars that young Abbas and his brother found scattered across the floor of *L'Orient*), that Napoleon had taken the defeat at Aboukir badly, had struck eastward toward Palestine, and been halted at the fortress of Acre. Thereupon the emperor, as he was now, slipped back to France in a smaller ship and recommenced his conquests. And the British would fight him, again and again, and never give up. Allah be praised! The infidels could continue to slaughter each other in Europe and leave Aboukir Bay alone. Years later Abdullah learned that the great English admiral, Lord Nelson, had been killed, and Abdullah was sad.

But not for very long. For Abdullah and his brothers, including the one with the spyglass, were by now rather rich men. They were no fools. Every morning they would go out to fish in the bay. They would catch eels and flounders, along with their cousins. It had been made plain, in no uncertain terms, to fishermen in the neighboring villages that this area of the bay was fishing grounds for the Hourani family alone. As they duly fished, young Abbas and his brothers and cousins would quietly dive into the waters, down to *L'Orient,* and bring up a few more items: coins, urns, porcelain. Then they would all move to the island, as in days of yore, and dry the fish, leaving behind a couple of very strong cousins to do "night fishing" over the family area. Each Saturday Abdullah's cousin, with a powerful and armed friend, would come and stay with them, then head back to Alexandria with the coins and other relics hidden in the camel's water bottles. The local tax collector for Aboukir had been paid off and, in any case, had married one of Abdullah's cousins. The Jewish jewelry and coin dealer in Alexandria could be relied upon. Gradually the houses and gardens inhabited by Abdullah and his extended family were no longer mud shacks and offal heaps. They became grander, cleaner, with their own vines and figs and flowers. But nobody noticed; if they did, they did not ask. Truly, God was good.

And it all began when young Abbas had called out, "Uncle, uncle, look to the west!"

Further Reading

Oliver Warner, *The Battle of the Nile* (London, 1960).

G. J. Marcus, *A Naval History of England*, vol. 2 (London, 1961).

Nicholas Rodger, *The Wooden World* (London, 1986).

ROSS KING

The "Uncouth Riddle" of Édouard Manet: Le Déjeuner sur l'herbe *at the 1863 Salon des Refusés*

Ross King lives in Woodstock, England, and is the author of two novels, *Ex Libris* and *Domino*, as well as three books on art and architectural history: *Brunelleschi's Dome: How Renaissance Genius Reinvented Architecture, Michelangelo and the Pope's Ceiling,* and *The Judgment of Paris: The Revolutionary Decade That Gave the World Impressionism.* His most recent work is a biography of Niccolò Machiavelli.

In this essay King joins seven thousand other visitors at the tumultuous opening of the Salon des Refusés, the "Salon of the Rejected," on May 15, 1863, in Paris. He is particularly interested in the work of an obscure young painter named Édouard Manet, who is represented by a large canvas titled *Le Bain.*

The "Uncouth Riddle" of Édouard Manet: Le Déjeuner sur l'herbe *at the 1863 Salon des Refusés*

On May 15, 1863, more than seven thousand people pressed into a cavernous exhibition hall on the Champs-Élysées in Paris to see an art exhibition. The Palace of Industry was used to hosting large crowds, and the Paris Salon there, a juried art exhibition, never failed to attract hundreds of thousands of people over its six-week run in May and June. Yet this particular exhibition, as everyone knew, was no ordinary Salon. For the previous few weeks the French press had been whetting appetites with descriptions of what they dubbed the "Salon of the Heretics" and "Salon of the Pariahs." The name that eventually stuck, the *Salon des Refusés,* or "Salon of the Rejected," alluded to the fact that all of the more than eight hundred canvases, statues, and engravings put on show had been rejected by the jury from having a place in the regular Paris Salon. They were works of art, in other words, that the Salon's Selection Committee, composed of France's most successful and esteemed artists, deemed unfit for public display.

The Selection Committee was unusually harsh in 1863, giving a thumbs-down to more than two-thirds of all artists. The spurned artists voiced such angry complaints at their exclusion that no less a figure than the Emperor of France, Napoleon III, ordered an exhibition of the rejected works. The people should decide, he declared, whether or not the jurors had been too stringent. And so, on May 15, the crowds in their thousands began thronging the Palace of Industry. I would love to have been among them. How astonishing it would have been to see the paintings and also to witness the reactions to them—everything from howls of outrage voiced by indignant men in top hats to the awestruck appreciation of young artists who realized that they were seeing the future of art.

Most people came, of course, to taunt and laugh. Pushing through the turnstiles, one would have heard incredulous, mocking laughter coming from within. One critic complained that visitors showed all the decorum of tourists entering the Chamber of Horrors at Madame Tussaud's. The jurors who oversaw the hanging of the paintings certainly did their best to serve up some frights. It was in their interests that the Salon des Refusés should be seen as a failure, and so they placed the most outrageous offenders—and there were some truly unusual works from which to choose—in highly conspicuous locations. The tactic seemed to have worked. One of the paintings prominent near the entrance, *The White Girl*, a seven-foot-high canvas by an unknown young American named James McNeill Whistler, provoked much raucous mirth. Whistler had chosen to explore subtle harmonies of color by depicting a young redhead in a white dress standing in front of a white curtain—but the public, it seems, saw only a sloppily painted canvas featuring a dazed-looking woman.

Even more derision was heaped on a painting by an equally obscure painter, a friend of Whistler named Édouard Manet. His canvas was entitled *Le Bain*, or *The Bath*, which the public quickly rechristened *Le Déjeuner sur l'herbe*, *The Luncheon on the Grass*. It was a deceptively simple scene featuring a young woman seated on the grass flanked by two young men and a picnic basket. The young men were dressed in hats and frock coats; the young woman—not unusual for a painting at this time—was nude. Most of the public found the scene ridiculous: What was this shameless young woman, whose clothes lay piled beside her, meant to be doing in the company of this pair of dandies?

The critics, predictably, threw up their hands in horror and despair. Manet was denounced for choosing deliberately scandalous subjects and for his supposed obsession with the bizarre. He was even accused of being unable to paint or draw properly.

The offending artist was thirty-one years old. To the surprise of many, Édouard Manet was not a longhaired, wild-eyed lunatic, but rather, as a critic would later put it, "a peaceful and distinguished man." He came from an affluent Parisian family: His late father had been a magistrate, his mother the goddaughter of one of Napoleon's generals, who became King of Sweden. Young Manet grew up in a well-appointed house that stood across the river from the Louvre and across the street from the École des Beaux-Arts, the state-sponsored art school. He began studying art not at the École, however—his lackadaisical nature would no doubt have chafed under its strict regime—but with a respected teacher named Thomas Couture. Manet spent six years learning how to draw and paint in Couture's studio. He also spent much spare time in the Louvre, setting up his easel in its galleries and making copies of Old Masters; and he made three trips to Italy in the 1850s, visiting Venice, Florence, and Rome, and making drawings in their churches and museums.

Manet's artistic education was therefore irreproachable. Far from being unable to paint or draw, he was in fact a superb technician with both talent and expert training. Yet *Le Déjeuner sur l'herbe* was executed in a style utterly different from how Couture or the Old Masters had taught him to paint. Both enigmatic in its subject matter and eccentric in its execution, it was a shocking work that seemed to violate all the rules of painting. No one who saw the painting in the Salon des Refusés could have failed to be dumbfounded. What, indeed, was the meaning of the scene? What was the logic behind the strange style in which it was painted?

In some respects, Manet was as enigmatic as his painting. An

Today, Édouard Manet's *Le Déjeuner sur l'herbe* is considered one of the most influential works of its era and a departure point for modern art. In 1863, however, the painting (exhibited as *Le Bain*) generated both laughter and scandal. The presence of a naked woman among clothed men in contemporary dress was justified neither by mythological nor by allegorical precedents and was considered bold and obscene. As to his painting style, Manet was accused of "seeing in blocks," as he abandoned the traditional subtle gradations between light and dark in favor of sharp contrast.

articulate conversationalist with very determined views about art, he gathered nightly with artist friends in Paris cafés to discuss what he called "Art with a capital A." But few of his theories and opinions would ever find their way into print. We have no firsthand comments from him about *Le Déjeuner sur l'herbe*: what he intended to show, what he hoped to achieve, what he thought about the outrage it caused at the Salon des Refusés. What led him to adopt such a radical style of painting? Did he expect to scandalize the public in the way he did? And what precisely did he hope to convey? To have been at Manet's side as he gauged the baffled reactions to the work, or as he opened the newspapers each morning to read the blistering reviews, would have been a rare and wonderful opportunity to get an insight into one of the world's most inscrutable paintings.

One person who probably knew more about the painting than most was Manet's friend Antonin Proust. Many years later, in 1897, Proust would write a memoir describing the genesis of the painting. He claims that in the late summer of 1862, he and Manet traveled a few miles west of Paris to Argenteuil, downstream along the Seine, near to where the Manet family had a second home at Gennevilliers. Easily reached by train, Argenteuil and Gennevilliers were favorite locations for Parisians to spend their Sunday afternoons in pleasant outdoor recreation: They picnicked or promenaded on the riverbank, played *boules,* rowed skiffs, swam in the Seine, and drank in the cafés and restaurants. It's easy to picture the two young men lounging on the riverbank, watching the scene before them, and talking about art. Inspired by "the flesh of the women leaving the water," Manet apparently announced that he intended to paint a modern scene for the next Salon, a female nude that he promised would shock the critics. He then climbed to his feet, brushed off his top hat—he was always impeccably turned out— and returned to his studio in Paris.

Nudity was certainly taboo in French society at this time. The French were every bit as prudish as the Victorians across the Channel. Manet could have enjoyed only the most fleeting and distant view of "women leaving the water," since male and female bathers at Argenteuil were kept apart by barriers and uniformed inspectors. Strict penalties awaited anyone swimming either naked or in an improper costume; even men faced arrest if they swam without a top. The ludicrous fear of physicality was reflected in the fact that women were forbidden to ride on the upper deck of Paris's omnibuses in case the male passengers should glimpse their ankles as they climbed the stairs. Nudity was on offer, of course, for those who sought it out. The invention of photography a few decades earlier inevitably led to a flourishing trade in pornographic images; but the authorities were vigilant in prosecuting offenders, and by the early 1860s literally hundreds of photographers and dealers had been arrested for peddling indecent images.

In the midst of all this anxiety about naked flesh there was one place in Paris where nudity was both lawful and profuse: the Palace of Industry. Painting a nude woman was not in itself shocking or rebellious. On the contrary, both the public and the critics celebrated idealized, soft-focus nudes, and a Venus or a Psyche, "tastefully" done, was virtually guaranteed to attract large crowds and favorable reviews. These paintings were not meant to be erotic; they showed instead (so the theory went) ideals such as beauty and chastity embodied in physical form. By Manet's time the undisputed champion of the genre was J. A. D. Ingres, whose *La Source,* a full-frontal female nude completed in 1856, was hailed by the critic Charles Blanc as the most beautiful figure in the history of French art. There was a great difference, naturally, between an Ingres nude and the illicit images sold by disreputable photographers. Ingres urged painters not to show too much detail, and the limbs of a nude, he stressed, "must be, so to speak, like shafts of columns." The result was that the walls of the Palace of Industry swarmed with nude flesh—but bloodless flesh, for the most part, from which the fevers of desire were almost surgically removed.

There was no better way to execute a nude, painters like Ingres believed, than to look at how painters of the Italian Renaissance worked. French art at this time was very much in the thrall of the past, with the École des Beaux-Arts a shrine to Italian art of the Renaissance. Its collection included hundreds of casts of statues and copies of paintings, including fifty-two Raphaels and a full-scale replica of Michelangelo's *Last Judgment* from the

Sistine Chapel. Pupils were instructed to study these works in order to perfect the style of the Old Masters. They were also encouraged to take as their subjects the same scenes from Greek and Roman mythology and biblical history. The Salons abounded, as a result, with endless images of Venus, Bacchus, Abraham and Isaac, frolicking nymphs, and toga-clad warriors.

There was a strange incongruity about these images of the past appearing at the Salon. I wish I could have walked the boulevards of Paris in 1863, since it would have been fascinating to see how the city was reinventing and rebuilding itself. In the dozen years since Napoleon III seized power in a coup d'état in 1851, Paris had turned into a modern-looking metropolis. The cityscape featured steam-cranes, telegraph lines, and cast-iron train stations and soaring railway bridges. Many of the city's twisting cobblestone streets had been replaced by wide boulevards paved in asphalt and macadam; and these new boulevards were lit not with the old eighteenth-century oil lamps but twenty thousand new gas lamps whose bright, steady light was conducive to strolling and socializing. Street life was further enhanced by the two hundred miles of underground sewers, which vastly improved the city's sanitation. There was even a department store, Le Bon Marché, that opened in 1852.

To stroll these boulevards and see these new sights, therefore, would have been to appreciate the exhilaration of young artists like Manet who wished to paint "modern" scenes of the exciting new world in which they lived. The irony of displaying so many regurgitated images of the past in the Palace of Industry—itself a newfangled cast-iron and glass construction—was not, of course, lost on everyone. A number of younger painters and critics believed the mythological whimsies on which painting had nourished itself for the previous four or five centuries were obsolete and pointless in an age of electricity and steam. They began calling for the depiction of what they regarded as the beautiful triumphs of Parisian life—the tree-lined boulevards, landscaped parks, and cast-iron, smoke-spewing monuments to progress and industry. The greatest poet of the age, Charles Baudelaire, coined a term for this brave new world: *la vie moderne,* or "modern life." In a work entitled *The Painter of Modern Life,* written in 1859 but not published until 1863, he advised artists to take their subjects from this new-sprung world, admonishing them to abandon the fripperies of period costume and paint instead people in frock coats and top hats—the modern but decidedly unheroic uniform of the nineteenth century.

Manet was a close friend of Baudelaire. They had known one another since the mid-1850s, and most evenings found them warming the benches of cafés such as Tortoni, a fashionable Right Bank establishment where Manet was conspicuous for his sarcastic wit and dandyish apparel (he wore what one friend called "intentionally gaudy trousers"). Even so, Manet must have seemed an unlikely convert to Baudelaire's theories of art given how he usually turned for inspiration to the walls of the Louvre rather than the streets of Paris. A work by the eighteenth-century painter François Boucher entitled *Diana at the Bath* provided the model for his biblical scene, *The Finding of Moses,* begun in 1859. He also painted a work called *La Pêche (Fishing),* an idyllic landscape based on a painting by Peter Paul Rubens in the Louvre called *Landscape with Rainbow.* The couple in the foreground of the painting—one of whom is Manet himself—wear distinctive seventeenth-century costume, with Manet depicting himself in a lace collar, knee breeches, red hose, and gold-buckled shoes. An image of *la vie moderne* it certainly was not.

This fascination with museums set Manet apart from a number of his contemporaries. In 1856 one of his friends, a writer named Edmond Duranty, called for the burning of the Louvre. Though no doubt speaking metaphorically, Duranty believed that progress in the arts could come about only through a collective act of cultural obliteration. This sort of injunction would be revived periodically by other artists, most famously in the Italian futurist Filippo Marinetti's overheated command to "demolish the museums and libraries." For Manet, nothing could have been more retrograde. He didn't regard museums as the musty repositories of outworn images that Marinetti was later to dismiss as "cemeteries of wasted effort." It's an intriguing paradox that a true break with the past came not from the museum-burning zealots of progress, but rather from the brush of someone who had spent his spare time learning his craft inside those very museums. New forms of expression could best be explored, Manet believed, within the existing monuments of artistic tradition. This reverence for the art of the past, coupled with a definitive break from its values, is what makes him so fascinating, enigmatic, and complex. And that's why one needed to be in Paris in 1863—sharing a drink with him in the Café Tortoni, perhaps—to understand what exactly he intended with *Le Déjeuner sur l'herbe*.

Manet's esteem for tradition was not the timid faithfulness and conspicuous imitation taught at the École des Beaux-Arts. Rather, he experimented with masterpieces in the Louvre to give them a personal interpretation and an invigorating contemporaneity. Thus, although he started *The Finding of Moses* in 1859, a year or two later he made a number of alterations—including the removal of the infant Moses and the addition of a satyr—and renamed it *Nymph and Satyr*. A year or so later, more changes: The satyr was overpainted and the canvas, now featuring only a modern-looking female figure, was rechristened *The Surprised Nymph*. The biblical and mythological references were lopped from everything but the title; all that remained was the female nude inspired by Boucher's *Diana at the Bath*. Manet still followed the lead of Boucher and other Old Masters, but out went the buckles and knee breeches, and in came new perspectives and a fresh sensibility.

Manet used a similar approach in 1862 as he worked on *Le Déjeuner sur l'herbe*. Antonin Proust claims Manet specifically mentioned using Titian's *Le Concert champêtre (The Pastoral Concert)*—another masterpiece from the Louvre—as the model for his canvas. Executed about 1510, Titian's painting, then believed to have been the work of Giorgione, features two men and two women set against an idyllic landscape of sheep, shepherds, and shady groves. The men are dressed in contemporary sixteenth-century costume; one wears voluminous scarlet knee breeches and strums a stringed instrument called a rebec. The two women, by contrast, are nude: One sits on the grass playing a flute, while the other draws water from a well. The painting is a good example of the genre known as the *fête champêtre* ("country fair"), which characteristically features bevies of musicians, rustics, and courting couples blissfully disporting themselves in leafy bowers. If Proust is right, Manet wanted to superimpose this vision of Arcadian pleasure onto the more rampant delights of the riverside at Argenteuil. A Venetian daydream of the Golden Age would become a Sunday outing in modern-day Paris.

As models for his painting Manet used his brother Gustave; a young sculptor named Ferdinand Leenhoff (his future brother-in-law); and Victorine Meurent, a nineteen-year-old model nicknamed "The Shrimp," who had recently posed for several of his other paintings. The two young men were attired in thoroughly modern dress: cravats, frock coats, trousers, and, on the head of the young man to the right, a bohemian-style hat worn by Left Bank students. Victorine was painted in the nude—or, rather, she was painted naked, since Manet's canvas neatly illustrates the distinction between nudity and nakedness. She has none of the powderpuff complexion and shy demeanor of an Ingres nude. Rather than an idealized figure of a nymph or goddess, she is portrayed as a flesh-and-blood woman whose skin might still bear the imprint of her corset and garters. And, as many critics and members of the public recognized, she is undoubtedly meant to be a prostitute consorting with two young men in the kiss-me-quick purlieus of Argenteuil.

Altogether, work on the painting took three or four months. Manet must have made a number of drawings and studies, though only one of them survives, a smallish sketch of the scene done in watercolor, pencil, and India ink. He probably made outdoor studies of the landscape alongside the Seine at Argenteuil, but the entirety of the canvas—a whopping eight feet, eight inches wide—was painted in his studio in the Rue Guyot. The sheer size of the canvas reveals the scale of Manet's ambitions.

It would have been intriguing to watch Manet at work. One of his other models was later to marvel at how he was "engrossed in his work . . . with a concentration and artistic integrity that I have seen nowhere else." He had no time for small talk as he worked, so I suspect he told his sitters very little of his plans or intentions for the painting. I can't help wondering what they made of it, especially Victorine. Did she object to her unorthodox portrayal? A year or two earlier a woman named Madame Brunet had fled Manet's studio in tears after seeing her unflattering portrait. I'd love to know if Victorine was ever among the crowds at the Salon des Refusés, hearing the mocking laughter and seeing the fingers pointed at her image on the canvas. Was she bothered by the critics who called her ugly and indecent? Or did she revel in her sudden notoriety?

Victorine certainly had cause for concern if she was as vain as the unfortunate Madame Brunet. Manet applied his paints in a remarkable manner that was by no means guaranteed to beautify his subjects. Artists almost always added their dark and light colors in different thicknesses and consistencies, with the high-

James McNeill Whistler's *Little White Girl* was among the artworks meeting with severe public derision at the Salon des Refusés. Clearly, Whistler was far more interested in creating an abstract design than in capturing an exact likeness of the model (his mistress Joanna Heffernan). His radical espousal of a purely aesthetic orientation and the creation of "art for art's sake" became a virtual rallying cry of modernism.

lights spread more thickly over thinner layers of dark paint. This technique made use of the optical illusion that makes light colors seem to advance and dark ones recede. But Manet forfeited this natural perspective by applying his paints in the opposite way to how he was taught, adding his darks in thick layers and his highlights very thinly. He also abandoned most of the half tones, the gradations of color that managed the transitions between light and shade. The result was a painting with abrupt contrasts and a lack of spatial recession—the illusion of three dimensions that for the previous four hundred years was the aspiration of all painters. Victorine, as a result, looked curiously flattened, with none of the sensuous lineaments and diaphanous beauty of the average Salon nude.

What led Manet to adopt his revolutionary technique? Clearly he was indifferent to creating either an illusion of depth or a "realistic" and convincing scene. Since the Italian Renaissance this supposedly lifelike quality—an approximation of the world we see around us—was one of the highest aims of art, a standard by which a painter or sculptor was judged. There's a funny but revealing anecdote about the fifteenth-century Florentine sculptor Donatello. While carving the marble sculpture known as *Lo Zuccone (The Pumpkinhead)*, Donatello would mutter to himself over and over again, "Speak, damn you, speak!" For the next four hundred years no artist could expect a higher compliment than being told how his characters were so alive they looked as if they could move or speak. The unsurpassed master of this style of painting in Manet's day—some claimed the greatest of all time—was Jean-Louis Ernest Meissonier. In 1857 a leading critic wrote that Meissonier painted with such amazingly lifelike detail that viewers believed they could see his figures moving their lips. But Manet, later to become a fierce opponent of Meissonier, was clearly concerned with something other than this lip-moving realism.

There are certainly no moving lips in *Le Déjeuner sur l'herbe*. It's a cryptic painting that does not in any way speak for itself. At least as unsettling as the innovative technique is the way the subject matter is handled. The work simply didn't fit into any of the traditional genres with which Salon-goers were familiar, such as the landscape, the portrait, the still life, or even, in any straightforward or conventional way, the nude or the *fête champêtre*. Nor did it tell a recognizable story. In the 1860s people went to the Salon expecting to see various well-known legends and historical episodes illustrated on the walls. But Manet's canvas defies any clear narrative. It seems pregnant with meaning, yet the ambiguous gestures of the participants, their lack of interaction, the allusions to other paintings, the small details that might or might not hold significance—all conspire to frustrate an easy or unequivocal reading of the painting. Small wonder that one critic, reviewing the Salon des Refusés, dismissed the work as an "uncouth riddle."

Not everyone, though, had such an adverse reaction. How thrilling it would have been to watch the electrifying effect of the painting on more discriminating visitors to the Palace of Industry. One reviewer at the Salon des Refusés claimed that Manet's "strange new style . . . caused many painters' eyes to open and their jaws to drop." Among these painters were young men like Claude Monet, Paul Cézanne, Edgar Degas, and Pierre Auguste Renoir. They quickly recognized Manet as the kind of the painter of *la vie moderne* called for by Baudelaire. A friend praised him as the first artist to assert "a sense of modernity" in painting. They and other young artists and writers would soon begin gathering with Manet at the Café Guerbois to discuss "Art with a capital A" and how best to overcome the intransigence of the critics and the conservatism of the Salon juries. An art critic was later to claim that Manet played for these younger artists the role of "the heroic annunciator, the initiator of a new art," and for Renoir he would be as important to impressionism as Cimabue and Giotto had been to the Italian Renaissance.

Manet may well have been a kind of John the Baptist figure for the emerging impressionists as well as their vigorous successors in twentieth-century art. Only those of us who know what was to follow, though, could truly appreciate what it meant for the modern world to see his "uncouth riddle" hanging in the Salon des Refusés on that fifteenth of May in 1863.

Further Reading

Beth Archer Brombert, *Édouard Manet: Rebel in a Frock Coat* (New York, 1996).

Robert Hughes, *The Shock of the New: Art and the Century of Change* (London, 1991).

Émile Zola, *The Masterpiece,* trans. Thomas Walton and Roger Pearson (Oxford, 1993).

RICHARD PIPES

Nicholas 2 Signs the October Manifesto

Richard Pipes is the Baird Professor of History, Emeritus, at Harvard University. Born in 1923 in Ciestyn, Poland, he arrived in the United States in July 1940 and completed his BA at Cornell University in 1945, even while on active service with the U.S. Air Force from 1943 to 1946. He was on the Harvard faculty from 1950 to 1996, where he was also Director of the Russian Research Center. In addition, he was the Director of East European and Soviet Affairs in President Ronald Reagan's National Security Council. In 1992 he served as Expert Witness in the Russian Constitutional Court's Trial of the Communist Party of the Soviet Union. His principal publications have been *Formation of the Soviet Union, Struve* (2 vols.), *Russia under the Old Regime, The Russian Revolution, Russia under the Bolshevik Regime,* and *Communism: A History.*

In his essay he has chosen to return to an unexpected moment amidst the ominous tensions of autumn 1905 in Russia.

Nicholas 2 Signs the October Manifesto

By tradition, Russia was until October 17, 1905, an autocracy: Her tsar was constrained neither by a constitution nor an elected legislature, ruling his vast empire as he saw fit by means of a bureaucracy, police, and army. This political arrangement enjoyed the support of the great majority of the population. The peasants, who in the nineteenth century began to suffer from an acute shortage of land, firmly believed that the tsar, as the patrimonial owner of the realm, would someday confiscate all privately owned land and distribute it to them. Conservative thinkers, who dominated Russian political culture even if the radicals with their violence attracted greater attention, supported autocracy for a variety of reasons, the principal one of which held that the Russian Empire was too vast and its population too diverse to be governed in any other manner.*

The reigning tsar, Nicholas II, derived no pleasure from the privileges of absolute power. As he told one of his ministers, "I maintain autocracy not for my personal pleasure. I act in its spirit only because I am convinced that it is necessary for Russia. If it were for myself, I would gladly renounce all of it." He considered his political responsibilities a disagreeable duty, at best boring, at worst vexatious, and he simply could not understand why ordinary people did not mind their own business and leave politics to professionals. But he had convinced himself—and in this he had the full support of his spouse—that he had a

---

*This is the subject of my recent book *Russian Conservatism and Its Critics* (New Haven, CT, 2006).

sacred duty to uphold the autocratic regime he had inherited from his father and to pass it on intact to his son.

And yet this regime was in many ways an anachronism, was becoming more so with each passing year. By the end of the nineteenth century every European country—and Russia considered herself one of them—had abandoned absolutism in favor of either republicanism or constitutional monarchy. Moreover, the tsarist government itself had quietly yielded some of its powers, as if unaware that by so doing it undermined the principle of autocracy. Foremost among these concessions was the creation in 1864 of an independent judiciary with irremovable judges and trial by jury. With the rapid development of industry, encouraged by the monarchy, Russia ceased to be an exclusively agrarian country inhabited by peasants who took no interest in politics. As the century was drawing to a close, a kind of millenarianism spread among the educated elite expressed in the conviction that "things cannot go on like this," that in the coming century Russia would have to abandon its autocratic system of government. This conviction became something of an axiom among the liberal intelligentsia, which in 1902 formed abroad the Union of Liberation committed to the introduction in Russia of a constitutional order. The two radical parties—the Socialists-Revolutionaries and the Social Democrats, organized at about the same time—had far more ambitious goals, yet of necessity lent support to their liberal rivals in their struggle for a constitution.

Russia may have escaped fundamental change for some time longer were it not that in 1904 the tsarist regime unwisely provoked a war with Japan, a war that went badly from the start and ended in defeat. Russians never pardon their governments for losing a war, and this war was no exception. The public expected an easy victory over the Japanese, whom it treated with unconcealed contempt: Our troops will "blanket them with their caps" was a common boast. But as the news from the front reported one humiliating reverse after another, the mood turned grim and incidents of disobedience became commonplace.

The most dangerous challenge to the government was the hostile front organized by the liberals who, with increasing boldness, demanded political change. What they wanted was a constitutional regime on the English model under which a parliament would have the authority to appoint ministers. The radicals, who were both their allies and rivals, had more far-reaching demands, calling for the convocation of a "constituent assembly" elected on a universal franchise which, in their judgment, would inevitably abolish the monarchy and replace it with a republic based on the communal principle. In November 1904 there took place in St. Petersburg a congress of leaders of the organs of local self-government, the so-called *zemstva*, a gathering that was illegal yet tolerated by the disoriented authorities. With a sizable majority it adopted a resolution calling for the creation in Russia of an elected legislature to oversee the bureaucracy and participate in the drafting of the state budget.

This challenge, initially confined to the liberal intelligentsia, could have been contained were it not that on January 9, 1905, there occurred a tragic event known ever since as "Bloody Sunday." A large body of industrial workers in St. Petersburg, acting under the influence of the Union of Liberation and headed by a priest, Father Gapon, who had police connections, marched in several columns in a peaceful procession to the imperial palace, intending to present the tsar with a petition calling for the convocation of a constituent assembly and other political reforms. The authorities, powerless to prevent this manifestation, which they feared could get out of control, tried to contain it by placing military detachments on the approaches to the Winter Palace. When the unarmed demonstrators kept on advancing toward them, the troops fired, killing some 200 persons and wounding 800.

News of this outrage produced a nationwide reaction. In St. Petersburg, Russia's most industrialized city, 400,000 workers stopped work in what was the country's greatest strike until then. University students also struck. In the port city of Odessa the sailors of the battleship *Potëmkin* mutinied; they were joined by local workers. In the ensuing confrontation with the authorities, some 2,000 Odessa inhabitants lost their lives.

The government tried to calm the spreading unrest with palliative measures, but these only whetted liberal appetites. Nicholas's ablest advisers realized that the game was up: With the army thousands of miles away in the Far East, there was no

The first blood of the revolution was shed in St. Petersburg on January 9, 1905, a day that would enter history as "Bloody Sunday." Unarmed demonstrators carrying a petition for the tsar advanced toward the admiralty building and were met by the military repulsing them with swords, whips, and gunshots.

way of quelling the turmoil by force. The only means of arresting the incipient revolution was to grant society an effective voice in the formulation of policy.

The main advocate of such a course was Count Sergei Witte, the Chairman of the Council of Ministers. A convinced monarchist, Witte realized that without major concessions the situation would spin out of control. He had spent the summer of 1905 in Portsmouth, New Hampshire, where, under the auspices of President Theodore Roosevelt, the Russians and Japanese had engaged in peace negotiations. By exploiting American anti-Japanese sentiments and Japan's eagerness for peace, Witte secured for his country unexpectedly good terms, surrendering minimal territory and avoiding the payment of an indemnity. But by the time he returned home in September, a nationwide general strike was in the offing.

One month after his return, on October 9, Witte had an audience with the tsar. He carried a memorandum in which he summarized his view of the situation: It bore all the earmarks of having been influenced by the Union of Liberation. "The advance of historical progress is unstoppable," he wrote:

> *The idea of civil freedom will triumph, if not by way of reform then by way of revolution. But in the latter event it will come to life on a thousand years of destroyed history. The Russian rebellion* (bunt), *mindless and pitiless, will sweep everything, turn everything to dust. What kind of Russia will emerge from this unprecedented trial exceeds human imagination: the horrors of the Russian rebellion may surpass everything known to history. A possible foreign intervention will tear the country apart. Attempts to put into practice the ideals of theoretical socialism—they will fail but they will be made, no doubt about that—will destroy the family, the display of religious faith, property, all the foundations of law.*

To prevent such a catastrophe, Witte proposed measures that would detach the liberals from the revolutionaries: The liberals called for a constitutional charter and the convocation of a legislative assembly with authority to appoint ministers, or at least confirm them. Such a legislature would be elected on a democratic franchise. Witte further proposed guarantees of speech, press, and assembly. Rather disingenuously, he assured his skeptical sovereign that none of these measures would diminish his authority. The empress, an even more ardent proponent of autocracy than her husband, listened to Witte's arguments without uttering a word. In such situations, she felt it her duty to bolster her irresolute husband. She tried to inculcate in him the conviction that as autocrat he "had the right to do anything, constrained by nothing and no one."

While Nicholas was mulling things over, events were coming to a head, for the initiative of the anti-autocratic movement now passed to the radicals. On October 15, by which time all railroad traffic and postal services had ground to a halt, the St. Petersburg Soviet came into being. It was the offspring of a workers' council authorized by the government in February 1905 for the purpose of giving workers an opportunity to voice their grievances. It now acquired a revolutionary coloring headed by an Executive Committee, in which the Socialists-Revolutionaries and the Social Democrats, both of the Bolshevik and Menshevik variety, played a dominant role. On October 17 this body renamed itself the Soviet of Workers' Deputies. Similar soviets sprung up in other cities of the empire. They in turn were forerunners of the soviets that would reemerge in 1917, and in whose name Lenin and Trotsky would fraudulently seize power.

While this was happening, Nicholas studied the text of an imperial manifesto that Witte (with the assistance of Alexis Obolensky) had drafted at his request. It was a bold document that committed the government to a set of policies adopted by the Zemstvo Congress held in Moscow the preceding month. Having read it, Nicholas consulted several advisers. He had a hard time deciding. He mistrusted the intellectuals who were certain to control the proposed legislature: Aware that they lacked administrative experience, he believed they would bring ruin to the country. He much preferred a military dictatorship as a means of restoring internal order, but was told that the forces for such a measure were lacking: The St. Petersburg garrison at this time, reduced to a skeletal force by the exigencies of war, numbered a mere two thousand troops.*

Nicholas was quite unaware of how profound were the causes of the unrest, which he tended to attribute to troublemakers, especially Jews. On October 17, Witte tried to explain to him that they ran deep, and that the application of force, even if it were possible, would solve nothing. The riots convulsing Russia, he advised Nicholas,

> *undoubtedly resulted from the upsetting of the equilibrium be-tween the ideological strivings of Russia's thinking society and the external forms of life. Russia had outgrown the forms of the existing regime. It desires a law-abiding regime based on civil freedom.*

Nicholas made one more attempt to avoid the seemingly inevitable by meeting on this very day with his cousin, Grand Duke Nikolai Nikolaevich, governor-general of the capital city, and urging him to assume the post of military dictator. It was to be a critical encounter in the history of the revolution, and it would have been fascinating to be a silent spectator as it unfolded. We learn from Witte's memoirs that the Grand Duke

---

*Abraham Ascher, *The Revolution of 1905* (Stanford, CA, 1988), p. 225.

was convinced that there were no forces available to sustain such a dictatorship, and that unless the tsar signed Witte's manifesto, he had made up his mind to shoot himself with the revolver he had on him.

The Grand Duke was known to be a staunch monarchist, indeed, a reactionary. What caused him to veer to the left and align himself with the liberals? There is evidence that he did so under the influence of a certain M. A. Ushakov. Ushakov was one of those peculiar people who populated late imperial Russia: a worker—he was employed by the government printing office—and an active labor leader who, like the better-known Sergei Zubatov, had connections with the tsarist police, which used him in an attempt to divert labor from politics.

Introduced to the Grand Duke, Ushakov sought to persuade him that it had become imperative for the tsar to grant a constitution: It was the only way of calming the country and frustrating those who wanted to replace the monarchy with a republic. According to accounts that have come down to us,* Nikolai Nikolaevich at first contradicted him, insisting that autocracy was the only suitable regime for Russia. But he gradually yielded to Ushakov's arguments and agreed to present them to the tsar.

Which he did very forcefully. Nicholas did not give him a firm answer, but it seems that the Grand Duke's reaction played a decisive role in his decision to sign Witte's manifesto. He did so at 5:00 P.M. after having said his prayers.

As a historian, I would give a great deal to have been an invisible guest at this encounter between Russia's last tsar and his cousin, an encounter that persuaded Nicholas to surrender his autocratic prerogatives and transform Russia into a constitutional monarchy.

---

*Iurii N. Danilov, *Velikii Kniaz' Nikolai Nikolaevich* (Paris, 1930), pp. 54–56; Witte, *Vospominaniia*, vol. 3, pp. 43–45.

The October Manifesto was a watershed in Russian history, for it recognized for the first time society as a partner of the crown and granted Russian citizens basic rights they had never before possessed. It had three short articles. Article 1 granted the population civil liberties based on the principles of "genuine inviolability of person, freedom of conscience, speech, assembly, and association." The second article provided that the new legislative body, the State Duma, would be elected on the basis of universal franchise. The final article pledged that no law would acquire force without the Duma's concurrence, and that the Duma would have the authority to supervise the legality of the actions of officials appointed by the crown.

In his diary for that day Nicholas wrote: "After such a day the head has grown heavy and thoughts grew confused. Lord, help us save and pacify Russia." In a letter to his mother he was more effusive:

> *My dear Mama, you cannot imagine what I went through before the moment [of signing]! I could not explain to you by telegraph all the circumstances which led me to this terrible decision, which, nevertheless, I made in full consciousness. From all over Russia, they shouted, they wrote, and they begged only for this. Around me many—very many—told me the same. . . . There was no other way out than to cross myself and give what everyone was asking for. The only consolation is the hope that such is God's will, that this difficult decision will lead dear Russia out of the insufferable chaotic condition in which she has found herself for nearly a year.*

The October Manifesto, greeted with enthusiasm across the country, did not immediately pacify Russia, although it helped to do so in the long run. The blame for this must be apportioned equally between the government and the opposition.

Nicholas was under the illusion that having granted a constitution but not sworn an oath to uphold it, he could change or even revoke it at will. He dissolved the First Duma in 1906 after it had sat in session for a bare three months because the liberal (Constitutional-Democratic) party that dominated it had adopted an extremely belligerent course, which made cooperation impossible. He similarly dissolved the Second Duma in 1907 and then, in a flagrant breach of the constitution, changed the franchise to secure a more conservative legislature. In the years to come, on more than one occasion, when unlikely to obtain the Duma's approval for a bill, the crown prorogued it and passed laws under Article 87 of the constitution, which provided for the passage of emergency legislation by edict when the Duma was not in session.

The political parties of the left and center bore no less responsibility. The liberals, displeased by the provision of the constitutional charter that gave the crown the power to appoint ministers, demanded the introduction of parliamentary government. They resolutely rejected Witte's invitation to join the post-October cabinet of ministers. After the crown had dissolved the First Duma, which it had a perfect right to do, the liberal deputies adjourned to Viborg in Finland (a Russian dependency but beyond the reach of the Russian police) and from there called on the citizens to refuse to pay taxes. The socialist deputies, after initially boycotting the elections to the Duma, subsequently used their membership in it to sabotage legislative procedures and demand the convocation of a constituent assembly. Eventually, a modus vivendi between crown and parliament was worked out and the last two Dumas functioned reasonably well.

Nor did the manifesto pacify the countryside. Rural disorders continued without letup. The peasants, interpreting it in their own way as giving them license to do what they wanted,* seized land from private landowners and burned down manors. These were quelled with the introduction of field court-martials under Prime Minister Peter Stolypin the following year.

But if the October Manifesto and the constitution that issued from it failed to give the country a stable political order, it did give Russians civil liberties such as they had never enjoyed before and were to lose a decade later. Censorship was abolished (though partly restored during World War I), and one could publish as freely as in the Western democracies. Citizens were no longer arrested and exiled to Siberia on suspicion of political dissent. They could assemble and form associations at will. This was no mean achievement for a country in which the population had lived for centuries without any rights save the right to obey.

Further Reading

Abraham Ascher, *The Revolution of 1905*, vol. 1 (Stanford, CA, 1988).

Sidney Harcave, ed., *The Memoirs of Count Witte* (Armonk, NY, 1990).

Richard Pipes, *Russian Conservatism and Its Critics* (New Haven, CT, 2006).

---

*Roberta T. Manning, *The Crisis of the Old Order in Russia: Gentry and Government* (Princeton, NJ, 1982), p. 147.

MARGARET MACMILLAN

Tunnels, Territory, and Broken Promises: France Betrayed by the Anglo-Saxons?

Margaret MacMillan was the Provost of Trinity College and Professor of History at the University of Toronto. She is now Warden of St. Antony's College, Oxford. Her books include *Women of the Raj* and *Peacemakers: The Paris Conference of 1919 and Its Attempt to End War*, published in the United States as *Paris 1919: Six Months That Changed the World.* Her most recent book is on President Nixon's trip to China, published in the United States as *Nixon and Mao: Six Days That Changed the World.* Professor MacMillan is a Fellow of the Royal Society of Literature and an Officer of the Order of Canada.

In her book *Paris 1919*, the author provides a comprehensive, engaging account of the conference that produced the peace treaty that ended World War I. In this essay, she transports herself back in time to two private meetings: one in November 1918, and another in March 1919, that may have substantially affected the outcome of the Paris Peace Conference.

Tunnels, Territory, and Broken Promises:
France Betrayed by the Anglo-Saxons?

At the end of November 1918, Georges Clemenceau, the French prime minister, paid a visit to London. There was much to celebrate. The Great War was finally over and Germany lay defeated, abandoned by its former allies. The great German armies that had menaced France had shattered in the face of Allied attacks that August. The Kaiser's beloved navy, which had threatened the British Empire and its command of the seas, was safely interned in British ports. Germany itself was in turmoil; the Kaiser had fled into exile and many of its cities were under the control of self-appointed councils of workers and soldiers.

There was much also to mourn. The millions of men lost in battle and the damage to those who had survived: the devastation of much of the north of France and of Belgium, of little Serbia, and the territories along Germany's and Austria-Hungary's frontiers in the east. The waste was tremendous, the questions unanswerable. How had Europe, the mighty continent that had so confidently dominated the world in 1914, turned on itself so savagely? What did the future hold when revolution seemed to be spreading westward from Russia, itself in the grip of civil war as its new Bolshevik rulers battled their many enemies? What was going to happen in Central Europe now that Austria-Hungary had fallen to pieces? Or in the Middle East as the Ottoman Empire slid rapidly toward its own end?

Clemenceau was in London to savor the triumph but also to plan the future with his counterpart, British prime minister

David Lloyd George. The two men had been partners in the war and in some ways they resembled each other. Both were vigorous, impetuous, and bold. Both had come into their offices in the darkest days of the struggle, when it looked like the Germans might win, and both had led their countries to victory. Their relationship was an uneasy one, though. On a personal level, for all their similarities, Clemenceau and Lloyd George were not destined to be close friends. The French leader was an intellectual; Lloyd George, for all his quickness, was not. Clemenceau came from a family with a distinguished pedigree; Lloyd George was proudly middle class. Nor did their two peoples entirely trust each other. The friendship between France and Britain was a very recent one and could not entirely eradicate the memories of old rivalries and enmities. Each man, moreover, represented a country that had a strong sense of itself and its own national interests. France was consumed by the need to defeat Germany and liberate French soil. During the war, when the British had planned expeditions in the east against Austria-Hungary or the Ottoman Empire, the French saw those as a diversion of much-needed resources from the Western Front. On the other hand, the French had not shared the British concern to defeat the German navies.

Nevertheless, the two men greeted each other warmly as Clemenceau descended from his train in London that cold winter day. As their car pulled out of the station, wildly enthusiastic crowds cheered and threw their hats in the air. The French were impressed by such a warm welcome from a people they considered cold and reserved. That night, though, the mood turned more businesslike as the Allies got down to the serious issues confronting them. During the next three days they covered a range of subjects, from what to do about the Kaiser (should he be tried for war crimes, perhaps?) to what each hoped to get out of the peace settlements. We have records of

The cartoon above was published in the German magazine *Simplizissimus* on March 11, 1919, under the title "The foundation for the League of Nations." David Lloyd George, Georges Clemenceau, and Woodrow Wilson appear as avenging angels standing on a dead body representing Germany. *"Nur so kann Deutschland darin geduldet werden"* ("The only way Germany can be tolerated in it," *it* being the League of Nations).

all the formal talks, but there is one conversation that was not recorded, and it is that one at which I wish I had been present.

At some point Lloyd George and Clemenceau met for a private conversation at the French embassy. We do not know who else, apart from Sir Maurice Hankey, the extremely efficient and discreet secretary to the Imperial War Cabinet, was there. We have only two references to what was said, the first in Lloyd George's memoirs, *The Truth about the Peace Treaties,* and the second in a note Hankey scribbled two years later in his diary. According to Hankey, the conversation included the following exchange. Clemenceau spoke first. "Well. What are we to discuss?" Lloyd George replied, "Mesopotamia and Palestine." Clemenceau: "Tell me what you want." Lloyd George: "I want Mosul." Clemenceau: "You shall have it. Anything else?" "Yes," said Lloyd George, "I want Jerusalem, too." Clemenceau: "You shall have it, but Pichon [the French foreign minister] will make difficulties about Mosul." Lloyd George's recollection is substantially the same.

What neither English account mentions is the impression that the French were left with: that by making concessions in the Middle East, they had won British support for their claims against Germany, especially when it came to the Rhineland. France had been invaded by German troops twice in forty years, a period short enough that many French, including of course Clemenceau himself, could remember both invasions. If France could somehow detach German territories west of the Rhine, the river would provide a marvelous natural barrier to German troops.

I wish that I had been there. Did Lloyd George, perhaps merely with a nod and a wink, give Clemenceau the impression a firm bargain had been struck? Knowing Lloyd George's propensity for telling people what they wanted to hear and, to be unkind, his talent for being devious, it is quite likely that he did. I would like to have seen the Welsh charmer at work for myself. I would also love to know whether either man ever hesitated for a moment, as they cheerfully doled out territory in the Middle East, to wonder, perhaps out loud, whether they were doing the right thing. That conversation, brief as it was, contained the seeds of much future trouble, between Britain and France, and more generally between the West and the Middle East. It also helped shape the international relations of Europe in the 1920s and 1930s and those of the Middle East right down to the present.

Clemenceau's main concern was always the situation in Europe. He had never been an imperialist and had no interest in _expanding the French Empire into the Middle East. Its growing importance as a source of oil had largely passed him by. As he had once famously said, "When I want some oil, I'll find it at my grocer's." His attitude infuriated the French colonial lobby, including his foreign minister, but in 1919, Clemenceau, as the *Père de Victoire*, was in an unassailable position. He was determined, as much as lay in his power, to provide for France's safety. If he did not loathe Germans as a people in the way that many French now did in 1919, he still saw Germany as the chief threat to France. (There is a story, probably untrue alas, that he left orders that, on his death, he should be buried standing up facing the frontier with Germany.) Always a realist, he knew that even in defeat Germany remained strong; its infrastructure was largely undamaged and its military was capable of rapidly rebuilding itself. Moreover, the demographics were against France. The French birth rate was static, even declining, while Germany's was rising. There were already more potential soldiers in Germany than in France, and the gap was going to grow. By the mid-1930s, French demographers predicted, France would have a severe shortage of men for its military.

Many French, and perhaps even Clemenceau himself, toyed with the idea of dismembering Germany, after all a very new country, but the British and the Americans made it clear that they would not go along with that. German nationalism had troubled Europe in the nineteenth century until it achieved its own nation-state, as Lloyd George rightly pointed out, and to break Germany down into its components such as Bavaria and Prussia would only start the whole cycle over again. The most France's allies would contemplate was taking away some of Germany's territory: its colonies certainly; and, in Europe, Alsace-Lorraine, the two provinces Germany had taken from France in 1871; a few scraps along German borders with Belgium and Denmark; and, in the east, land seized by Prussia from Poland at the end of the eighteenth century.

Germany did shrink a little after the Paris Peace Conference had done its work, but it still remained the largest country in Europe west of Russia. And, such are the vagaries of war, it was, although few Germans could see it at the time, in a stronger strategic position than in 1914. Where it once had a common border with Russia, something that had given the German high command nightmares for decades, it now had a buffer in the shape of the newly reborn Poland. In the east, too, Austria-Hungary, that great multinational empire, had disappeared, leaving in its wake shaky new states that rapidly fell to quarreling with each other. The 1920s and 1930s would give Germany many opportunities to play off its eastern neighbors against each other.

How to ensure France's security was one of the great issues at the Paris Peace Conference. The French, of course, wanted to weaken Germany as much as possible. Their allies, particularly the United States and Great Britain, disagreed. There were also prolonged arguments at the peace conference over the reparations to be extracted from Germany. In French eyes, these were not just about making good the damage that the German occupation of French territory had done, but were a way of keeping the formidable German economy weak. President Wilson had said firmly, though, that he would not support punitive damages being levied on the defeated nations. The British, who had traded extensively with Germany before the war, saw a threat to their postwar recovery if Germans could not buy British goods. Furthermore, as the young adviser to the treasury, John Maynard Keynes, pointed out, driving Germany into economic collapse would not only damage the world's economy but add to the already serious political and social unrest in the center of Europe. In the end Clemenceau backed down, significantly lowering the total amounts France was demanding and accepting a schedule of payments that made it very unlikely Germany would ever pay more than a fraction of what it owed.

He also backed down on the question of Germany's borders. He argued strongly for detaching the Rhineland from Germany as well as the Saar, which contained valuable coal mines. Lloyd George and Woodrow Wilson would not agree. The former, like many of the British, was becoming impatient with what he saw as unreasoning French vindictiveness. Wilson, who had loudly proclaimed the importance of self-determination of peoples as a guiding principle in international affairs, was not prepared to hand over reluctant Germans to French rule. The most they would agree to was that the Rhineland should be demilitarized for fifteen years: Germany would not be allowed to have troops there, and Allied forces would hold crucial bridgeheads over the Rhine. As for the Saar, France could take its coal, but at the end of fifteen years its inhabitants would decide in a plebiscite which country they wanted to belong to. In the event, they voted overwhelmingly to join Hitler's Germany.

The Allies wrote a number of other provisions into their treaty with Germany that might, in theory, have helped to keep it weak. The Treaty of Versailles's military clauses, for example, limited Germany to an army of only one hundred thousand men and prohibited it from having an air force, certain types of heavy weapons such as tanks, and large battleships. The problem was that there were no mechanisms to really ensure that Germany was adhering to the clauses and no willingness, certainly on the part of Britain or the United States in the interwar years, to enforce the limits.

So why did Clemenceau, an astute and wary statesman, agree to a treaty with Germany that did not give France the security it craved? He gave way partly because he felt he had no choice. France was still a power, but even before World War I it had never been on a par with Great Britain. Much of the war in the West had been fought on French soil, and up to 40 percent of France's industry and its mines had been destroyed. If his country was going to have a hope of coping with Germany in the future, France needed allies. Italy was not strong enough and was an unreliable friend. Russia had been a great counterweight to Germany before 1914, but with the revolutions of 1917 it had set off on a new path. What the new Bolshevik regime would be like when it finally established itself securely in power was anybody's guess, but this much at least was clear: The Bolsheviks loathed capitalists and liberal democracies and confidently hoped that they would all be swept away in a series of triumphant revolutions. One of the new Bolshevik government's first actions had been to cancel all its foreign debts, a serious blow to the French government, French banks, and all the thousands of middle-class investors who saw their savings disappearing. That left Great Britain and the United States as France's potential partners.

For Clemenceau, keeping the wartime alliance with the Anglo-Saxon powers alive in peacetime was therefore paramount in his thinking at the peace conference. He was also encouraged to place his hopes in it by what his colleagues in the Supreme Council told him. Lloyd George had already given, or so Clemenceau thought, his assurances in that conversation in London. Now, in March 1919, Wilson and Lloyd George met Clemenceau at the Crillon Hotel and offered him a deal. That conversation was never recorded, either, and if I could pick another moment, I wish I could have been there as well.

We know the outline of what was agreed. Britain and the United States undertook to give France a guarantee that if it were attacked by a third party, Germany almost inevitably, the two of them would come to France's defense. Perhaps on this occasion, Lloyd George, who loved dreaming on a grand scale, also held out a marvelous project: a tunnel under the Channel. (He had certainly done so and would continue to do so in other conversations with Clemenceau.) British troops could then dash across to France whenever they were needed. Clemenceau was apparently very moved by the prospect.

What had brought Wilson round to offer what was for the United States a virtually unprecedented guarantee? Ever since George Washington had uttered his famous warning to his new country against getting involved in "the toils of European ambition, rivalship, interest, humor, or caprice," the United States had stood aloof from great-power politics. And Wilson himself had told the Senate on the eve of the United States entry into the war, "I am proposing that all nations henceforth avoid entangling alliances which would draw them into competitions of power, catch them in a net of intrigue and selfish rivalry, and disturb their own affairs with influences intruded from without." Yet now, in this famous meeting at the Crillon, Wilson was apparently prepared to see his country entangled with a commitment to come to France's defense.

Wilson was an idealist, but he was also a seasoned politician, and perhaps he felt that only by such a promise would Clemenceau and France support the whole package being put together in the treaty for Germany. The most important part of that treaty, for Wilson, was the opening part, which set up the League of Nations. Wilson had thought long and hard about how the world could avoid the dangerous national rivalries and alliance systems that had led to the war that was just over, and he had concluded that the way ahead for humanity was to set up an association of nations that would offer each other protection—collective security—and work together for common aims such as disarmament and international justice and prosperity. Once the League was in place, he confidently thought, there would be no need for the old-style international diplomacy. The guarantee he was offering would no longer be necessary, but its offer would keep Clemenceau on his side. "When you have hooked him," Wilson told one of his confidants, "you first draw in a little, then give liberty to the line, then draw him back, finally wear him out, break him down, and land him."

Sadly, Wilson was wrong about the League. It never became the international force he had envisioned, partly because the United States itself never joined. From France's perspective, the guarantee in the end proved to be worthless. When Woodrow Wilson took it back to Washington along with the Treaty of Versailles, he failed to get the necessary approval from the Senate. The United States later signed a separate peace treaty with Germany, but it never revived the Anglo-American guarantee. When the French turned anxiously to the British to ascertain that Great Britain still stood by its commitment, the response was cold. Without the United States, the British regretted, they did not see themselves as bound by their agreement. As memories of the war faded, the British turned back to their primary interests: trade and their empire. As long as Europe remained quiet, with no single nation dominating it, the British were disinclined to get involved. Clemenceau and the French leaders who succeeded him were bitter at what they saw as a betrayal at the hands of the British, but there was little they could do. France tried to find allies elsewhere, looking to the other side of Germany for allies among the states in the center of Europe such as Poland, Czechoslovakia, Rumania, and Yugoslavia. An unfortunate consequence of French policy was to reawaken German fears of being encircled. In reality none of France's new allies were sufficiently reliable or strong, and in 1930, in a move born out of pessimism, France started construction of the Maginot Line to defend against a future German invasion. More far-sighted statesmen such as Aristide Briand, who formed a number of governments in the 1920s, hoped to bring Germany into a closer relationship with Europe and render it harmless. For a time it seemed as though that might work: Germany joined the League of Nations in 1925 and agreed at Locarno to respect all borders in the West. The Great Depression, sadly, fueled extremists, including of course the Nazis, who seized power in 1933. Britain reluctantly moved toward confrontation with Germany, but it is not surprising that France never really trusted its ally again. When war came in 1939, their alliance proved to be no match for Hitler's Germany. That conversation two decades ago between Clemenceau and Lloyd George is a small part of that sad story.

The other issue that came up then of course was the fate of the Middle East. Clemenceau may not have been interested in colonies, but, as a French statesman, he was obliged to protect his country's interests. France had long-standing ties to the Middle East, from trade and investment to claims to protect the area's Christian minorities. For Britain the paramount consideration was the Suez Canal, its link with its Asian possessions, including, above all, India, the jewel in the crown. Before the First World War, the British navy had switched from using coal to oil as fuel, and already it was clear that parts of the Middle East, Iran certainly and Mosul probably, contained major deposits of oil. In the course of the nineteenth century, the Ottoman Empire, which controlled a huge area stretching westward from the borders of Iran to the Mediterranean, was slowly collapsing. Britain and France were already moving in—Britain to take over Egypt, and France into North Africa. In 1914 the Ottoman Empire made the fatal mistake of joining in the war on the German side. Its soldiers fought bravely and, at Gallipoli, very well, but the war proved too much for a moribund political structure. By the time the armistice came in 1918, the British, along with a much smaller French contingent, were in occupation of virtually all of the Ottoman's Arab territories.

As they calmly divided the spoils of war, Clemenceau and Lloyd George sounded as much like imperialists as their predecessors in earlier generations. The world outside Europe had been, in the eyes of most Europeans, unclaimed real estate, destined to be grabbed by one empire or another. And so they had been. By the twentieth century, however, imperialism was under attack both by those in Europe who thought it unjust or inefficient, and from within the empires themselves as the subject peoples demanded a greater share in their own government. Wilson had made it clear that he would not stand for the parceling out of peoples without any consideration for their own wishes and so had insisted that the possessions of the defeated powers must be run as mandates under his new League of Nations. Clemenceau and Lloyd George had publicly gone along with this—indeed they had little choice—but in private, as their conversation shows, they continued to treat much of the world beyond Europe as though the wishes of its inhabitants did not count.

During the war itself, their two countries already had made a quiet deal about the Middle East. The famous, or infamous, Sykes-Picot Agreement of 1916 parceled out the Ottoman Empire's Arab territories. Britain was to have direct control of the two southern provinces of Baghdad and Basra while France would get the coast of what later became Lebanon and, farther north, part of the Ottoman province of Syria. Arab chiefs would rule the rest, but under the suzerainty of the great powers. Britain's zone of what was euphemistically called "influence" was to stretch in a great arc from the eastern border of Egypt over to the Arabian Gulf, taking in much of what later on became Transjordan, Iraq, and Saudi Arabia. France's zone of influence reached inland from Lebanon to take in much of today's Syria and the old Ottoman province of Mosul. Palestine presented a particular problem because not only did each power have claims there on religious and other grounds, but so too did the world Zionist movement, which was dedicated to creating a Jewish home there. So it was agreed that Palestine would be under some form of international control.

Almost as soon as the deal was signed, the British had second thoughts. France stood to gain too much and, for all that it was an ally, it remained a rival to Britain in the Middle East. For strategic reasons, Palestine should be under British control, abutting as it did on Egypt with its vitally important Suez Canal. The province of Mosul probably contained oil (and indeed it did) and Britain, not France, should manage what was a key resource. In the last years of the war, the British did their best to modify the terms of what the statesman Lord Curzon called "a millstone around our necks." In that December 1918 conversation in London, Clemenceau conceded everything the British wanted. It took some time and considerable argument to work out the details. In the end, because of American opposition to outright colonies, the two European powers acquired their new possessions in the form of mandates from the new League of Nations. I have always wondered whether either Clemenceau or Lloyd George ever paused for a moment to ask themselves whether lands and peoples of the Ottoman Empire should or could be disposed of quite so freely.

They should have had some inkling of future problems because there were two other wartime agreements on the Middle East that complicated any peacetime settlement. In their anxiety to safeguard the Suez Canal and to undermine the potential threat of the Ottoman sultan calling on all Muslims to wage a holy war against the infidel Allied powers, the British had started their own small war in the Middle East by encouraging the Arabs to rise up against their Ottoman overlords. The

Arab forces had been led by Faisal, a son of the Sharif of Mecca, who, as Guardian of the Holy Places, had a considerable amount of authority. With British guns and gold, and British advisers such as T. E. Lawrence, the Arabs inflicted a considerable amount of damage on the Ottomans. In return, or so Faisal and many other Arabs thought, they would get an independent Arab state, or possibly states, at the end of the war. When Wilson talked about self-determination and when Britain and France issued a proclamation in the autumn of 1918 saying that their war aims in the Middle East had always been the "complete and definite emancipation" of all Ottoman subjects, Arab nationalists, by now a growing force, saw a new era dawning, not a new empire.

The second promise was of course the one the British foreign secretary Arthur Balfour made to the Jews in 1917 on behalf of his government. The Balfour Declaration very carefully talked only about a "Jewish homeland" in Palestine, but it was in its effects to be the foundation of the modern state of Israel. To have the backing of the world's largest power (and France and the United States, which later added their approval of the Balfour Declaration) gave the Jewish presence in Palestine an official status. In the interwar years, as Jewish immigrants arrived and Jewish institutions from businesses to schools opened up, the Jewish agency increasingly behaved like a state within a state. Britain, as Clemenceau had promised, got control of the territory in the shape of the mandate for Palestine. But the British— and experts such as Curzon had warned Lloyd George of this—found that they had also gained a permanent and expensive headache. The Arab inhabitants of Palestine began to awaken politically as the Jewish presence there grew. By the start of the 1920s the British authorities had to deal with outbreaks of Arab violence directed both against themselves and against the Jews as well as growing criticism and hostility from the Jews themselves when Britain tried to limit Jewish immigration and influence. Looking back, it is sadly very easy to see in those years right at the end of the war the roots of the bitter and almost insoluble struggle between Israel and the Palestinians.

What is more, the rest of the Arab world seized on the Jewish presence in Palestine as evidence of the meddling of the Western powers in the Middle East. When Israel was born after the Second World War, it came into the world with many of its enemies already in place. This might not have happened if the Arabs had gained their independence after 1918, but they did not. Instead they saw it snatched away. The British and French mandates took in virtually all the Arab territories of the Ottoman Empire (with the exception of the Saudi Arabian peninsula, which appeared to have little value anyway), and mandates meant supervision and control by the mandatory power over local governments.

Faisal did get an Arab kingdom in 1919, but it was not the one he and his supporters had hoped for. Instead of a large independent Arab state with a coast on the Mediterranean and including Palestine, his new kingdom was a landlocked Syria. Even more galling, as his British friends made clear to him, Syria lay in the French zone of influence, and he was expected to accept French guidance and assistance. When Faisal arrived in Syria's capital Damascus in the spring of 1919 to take up his new throne, he found a city seething with Arab nationalism. When he made it clear that he intended to assert Arab independence in the face of the French mandate, the French authorities cracked down. Just over a year later, Faisal went into exile. The French tried to make Syria more manageable in part by making it smaller and giving chunks of its territory to Lebanon, also a French mandate. The Syrians have never forgotten this, which helps explain why Syria sent its troops into Lebanon in the 1970s and why it continues to meddle, usually with disastrous results, in Lebanon's affairs.

The British proved to be less authoritarian than the French, but they too kept a guiding hand on their mandates. They split Palestine in two, creating the new kingdom of Transjordan, which they gave to Faisal's brother, Hussein. Until the 1950s, the army of Transjordan, or Jordan as it became, had a British officer in command. Faisal received his own compensation in the shape of a new country, Iraq, which the British created out of their remaining pieces of the spoils. Iraq was an administrative convenience, not a real country, and its ethnically and religiously diverse peoples had little shared history. In the south, a mixed population of Arabs and Persians looked eastward to Persia, now Iran, or southward toward the Gulf and India. The territories around Baghdad were more predominantly Arab, and the dominant forces, mainly Sunni Arabs, were in those days Arab nationalists, looking westward toward their Arab compatriots. The north of Iraq housed a concentration of Kurds, non-Arabs who, although they were largely Muslim, had little in common with their fellow Iraqis. In addition there were significant minorities of Jews, Christians, and unorthodox Muslim sects. It is scarcely surprising that Iraq has always proved to be a fractured and perhaps unworkable state. What would Lloyd George or his colonial secretary Winston Churchill have replied if they had heard the warning an American missionary gave in 1920 to a British adviser as they chatted in Baghdad? "You are flying in the face of four millenniums of history," he told the famous Arab expert Gertrude Bell, "if you try to draw a line around Iraq and call it a political entity!"

Faisal inevitably chafed under British restrictions, as he had under the French, and he managed to achieve a degree of independence by the 1930s, but by then the damage was done as far as Arab memories of the postwar period were concerned. From the Arab perspective, the West had treacherously reneged on its promise of independence and, to add insult to injury, had planted a Western colony in the shape of the Jewish presence in Palestine on Arab soil. Increasingly, Arabs outside Palestine took up the cause of the Palestinian Arabs as their own, with the results that we have seen since the end of the Second World War.

I wish I had been there during that first confidential talk between Clemenceau and Lloyd George in London when they divided up the Middle East and when Lloyd George may have promised to support France's demands against Germany. I wish, too, that I had been there again a few months later in Paris when Wilson and Lloyd George seemingly guaranteed France's safety from Germany. I would have warned Lloyd George and Wilson that broken promises, especially when they involve the very survival of an ally, leave a damaging legacy of mistrust. France's search for security led it, among other things, to the fateful decision to place its faith in the Maginot Line. Their betrayal, as many French saw it, by the Anglo-Saxon powers fostered defeatism and, in right-wing circles, a willingness to come to an accommodation with Nazi Germany. After World War II, General de Gaulle, who as a young officer had witnessed the Paris Peace Conference, infuriated Britain and the United States by insisting that France could not trust them and that there must be an independent French foreign policy and a French nuclear deterrent.

The Big Three at the Paris Peace Conference were not able to see the future, but they could have made some good guesses. And perhaps I could have helped by reminding them to use their own eyes and to listen to their own advisers. They all knew that Germany was still a powerful and troubled country. Their spies and their newspapers kept them well informed about the turmoil in German society and politics. They feared that Germany might fall under a military dictatorship or, alternatively, that it might become Bolshevik. They were aware of the dangers of imposing too harsh a peace. Lloyd George argued repeatedly against taking away German territory. Remember, he told his colleagues, how German nationalism had disturbed Europe for a generation before Germany was created. And his economic adviser, John Maynard Keynes, sent warnings, which Lloyd George passed on to his colleagues, that trying to squeeze too much in reparations out of Germany would severely impede Europe's economic recovery.

It was not just German nationalism that was a problem for the future peace of the world. Talk of self-determination had fueled nationalisms everywhere, in the center of Europe, in the former Russian Empire, throughout the French and British empires, and in the Middle East. The peacemakers understood and respected nationalism's force in Europe, but they did not yet take it seriously in the non-European world. As a result, when they disposed of the Middle East, they failed to take into account the growing force of Arab nationalism. Lloyd George, Clemenceau, and Wilson were still prisoners of the nineteenth-century worldview, that most peoples outside of Europe and North America were not yet advanced enough to rule themselves and would not be for generations to come. Moreover, so they assumed, Western technology would continue to give the West the upper hand. Perhaps I could have reminded them that even great powers such as Britain, France, and the United States must too recognize that they cannot always settle the world as they wish, and that even great power does not last indefinitely.

Further Reading

Margret MacMillan, *Paris 1919: Six Months That Changed the World* (New York, 2001).

David Fromkin, *A Peace to End All Peace: The Fall of the Ottoman Empire and the Creation of the Modern Middle East* (New York, 1989).

Zara Steiner, *The Lights That Failed: European International History, 1919–1933* (Oxford and New York, 2005).

CHARLES A. RILEY II

Backstage at the Ballets Russes with Picasso

Charles Riley is a Professor of English at the City University of New York. He is also an arts journalist, a curator, and the author of fourteen books, including *The Jazz Age in France*, *Aristocracy and the Modern Imagination*, *The Saints of Modern Art*, *Color Codes*, and *Sacred Sister* (written in collaboration with theater director Robert Wilson). He is a former reporter for *Fortune* magazine and former editor in chief of *WE* magazine.

In this essay we accompany Professor Riley on a journey to Paris in May 1917. There we encounter the famous painter, Pablo Picasso, and share his involvement in what is, for him, an unusual enterprise.

Backstage at the Ballets Russes with Picasso

It is rare for an epoch-shaking artistic breakthrough to happen in public—these discoveries generally occur in the privacy of the studio or study, where, like in a laboratory, eureka is a solo cry of elation. But the worlds of painting, dance, and music all shifted ahead abruptly on the afternoon of May 18, 1917, when Pablo Picasso made his stage debut as cocreator of the ballet *Parade*. The high-profile encore to the heroic cubist period turned out to be a theatrical tour de force before a keyed-up audience composed of opposed camps of fashionable and artsy Parisians. They had reason to be apprehensive—the cannons of the advancing German army were pounding the French troops just three hundred kilometers away, while eastward the Russian Revolution was in its fourth month. That was the mise-en-scène as the sun shone across the façade of the massive Théâtre du Châtelet and the crowd milled in the ornate lobby, gathering well in advance of the 3:45 performance of what had been billed by the controversial impresario Sergei Diaghilev as a one-act *ballet réaliste* based on a story by society wit Jean Cocteau, set to music by Erik Satie with costumes and décor by Picasso. Lovely as it would have been to sip Veuve Clicquot and sit up front for the performance, I would have much preferred to hold a backstage pass. The mirrors in the company's dressing rooms reflected glances of tension in the heavily made-up faces of the Russian beauties, more for aesthetic than geopolitical reasons. Even as accustomed as the brave ballerinas of the Ballets Russes were to explosive arguments over modernism, they knew they were in for a wild night because the creators of the work had quarreled too much to finalize, during the tumultuous rehearsals, what was planned for the performance. As they danced, Picasso and Cocteau would soon come to blows behind the curtain, and afterward libel suits would land Satie in jail for eight days, labeling him and Cocteau "cultural anarchists" who were a threat to national security in a time of war.

OPENING NIGHT

The crowd was primed for shock treatment, and that is what they got from the start. The overture reeled drunkenly from atmospheric strings to boisterous anthems to jazz, and suddenly three of the most outrageous creatures ever seen in the theater lurched into view—towering apparitions in giant top hats, one dressed in what looked like the Manhattan skyline and smoking a blue pipe the size of a hockey stick. To those in the know about contemporary art, they seemed to have wandered straight out of cubist paintings. The giants stalked the apron of the vast stage bellowing nonsense ("Tilanic toctoc tic tadelboc tadeltac mic") in a broad, Dada parody of carnival barkers outside their booth. These "managers" introduced a sampling of the show inside, starting with a frenetic Chinese conjuror, danced by the incandescent Léonide Massine, the choreographer, who in turn brought on "the American Girl" clad in a sailor suit. Her movements thrilled schizophrenically between the fluid arabesques and *fouettés tournants* of classical ballet and angular, knee-knocking stomps or bow-legged shimmies to ragtime. She was routed by a troupe of acrobats, with a pantomime horse that was pathetically inept (enough to draw gales of laughter). If the conservatives were baffled into silence by the hybrid completion of ballet gestures by jazz moves, they were jarred to protest by a sudden barrage of odd sound effects. The early tapping and faint chiming bell of a typewriter had been a distraction under the violins and flutes, but the pistol firing a blank straightened them in their box seats, and by the time they had looked around the theater to locate the sources of the whistle, siren, klaxon, cracking of a whip, and "dynamo," they were ready to make noises of their own. The hullabaloo onstage was nothing compared to the violent response that began well before the final curtain came down on the brief piece (less than twenty minutes long). Catcalls and booing started in the third of eight episodes, and the message was pointed. "Go back to Berlin!" bellowed a hefty baritone from the orchestra seats. "Shirkers! Draft dodgers! Foreign scum!" was the chorus from the xenophobic balcony. Recognizing rapidly that they were bombing, the angry creators started to bicker backstage. Cocteau was infuriated that some of his most bizarre ideas had been cut behind his back by Satie and Picasso, whom he started to berate noisily. That was when the artist delivered *une bonne paire de gifles* ("a good pair of slaps in the face") not far from where the novelist André Gide was standing, his mouth agape at the sight.

Onstage, the dancers were looking ever more nervous as the piece, fittingly enough, concluded with the chorus of boulevardiers refusing to pay for a show they couldn't fathom, the highlights of which they had enjoyed free anyway. By the time the hulking managers had collapsed to the floor in the finale of their fruitless last-ditch efforts to induce a ticket-buying audience inside the tent, it was clear that most of the disgruntled audience in the theater wanted the three main creators of the work to follow suit. A few of the more rabid boobirds stormed up the aisles toward the stage shouting for Diaghilev and his collaborators to appear. At the least, others were offended by the frivolity. "If I had known it was going to be that stupid, I would have brought the children," huffed one unsatisfied connoisseur on her way out. But the darkest anger was vented over "foreign Kubists" who had insulted the French with inscrutable yet violent strangeness. The papers the next day, from *Le Gaulois* to *Le*

Temps, proclaimed the spectacle a "scandal" and dubbed Picasso, Cocteau, and Satie "les trois boches." They failed to report that Diaghilev donated a share of the proceeds from the performance to aid refugees from the eastern provinces of France, still occupied by the Germans.

The outcry seems at this distance to be the typical bile of philistines who cannot handle avant-garde art, yet the rage of the moment stemmed from more widely held feelings, and we have to turn from the arts section to the front page to understand its source. The headlines were dominated by bad news from the front. Earlier that month, General Henri Philippe Pétain had replaced General Robert Georges Nivelle (who earlier had replaced Pétain) as commander in chief of the French forces after the disastrous offensive at Chemin des Dames had failed. Pétain had inherited a crumbling war effort that was leaving Paris more vulnerable by the day. Adding to the tension, an ally to the east was in turmoil as the Russian Revolution, which had started in February, was in one of its most obscure phases. Many in the audience were still bristling over the insensitive way that Diaghilev had paraded the red flag of the revolution onstage at the conclusion of a performance of *The Firebird* just a week earlier in the same theater. Cocteau certainly did not help matters by undiplomatically declaring to the press, as part of the public relations run-up to the debut of his collaboration with Picasso and Satie, that *"Parade* would be the greatest battle of the war." This was a theater riot of a different order from the one that had been sparked by Diaghilev and Stravinsky over the *Rite of Spring* in the nearby Théâtre des Champs-Élysées on May 29, 1913. This time it was their patriotism, not just their taste, that Parisians felt had been insulted.

Not all the critics agreed. Apollinaire, hardly a dispassionate observer, wrote, *"Parade* will upset the ideas of a fair number of spectators. They will certainly be surprised, though in a most agreeable way, but as its charm works they will gradually discover that modern movements have a grace which they had never suspected." What Apollinaire realized, no doubt in part because he was in the circle of Picasso and the "dream team" of creators summoned by Diaghilev, was that something very special had happened that night that would alter the course not only of modern dance, but art, literature, music, theater, and thought. That is why the story behind the making of *Parade* is one of our most remarkable narratives of creative collaboration. To have stood in the corner of the rehearsal room with the dancers, or peered over the shoulder of Picasso alone in his studio, would have offered an eyewitness experience of a crucial passage not only in his career, from the cul-de-sac of cubism into his own brand of realism, but in twentieth-century aesthetics. Eavesdropping on the extraordinary conversations among Picasso, Cocteau, Massine, Satie, and Diaghilev, I might have been able to clear up some of the lingering mysteries that dog the art historical and biographical accounts of this period of flux— questions of how and why Picasso retreated from his epochal invention (cubism) and which way the currents of influence flowed in the ever-dynamic, tidal interaction of the arts. Even the dancers may not have known what hit them, but to listen in on the decision-making process as this masterpiece was brought together would have been extraordinary.

ASSEMBLING THE CAST OF CHARACTERS

The whole project started with Jean Cocteau. The slender and ambitious teenage poet had joined Diaghilev's dazzling company in 1909, when the impresario challenged him on their first meeting: *"Étonnez-moi."* He did not disappoint the master, astonishing him at every turn with poetry, plays, drawings for the covers of the lavish programs for the seasons in Paris and Monte

Carlo, and, in an almost feline display of fealty, depositing on the doorstep of the Ballets Russes one useful artist or patron after another. Picasso was by far his greatest catch.

Cocteau realized early that Diaghilev, a minor nobleman and onetime art curator who had built an internationally known private dance company, could not trade forever on the Russian folklore and exoticism with which he had dazzled London and Paris audiences in the past. As he created the graphic look for the company, he suffused it with a cosmopolitan style based on art nouveau, and edged the impresario toward composers, including Richard Strauss, Claude Debussy, and Maurice Ravel, who employed the musical idiom of European modernism. In 1912, he and designer Léon Bakst created *Le Dieu Bleu*, based on Indian mythology. Although it was underwhelming at the box office and with the critics, it was just notoriously odd enough to assure Cocteau of insider status with the avant-garde Diaghilev and the artists already in his thrall, a circle that Cocteau was expanding through his society contacts. One of Cocteau's discoveries was the middle-aged satyr Erik Satie, whose light touch at the café piano and unerring sense of humor Cocteau admired from afar. He arranged to meet the composer at a soiree on October 18, 1915, hosted by Valentine Gross, prominent *salonnière*, and the plot to collaborate on a theater work was hatched. Just a week later he had deposited a pile of rough ideas for a new ballet at Satie's door. It took weeks before Satie wrote back, "It will be tough work. I'm starting to boil it all down." The most promising of the ideas Cocteau pitched, Satie felt, was the one about the "parade" of carnival players outside the entrance to their booth to drum up an audience for the show.

Who better to handle the circus subject than the maestro of harlequins, Picasso? Cocteau had been hankering for years to join the *bande à Picasso*, that fortunate and close-knit circle of poets and painters who had been gathering in Montparnasse for a decade. More materialistically, Cocteau also yearned to add a Picasso to his burgeoning collection of portraits by other art stars of the generation. He did not offer *Parade* as his opener. His original proposal for their collaboration was a patriotic, Francophone production of *A Midsummer Night's Dream* intended to upstage the Teutonic interpretation by Max Reinhardt. Even before he met Picasso, Cocteau was convincing friends that it would be "the greatest encounter of his life." And so it was.

Cocteau, by then twenty-six, was difficult to resist. Spectacularly multitalented and socially adept, he styled himself a poet but was a gifted draftsman and man of the theater. Even the staid Edith Wharton had written that she had "known no other young man who so recalled Wordsworth's 'Bliss was it in that dawn to be alive.'" Having secured the go-ahead from Diaghilev and talked Satie into taking part, he laid siege to Picasso. Cocteau turned up at the studio on the rue Schoelcher with an introduction from the composer Edgar Varèse and a harlequin costume that he offered to model, but Picasso somehow managed to house the costume while avoiding the portrait. Although he did draw Cocteau, in a spectacular imitation of the pencil portraits made by Ingres, he never actually painted him— despite the poet's feeling that Picasso's magisterial (but dark) *Harlequin,* completed in the fall of 1915, was a deeply disguised version of him in his costume (many say it was an encoded self-portrait reflecting the painter's grief after the death of his muse Eva Gouel, but this is yet another enigma that being a fly on the wall might have solved).

According to the eminent Picasso biographer John Richardson, the artist was ripe for the picking. Devastated by the death of Eva from lung cancer or tuberculosis, and bored by the familiar antics of his erstwhile co-cubists Braque and Gris, Picasso in the summer of 1915 needed Cocteau, a fresh and endlessly inventive new stimulus. Cocteau was also a first-class sycophant, who would address him as "Prince Pablo de Picasso." It was thanks to Cocteau that Picasso recovered from his elegiac mode and caught what the poet called "the red and gold disease" of the theater. It also marked the end of a lingering period of isolation after his friends, including Léger, Apollinaire, and Braque, went off to war and his dealer Kahnweiler fled to Switzerland. Cocteau himself had been to the front. He had been one of the more idiosyncratic members of an ambulance crew at the Somme, where he wore funny uniforms he concocted and very nearly had his head blown off not by the Germans, but by African soldiers who caught him spying on them with a camera while they showered. He managed to return to Paris on medical leave for what would today be called post-traumatic stress, and that was when he finally patched together a commission for a new work from Diaghilev. He covertly set it up so that he would receive the three-thousand-franc advance on royalties while Satie and Picasso, neither of them nearly as well off, did the work and got whatever Cocteau passed on to them.

There were cheerleaders on the sidelines who played their own vital roles in the genesis of *Parade,* including the powerful collector and expatriate tastemaker Gertrude Stein, the far more charming hostess Valentine Gross, wife of a prominent composer, and Eugenia Errazuriz, an art-crazy Chilean silver heiress who was in love with the much-younger Picasso and had been a backer of the Ballets Russes as well as an adviser on the acquisition of contemporary art to Diaghilev and Léonide Massine, the dancer and choreographer who had taken the place of Nijinsky in the company and would star in *Parade.* In addition to helping the ballet, she was the principal supporter of Igor Stravinsky, who lived on a monthly allowance of a thousand francs a month, and she was the patron who commissioned Le Corbusier to create a villa for her at Viña del Mar, a Chilean resort. She exerted her pressure on both Diaghilev and Picasso to make Cocteau's dream into a real theater piece.

It took the combined coaxing of Eugenia and Cocteau to overcome Picasso's initial qualms about "going over" to the socially acceptable medium of ballet. He correctly predicted that the hard-core bohemians in his circle would scoff. Cocteau also realized he was playing with strong passions when he lured Picasso to the Ballets Russes. The *bande à Picasso* was so dedicated not just to painting, but to the strict asceticism of cubism, that it regarded any figural depictions as heresy. They also had problems with the way in which Picasso was turning his back on their bohemian style and embracing high society—he had moved from a studio-home in Montparnasse to a suburban villa in Montrouge that was the epitome of bourgeois respectability. "L'époque des duchesses," sneered the resentful Max Jacob. Cocteau boasted, "His entourage couldn't believe he would follow me. A dictatorship weighed on Montmartre and Montparnasse. They were passing through the austere phase of cubism. The objects that could stand on a café table, the Spanish guitar, these were the only pleasures allowed. To paint a décor, above all at the Ballet Russes . . . was a crime." But on August 24, Cocteau triumphantly wrote to Valentine Gross, "Picasso is joining us in *Parade*."

By September the pieces were in place for what Apollinaire would soon recognize, in a note for the Paris program, as "the first marriage between painting and the dance, between plasticity and mime which is the sign of the advent of a more complete art." Diaghilev bestowed his official blessing on the commission at a meeting in Paris with Satie and Picasso. They were given five months to devise a score and sets for Cocteau's scenario and then reconvene in Rome for rehearsals and the inimitable Diaghilevian collaborative experience of fine-tuning the piece with Massine "on" the dancers. Satie went straight to work, but made Cocteau wait until October to hear any of the score. Picasso was off to a slower start, in part because he was a notorious procrastinator but also because the formal contract was delayed. He had heard that Diaghilev had a spotty reputation in financial matters. By January, though, Picasso had a brilliant maquette that delighted Diaghilev (who had started to call him "Pica," just as he called Cocteau "Jeanchik"), and by February 12 they were ready for the next phase.

Another subplot was brewing, however. During the long walks home together to Satie's modest place at Arcueil and Picasso's comfortable villa at Montrouge, while they ambled through the outlying suburbs a couple of Métro stops from the old haunts in Montparnasse, the two colleagues enjoyed heady conversations about the direction in which their piece was going. It would have been fascinating to tag along. They were concerned that the brash sound effects, such as the offstage voice shrieking gibberish through a circus megaphone, would be too "unreal" and tax the patience of even a sophisticated Paris audience. Cocteau's notes called for stylized chaos: *Comme un accident organisé qui dure* ("Like an organized accident that lasts"). Behind Cocteau's back they devised a quieter, more stern plot. At one point the Chinese character was torturing missionaries, and the American girl drowned on the *Titanic*. A crucial aspect of Picasso's reconception was to have the huge managers mime their parts rather than shout. The two conspirators felt guilty about subverting Cocteau, but Picasso's astonishing enthusiasm for the project was translated into a daily barrage of new ideas. "Picasso tells me to go ahead and follow Jean's text, and he, Picasso, will work on another text, his own—which is astounding, prestigious. . . . Knowing Picasso's wonderful ideas, I am heartbroken to be obliged to compose according to those of the good Jean, less wonderful, oh yes? Less wonderful!" Satie wrote a friend in the fall. What he may have missed was the aesthetic method to Cocteau's madness—he was trying to use sound in the same way that Picasso would use clips of newspaper or bits of wallpaper in a collage, as fragments of reality amid the artifice of ballet, the most illusory of performance media. Eventually, Picasso and Satie would come clean and present their ideas for editorial changes to Cocteau, who resisted some but relented on most. For Picasso and Satie, *Parade* was more than a modernist joke with gimmicks that would play humorously in a massive theater.

WHEN IN ROME

The most exciting phase of the collaboration occurred during a now-famous road trip that altered the course of modern art. On February 17, 1917, Cocteau and Picasso boarded a train for Rome, where Diaghilev and Massine had assembled the dancers for rehearsals. In a funny letter to Gertrude Stein, who took great delight in noting Picasso's rookie enthusiasm for the stage, Cocteau called the trip their "honeymoon" and chortled over his success at absconding with Picasso, who "laughed when he saw our painter friends (I am only referring to the doctrinaire cubists) dwindling bodily as the train drew further and further away." This was one departure that no time-traveling historian would want to miss.

Thrilled to be ensconced among a corps of sixty dancers, Picasso proved to be particularly brilliant at improvisation, even to the extent of painting costume details on the stockings of the dancers or makeup on their faces as they patiently came up to him, bowed, and stood still for him to apply the colors. There were daily sessions with Massine, who had in 1914 been one of Diaghilev's recruits from the Imperial Theatre of Moscow. Massine arrived in Europe steeped in Russian nationalism, but quickly picked up the tempo of international modernism in the arts, thanks in part to the efforts of Natalia Goncharova and Mikhail Larionov, a husband-and-wife team of cubo-futurists who introduced him in turn to Giacomo Balla, who made the geometric sculptures that stood onstage in the "ballet of light" to the music of Stravinsky's *Firebird* in the 1917 season. Thanks to these revelatory experiences, Massine was ready for this pas de deux with Picasso, and in two intense months they prepared for tour dates in Rome, Naples, and Florence before heading to Paris with their new masterpiece.

When the collaboration is as tight as it was for *Parade,* with the partners as multifaceted as Cocteau (poet and painter), Picasso (painter and aspiring dramatist—he began writing plays soon after), Massine (choreographer and art collector), and Satie (composer and litterateur), it becomes a chicken-and-egg riddle to sort out who contributed what, and only if you had been there would you have known whose touches made it to the final cut for the opening night performance. The dance began with Cocteau's original notes for gestures, which were tweaked by Massine under the watchful eye of Diaghilev, who was not averse to editorial changes from the wings, and Picasso, who attended rehearsals even though he was mainly there to finish his designs for the scenery, which would be painted back in France, and see to the fabrication of the costumes. He had turned up with sketches for the décor and curtain, but tirelessly updated them amid a blitz of new collaborative ideas.

You can tell from the drawings and paintings he made in Rome during those magic months that Picasso was having fun. The cavorting line of his sketches from the wings, so like the investigation of dancers' lives by Degas, and the jolly grouping of the figures at the lunch table for a *fête champêtre* that became the design for the curtain, all testify to the enjoyment of the life with the dancers, who coyly flirt, drink, and pose. The very subject of Picasso's curtain and décor is the backstage drama of theater life, which he brought to the foreground with a realism that was sure to strike his fellow cubists back in Paris as too literal. As with the opera *I Pagliacci*, the result was a psychological punch that took many by surprise. Even Cocteau was impressed by the emotional appeal: "For only reality, even when well concealed, has the power to arouse emotion," he wrote in his notes. This realism was grounded in Picasso's life at the time, which he conducted at the theater and in the company of the dancers rather than alone in the studio. Theater companies are like families, and Diaghilev's corps was a particularly close-knit assembly of expatriates committed to an avant-garde agenda that doubtless resonated with the great painter, who had experienced the fervor of cubism just a few years before. The dancers, musicians, and stagehands embraced Picasso as one of their own, and historians of dance are quick to point out that they held him in great respect for his sure hand, his natural sense of what played well onstage, and the alert way in which he designed the décor and costumes with their freedom of movement in mind. Some artists in a similar role would conceive of the staged work as a straightforward, three-dimensional rendition of one of the paintings, through which the dancers must wend their way. Picasso's *Parade* was anything but this kind of subordination of movement to a static, primary work. Each element gave priority to character and kinesis, the dynamic forces of the dance.

Between rehearsal sessions in the Cave Taglioni, Picasso retired to his temporary studio in the Via Margutta, where he looked out the window at the Villa Medici. Under that window was a massive table crowded with the model of the set and the large sheets for the costumes of the managers, the Chinese conjurer, the American girl, and that poor horse with its boxy snout, swayback, and obviously human legs. Soon he was cutting up and painting cardboard boxes to assemble the managers' costumes. These grew taller and more fearsome as Picasso had more exposure to the tyrannical Diaghilev, whose punishing regimen for the dancers would bring rebellion in later years. The least "real" of the inventions Picasso put onstage were the managers. Like the fierce caricatures in the works of Fernand Léger that caricatured American business moguls, they display a wicked monstrosity that Cocteau detested because he felt they lacked the sophistication of the dancers. For Picasso they were the *carcasses* of his cubist paintings. He kept Gertrude Stein posted in a letter dated April 1917: "I work all day at my decors and the construction of the costumes as well as on two paintings which I have begun here. . . . I go to bed very late. I know all the ladies of Rome. I have done many rather naughty and fantastic things in a Pompeian manner, as well as caricatures of Diaghilev, Bakst, Massine and some of the dancers." There were side trips to Naples and Pompeii with Cocteau and Diaghilev, essential lessons in art history that not only filled some of Picasso's gaps, but propelled him on an important new tack in his painting, from the geometry of cubism to the more refined arabesques of neoclassicism. Discreetly omitted from this letter was any mention of Olga Kokhlova, the winsome prima ballerina and daughter of a "noble" Russian military officer who was the target of Picasso's laser gaze during rehearsal. Her soft, round face and trim physique drift into his numerous drawings and are more firmly and magisterially rendered in large pastel and oil portraits of the following year—when they married, with a honeymoon at the Errazuriz mansion in Biarritz.

Picasso had to briefly say good-bye to Olga when the troupe packed up for tour dates in Naples and Florence. The only job left for him was the construction of the sets and the execution of the backdrops. He headed back to Paris and joined the crew at the huge studios on the Buttes-Chaumont to paint the massive curtain that would greet the audience. There is a marvelous

Pablo Picasso (wearing his trademark hat) and his assistants are taking a break from creating the drop curtain for the ballet *Parade*. The canvas was spread on the floor for painting. After a light sizing of the surface with glue, the picture was outlined in charcoal, and distemper applied in a thin coat, highly diluted with water. This photograph reveals the enormous dimensions of the work; the painted harlequin seated on a bench is double the size of a man.

snapshot, taken from a stepladder, of Picasso surrounded by the Russian craftsmen on a break from work on the nearly finished drop curtain. Painting sets for the Ballets Russes became a badge of distinction for a whole generation of young expatriate artists who came through Paris in the years to come, and memoirs of the Jazz Age include many merry sessions enjoyed by the bon vivant Gerald Murphy, his friend the novelist (in those days, painter) John Dos Passos, and Fernand Léger; even e.e. cummings picked up the giant brushes to work on the flats, which were laid out on the floor of a huge hangar.

Back in Paris, concerned observers recognized that Picasso was suddenly pursuing two aesthetic avenues at once: in *Parade* and the paintings that he was feverishly producing under the influences of Olga and the dancers, and in the Mediterranean art and ancient sculpture he had seen. The sinuous lines of the dancers offered a curvy counterpoint to the angular, clunky giants who were holdovers from cubism. When they were back in Rome, the young Swiss conductor Ernest Ansermet, who would lead the orchestra on opening night, had asked Picasso how he could practice both styles in one sitting. "But can't you see? The results are the same," was the artist's response.

The stage was set for the debut of *Parade* and the art world's first glimpse of the new Picasso. Rumors were already buzzing that he had jettisoned cubism for the posh environs of the ballet. Even the choice of theater had historic resonance, holding special significance for Diaghilev's troupe. The Théâtre du Châtelet was the largest concert theater in Paris when it was built in 1862 and had seen the likes of Tchaikovsky, Grieg, Debussy, and others who conducted premieres of their own symphonies and concerti there. More important, under the directorship of the colorful impresario Gabriel Astruc, whose avant-garde derring-do embraced visual as well as performing arts, it had become the prime venue for scandal in an era that was particularly blessed for its succession of memorable theater riots. In 1907 there was the partial nudity in Richard Strauss's opera *Salome*, followed by the shocking erotic spectacle of Nijinsky pulling off the role of the faun in *L'Après-midi d'un faune* in 1911, the first of what was an animal rite—the Ballets Russes blowing into town with one or more outrageous tests of the Parisian public's capacity for moral outrage. Nothing in the history of music quite matches the fury released with Stravinsky's *Sacre du Printemps*, which ended in a full-scale riot that drove the performers from the stage in terror, just four years before *Parade*.

Many of those in the audience that unforgettable evening, including Cocteau, were back again on May 18, 1917, to see how far the Ballets Russes would push the envelope this time.

To be there and to know the prelude to the curtain-raiser was to grasp how *Parade* changed not only Picasso, but modern art, dance, music, and theater. The Ballets Russes had shaken him out of his Montparnasse aerie and taken him to Rome and Naples, where he was steeped in the art of Rome, Pompeian frescoes, Flavian portrait busts, the characters from Ovid, and the style from Michelangelo, a brush with Apollo that would not keep him permanently from returning to Dionysus. Picasso emerged from the experience with his bride, Olga Kokhlova, and a way of life that was domesticated—eventually it would grate on him to the extent that he would hang on his studio door a sign that asserted, *Je ne suis pas un gentleman.*

POSTSCRIPT

This was how the curtain came down on cubism and rose on neoclassicism, not just in painting, but in all the arts. Cocteau called the shift *la chute des angles,* "the fall of the angles," with a pun on "angels." It prefigured not only the syntheses of naturalism and abstraction in Picasso's later work, but in the work of Henri Matisse and others of the School of Paris. Choreography after Massine took the experiments in jazz and modern movement to new extremes, and Satie's score with Cocteau's sound effects echoed through the later works of John Cage and others. The next medium to capitalize on the breakthrough of *Parade* was film, and it is no coincidence that Cocteau, Satie, and Massine would become pioneers, along with Léger, in its exploration.

As for the principals in this drama, many had brief but brilliant epilogues left to play. Picasso was tapped four more times by the Ballets Russes to produce décors, for *Le Tricorne* (1919), *Pulcinella* (1920), *Cuadro Flamenco* (1921), and *Le Train Bleu* (1924). He and Olga, who quit dancing when they married in 1918, had a son, Paolo, in 1921, and the briefly happy family was the inspiration for a series of paintings on the theme of maternity. He was divorced from Olga in 1935.

Jean Cocteau continued on his rise to stardom not only in the theater but in poetry, graphic design, and film—his *Orphée* (1950) is a classic that still appears occasionally in art houses or museum festivals. Massine himself rode the Hollywood express to global stardom when *The Red Shoes,* loosely based on his own life with Diaghilev's company, became a box office smash in 1947. By then the Ballets Russes was long gone. Under Dia-

When the curtain rose on the first performance of *Parade* in Paris, the audience must have been surprised to see—instead of the dancers' stage—a second, painted curtain depicting a stage occupied by performers and animals surrounded by red curtains. The work was Picasso's most monumental canvas: 10.52 meters high by 16.2 meters wide. It consisted of nine horizontal panels made of cotton and jute sewn together, and it weighed some 40 kilograms.

ghilev they had proceeded in the twenties, season by season, to unveil many of the most daring and important dance works of the twentieth century, giving rise to a number of private ballet companies, including Sadler's Wells and the New York City Ballet under the aegis of one of Diaghilev's many protégés, George Balanchine, who had escaped from Russia with Diaghilev's help. But the company lasted only until Diaghilev's sudden death in 1929 from a fever—he was attended in Monte Carlo in his final hours by Coco Chanel, another of his collaborators. His company was pressed for cash, so the curtain that Picasso created for *Tricorne* was cut into pieces and the central panel was sold to a collector. Today it hangs in the hallway to the "pool room" of the Four Seasons Restaurant at the Seagram Building in Manhattan, where it is routinely ignored by hedge fund managers and media magnates en route to their power lunches.

Further Reading

Douglas Cooper, *Picasso Theatre* (New York, 1968).

Lynn Garaola, *Diaghilev's Ballets Russes* (New York, 1989).

Charles A. Riley, *The Jazz Age in France* (New York, 2004).

FREEMAN DYSON

Exorcising Aristotle's Ghost

Freeman Dyson was born in England and came to the United States to study physics with Hans Bethe at Cornell University. He spent most of his life as Professor of Physics at the Institute for Advanced Study in Princeton, where he is now Professor Emeritus. He has worked in a variety of fields, including particle physics, pure mathematics, nuclear engineering, climate studies, astrophysics, and biology. Besides doing his professional work as a scientist, he has written books for the general public on the human side of science and the human consequences of technology, the most recent being *The Scientist as Rebel* (New York Review of Books, 2006). In 2000 he was awarded the Templeton Prize for Progress in Religion. Among his other awards are the National Book Critics Award for Nonfiction and Rockefeller University's Lewis Thomas Prize, honoring The Scientist as Poet.

In this essay Professor Dyson transports us to a number of crucial moments in history that have formed our understanding of the universe.

Exorcising cAristotle's Ghost

"We must start from this, that everything which has a function exists for the sake of that function. The activity of a god is immortality, that is, eternal life. Necessarily, therefore, the divine must be in eternal motion. And since the heaven is of this nature [i.e., is a divine body], that is why it has its circular body, which by nature moves for ever in a circle." "Since, then, the heaven must move within its own boundaries, and the stars must not move forward of themselves, we may conclude that both are spherical. This will best ensure to the one its movement and to the others their immobility."

These are typical passages from Aristotle's treatise "On the Heavens." In other books he describes the sublunary world, the world in which we live, constantly changing, filled with irregularly moving objects, winds and waterfalls, animals and plants. The sublunary world is built out of the classical four elements of earth, water, air, and fire. The interactions of the four elements give our world its disorder and diversity. Aristotle imagined the sublunary world and the heavens to be different in substance as well as in behavior. The heavens have no disorder and no diversity. They have no earth, water, air, or fire. The heavenly bodies and the spheres on which they ride are made of a single fifth element, quintessence, which is changeless and indestructible. The heavens are the realm of perpetual harmony and perpetual peace. The sublunary world is the realm of dissonance and discord. The sublunary world is the home of animals and humans. The heavens are the home of gods.

We do not know how Aristotle came to believe with such confidence in his vision of the heavens. Why should an immortal god necessarily move in circles? Why was Aristotle so firmly convinced of the divine virtue of circular motion? His way of thinking was heavily influenced by Plato, with whom he studied and taught for twenty years. His books were not written like Plato's dialogues, as literary works of art. They are lecture notes, summarizing the talks that he gave at the Lyceum in Athens at the end of his life. Long after Plato's death, Aristotle founded the Lyceum as a rival institution to Plato's academy, because he liked to be independent. His students at the Lyceum were called peripatetics because they did most of their studying on foot. It never entered their heads that they might test their beliefs about physics or metaphysics by sitting down and doing experiments. Aristotle did not write like a scientist. He wrote like a theologian.

It was an unhappy accident of history that Aristotle's writings became known in Western Europe during the cultural revolution of the Middle Ages, when universities were founded in Bologna and Paris and Oxford. There was a striking affinity between Aristotle's view of the heavens as the home of gods and the traditional Christian story of Jesus ascending into heaven to sit at the right hand of God after his resurrection. There was also an affinity between Aristotle's style of thinking and the style of Christian theology. Perhaps these affinities were not entirely accidental. After all, the style of Christian belief and theology were heavily influenced at the beginning by Saint Paul, who was educated in Greek philosophy and was probably familiar with at least some of Aristotle's ideas. These affinities were powerfully strengthened by Saint Thomas Aquinas, who wrote his *Summa Theologica* in 1265, incorporating Aristotelian doctrines wholesale into a Christian context. The *Summa* became an official statement of theological belief for the Catholic Church, and as a consequence Aristotle's speculations about heaven and earth became a part of Christian dogma. Throughout the later Middle Ages, the Aristotelian worldview was taught in the schools and universities of Europe and accepted by all educated and right-thinking Christians.

Aristotle spent twenty years in Athens as a young man studying in Plato's academy and ten years as an old man teaching in his own Lyceum. Between these two periods in Athens, he spent three years in Pella, capital city of the kingdom of Macedon, invited by King Philip to be tutor to his son Alexander. Alexander was thirteen when Aristotle arrived and sixteen when he left. Four years later, Alexander became king and set out to conquer the world. No records exist of what Aristotle thought of the young prince or what the young prince thought of Aristotle. It is remarkable that two such powerful personalities were able to coexist peacefully for three years. I wish I'd been there as a fly on the wall to listen to some of their conversations. I would like to know whether either of them had any inkling of the enormous impact that they were to make on history, Alexander within a few years and Aristotle fifteen centuries later. But Alexander is not the subject of this essay, and I must reserve my time as a fly on the wall for other conversations more relevant to my theme.

My theme is the exorcism of Aristotle's ghost. This ghost haunted the intellectual life of Europe for many centuries. The exorcism was a long and difficult process, beginning with Copernicus in the year 1543 when modern science was struggling to be born, and ending four centuries later. At the beginning the ghost haunted the seats of power, in the minds of popes and inquisitors, giving them the fortitude to burn at the stake heretics who questioned the truth of Aristotelian cosmology. Since Aristotle had placed God in a material astronomical heaven, to question his arrangement of the heavenly spheres was to question the authority of God. Aristotle had written in "On the Heavens": "There is not now a plurality of worlds, nor has there been, or could there be. This world is one, solitary and complete." When Giordano Bruno publicly proclaimed that God had created many worlds with many forms of life inhabiting them, the authorities in Rome did not hesitate to burn him.

Three hundred years later, at the beginning of the twentieth century, nobody any longer believed in Aristotelian cosmology. Even in the official doctrines of the Catholic Church, the Copernican worldview was accepted. Catholic theologians understood that the arrangement of planets around the sun had no theological importance. Heaven was a spiritual and not a material realm. It seemed that Aristotelian cosmology had been swept into the dustbin of history. And yet, Aristotle's ghost was still alive, powerfully distorting our view of the astronomical universe. Up to the middle of the twentieth century, the old Aristotelian view of the celestial sphere as a place of perfect peace and harmony still dominated the practice of astronomy. This view had survived the intellectual revolutions associated with the names of Copernicus, Newton, and Einstein. It was still taken for granted that the universe was static. The job of an astronomer was like the job of a terrestrial mapmaker, to explore the universe and make a map of an unchanging landscape. Einstein himself shared the general belief that the universe must be static. After he had discovered the general theory of relativity, he found a cosmological solution of his equations describing a static universe. A few years later, when Alexander Friedman found solutions describing an expanding universe, Einstein did not accept them as valid. Einstein was still under the influence of Aristotle's ghost.

We now know that we live in a violent universe. Everywhere we look in the sky, we see violent events and rapid changes. The job of an astronomer today is to record and interpret the processes of change. Acts of violence dominate the evolution of astronomical objects of all shapes and sizes, from galaxies and stars to planets and comets. Since we began looking for acts of violence, we found them in abundance. We did not find them earlier because we did not look for them. We did not look for them because we were still wearing Aristotelian blinkers.

There were two turning points in the exorcising of Aristotle's ghost. The two decisive dates were 1610 and 1936. Both turning points were brought about by small pieces of glass used to focus light from celestial objects in novel ways. The names associated with the two events are Galileo and Zwicky. The name of Galileo is known to everybody, the name of Zwicky only to astronomers and historians. They are of roughly equal importance to our knowledge of the universe. Galileo was the first astronomer to imagine a coherent universe with celestial and terrestrial objects made of the same materials and subject to the same laws. Zwicky was the first astronomer to imagine a violent universe. Galileo saw Jupiter with four moons orbiting around it, like our moon orbiting around the earth, and understood that Jupiter and the earth must be in many ways alike. He also saw that our moon is not a perfect sphere made of quintessence, but an earthlike ball with some areas flat and some areas covered with mountains. Zwicky found that violent events, which he called supernovae, are occurring frequently all over the universe. Galileo broke the Aristotelian separation of heaven and earth. Zwicky demolished the Aristotelian universe of unchanging peace and harmony.

The decisive event of 1610 was Galileo making a telescope for himself out of two glass lenses and turning it to the heavens. He did not act alone. He belonged to a trio of adventurous spirits. In 1609, Hans Nippershey in Holland had invented the telescope, and Johannes Kepler in Austria had discovered that Mars moves around the sun in an elliptical orbit and not in a circle. Kepler's discovery proved that nature did not share Aristotle's love of circles. But Galileo's little telescope did far more. It opened the door to a new way of exploring the universe. Where the little telescope had shown the way, bigger and better telescopes would follow. Whatever questions one wished to ask about the heavens, the answers obtained by directly exploring with telescopes would be more reliable than those provided by Aristotle's philosophical reasoning. After Galileo, each generation of astronomers could see farther and more clearly than their teachers.

I'd love to have been a fly on the telescope at 11:00 P.M. on the night of January 28, 1613, when Galileo was observing Jupiter and its moons. That night, according to his custom, he drew in his notebook a sketch of the objects that he saw within the field of his telescope, namely Jupiter, three of its moons (the fourth moon was hidden by Jupiter), and two stars. Positions of the objects were accurately recorded. He remarks in the notebook that he had seen the same two stars the previous night and that they were then farther apart. One of the two stars had moved. We now know that the star that moved was in fact the planet Neptune, which had passed behind Jupiter on January 4 and was moving away from Jupiter on January 28 in precisely the direction where Galileo observed it. This well-recorded observation of Neptune, 233 years before it was discovered, demonstrates Galileo's skill and reliability as an observer. It is also one of the famous missed opportunities in the history of science. How would the history of astronomy have changed if Galileo had identified Neptune as a new planet far beyond the orbit of Saturn? We can never know. As a fly on the telescope, I could not have told Galileo that he had missed something important.

Like Galileo, Zwicky belonged to a trio of adventurous spirits. The other two members of his trio were the astronomer Walter Baade and the lens-grinder Bernhard Schmidt. They were all unusual characters, but Schmidt was the most unusual. Schmidt was born and spent his childhood on the island of Nargen in the Gulf of Finland, twelve miles north of Tallinn and forty miles south of Helsinki. In those days the island belonged to Russia. It now belongs to Estonia. His father was German and his mother Swedish, so that he grew up fluent in both languages. At the age of eleven he began experimenting with explosives, using gunpowder that he manufactured himself and packed into metal pipes to produce well-tamped explosions. One of his experiments was too successful and blew off his right hand and forearm. He successfully improvised a tourniquet to stop the bleeding. After that, he gave up chemistry and turned his attention to optics. Working with his left hand, he ground a lens out of the bottom of a beer bottle and used it to make a functioning camera. At the age of eighteen he enrolled as an engineering student at the Institute of Technology in Gothenburg, Sweden. There he attended classes in optics, but spent most of his time in the library. He was particularly impressed by the papers of Karl Strehl, an optician who was teaching in a technical school in Mittweida, a small town near to the Zeiss optical works in Jena. Schmidt traveled to Mittweida and liked it so much that he stayed there for twenty-five years.

Working with his left hand, he made mirrors and lenses that are optically more perfect than any that were commercially available. He supported himself by selling mirrors and lenses to astronomers, first to amateurs and then to professional observatories. The astronomers at the Bergedorf observatory in Hamburg were so pleased with his mirrors that they persuaded him to move to the observatory as a "voluntary colleague," with a workshop at the observatory but no fixed hours and no duties. He moved to Hamburg in 1926 and there he met Walter Baade, who was a kindred spirit. They became friends and talked about the problems of astronomical photography.

In those days, astronomical photographs were made on glass plates. The standard routine was to point the telescope at a par-

Walter Baade (right) and his colleague Albert G. Wilson are discussing a photograph from the Palomar Sky Survey, which started in 1950 and resulted in 1,758 plates of the northern sky taken by the 48-inch Schmidt telescope.

ticular patch of sky and expose the plate for several hours until images of faint objects could be recorded. Almost all interesting objects in the sky are faint. Two factors made this procedure grossly inefficient. The plates were too slow, and the field of view of the telescope was too small. Typically, only one or two pictures could be taken per night. And the images were optically sharp only within a small angle, less than a degree across. At the edge of the field of view the images were out of focus, smeared, and distorted. Toward the end of the nineteenth century an international committee of astronomers had organized a project known as the Carte du Ciel, the first attempt at a complete photographic survey of the sky. Each observatory was assigned an area of the sky to photograph. But the project languished. Few astronomers were willing to sacrifice their precious observing time to produce their quota of Carte du Ciel pictures. Because the plates were slow and the field of view small, a huge number of hours were required to cover the whole sky. Already in 1926 it was clear that the project had failed. The Carte du Ciel was never finished.

In 1929, Baade and Schmidt traveled to the Philippines with a couple of telescopes to observe a total eclipse of the sun. In those days every eclipse was an opportunity to test the deflection of light predicted by Einstein's theory of general relativity. They spent weeks together on the ship steaming across the Indian Ocean, with nothing to do but talk. One evening on the ship, Schmidt casually remarked that he had solved the problem of designing a telescope with sharp focus over a wide field of view. Baade urged him to build a telescope with the new design as soon as he got back to Hamburg. Schmidt said there was no hurry. He would get around to it as soon as he had thought of an elegant way to do the lens-grinding. After they returned, it took Schmidt a year to invent a new way of grinding a nonspherical lens and to put it into practice. Baade later described what happened next: "By the summer of 1930 he had completed his first 14-inch telescope. Schmidt called me one sultry Sunday afternoon to say it was ready. From an attic window of the observatory he trained it on a cemetery. 'Can you read the names on the tombstones?' he asked. 'Yes,' I replied, 'but I can see only one thing: the optics are absolutely marvelous.'" I'd love to have been a fly on the wall listening to the conversations between Schmidt and Baade, either on the boat or in Hamburg, or preferably both.

Schmidt's design produced sharply focused images with a field of view that had about ten times the diameter and a hundred times the area of the field of view of existing telescopes. This meant that the sky could be photographed a hundred times faster. Baade understood that it would now be possible to do a complete photographic sky survey in a few years with a single telescope dedicated to that purpose. He persuaded Schmidt to publish his design in the *Central-Zeitung für Optik und Mechanik*. That paper constitutes the entirety of Schmidt's published works. It is three pages long. The remainder of Schmidt's life was short and sad. He was a pacifist and saw clearly that the rise of Hitler would lead to war. He saw no place for himself in Hitler's Germany and felt too old to start a fresh life anywhere else. He bought a sufficient supply of cognac and quietly drank himself to death. He died in 1935 and is buried in the same cemetery where Baade read the names on the tombstones.

Baade found a better way out. In 1931 he accepted an invitation to join the staff at the Mount Wilson Observatory in California. He took with him a photograph of the tombstones, together with some photographs of the sky taken with the first Schmidt telescope in Hamburg. He showed the photographs to his new colleagues in Pasadena, Edwin Hubble and Fritz Zwicky. Both of them saw immediately that a new era in astronomy had begun. But they reacted in opposite ways to the new opportunity. Hubble was a pillar of the establishment, a promoter and practitioner of big science. Zwicky was a rebel, a promoter and practitioner of individual enterprise. Hubble asked, "What is the largest Schmidt telescope that we can build, to photograph faint objects in the sky as deeply as possible?" Zwicky asked, "What is the smallest Schmidt telescope that I can build, to photograph large areas of sky as quickly as possible?" Answers to both questions were soon forthcoming. The largest practical size for a Schmidt telescope was forty-eight inches. The smallest practical size for scanning the sky was eighteen inches. Both roads, the large and the small, the slow and the quick, were followed. The two Schmidt telescopes on Palomar Mountain, the forty-eight-inch, which started working in

1949 with Hubble in charge, and the eighteen-inch, which started working in 1936 with Zwicky in charge, are still in operation and still finding fresh problems to solve. They are monuments to Baade and Schmidt as well as to Hubble and Zwicky.

Baade and Zwicky quickly became friends and worked together fruitfully for several years. They published together in 1934 a classic paper with the title "Cosmic Rays from Supernovae," proposing that a supernova explosion is the result of a star using up all its nuclear fuel and collapsing gravitationally to become a tiny object made of pure neutrons. This paper was a big step forward in the conception of a violent universe. Later they became bitter enemies. Baade was German and Zwicky accused him of being a Nazi. When the United States went to war against Hitler, Zwicky enthusiastically joined the war effort and Baade did not. When the forty-eight-inch Schmidt was finally built, Baade was given time to use it and did not share his time with Zwicky. Each of them went his own way, Baade the meticulous observer pushing the art of photography to its limits, Zwicky the slapdash entrepreneur grabbing every opportunity to do something new.

Zwicky was trained in Switzerland as an x-ray crystallographer. When he came to the California Institute of Technology in 1925, he was an assistant professor in the physics department. He had no official credentials as an astronomer. The professional astronomers never accepted him as a colleague. They thought he was crazy and he thought they were stupid. In retrospect we can say that both judgments were partially correct. In 1928 the Rockefeller Foundation awarded a large sum of money to Caltech to build a major astronomical observatory. Caltech acquired Palomar Mountain as the site for the new observatory, and the professional astronomers made plans to build the biggest telescope in the world, the two-hundred-inch Hale telescope that began to operate in 1947. Meanwhile, in 1931,

Zwicky heard from Baade about the Schmidt telescope and decided to beat the professional astronomers at their own game.
He quickly persuaded Caltech to buy an eighteen-inch Schmidt
telescope and install it on Palomar Mountain. He made sure
that he would have full-time use of the telescope, which was at
that time the only wide-field telescope in the world at a site with
good astronomical views. His telescope was up and running
long before the bigger instruments on Palomar Mountain were
started.

Zwicky had a hunch that the universe was full of violent
events, unseen because nobody had been looking for them. He
published papers about neutron stars and supernovae and black
holes and gravitational lenses long before these subjects became
fashionable. Supernovae were new stars that occasionally shone

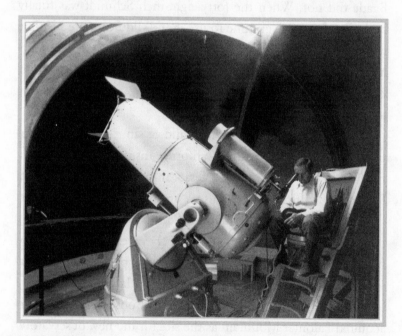

Fritz Zwicky peers into the 18-inch Schmidt telescope at Palomar Observatory,
ca. 1936. In order to accomplish his intended survey, which included photo-
graphing the entire northern sky, he had to spend hours in the exact same position.

in the sky for a few weeks with extraordinary brilliance. One had been seen by Kepler and Galileo in 1604, before the days of telescopes, and they viewed it as evidence that the heavens were not unchanging. Zwicky understood that supernovae were events of extreme violence, probably resulting in the disruption of an entire star. He understood that to see rare, violent, and short-lived events in the universe, it was necessary to photograph large areas of sky repeatedly. With his little Schmidt camera, he would have a unique opportunity to photograph the entire northern sky over and over again. Starting in 1936, with a single assistant to help him, he continued for four years to survey the northern sky repeatedly. He and the assistant discovered twenty supernovae, a large enough sample to allow him to classify them into several types and to infer their different modes of origin. He also discovered the uneven distribution of galaxies in space, with clusters and superclusters of galaxies in some places and empty voids in others.

After Zwicky's sky survey was finished, he proudly wrote: "For the construction of the 18-inch Schmidt telescope, its housing, a full-size objective prism, a small remuneration for my assistant, and the operational costs for the whole project during ten years, only about fifty thousand dollars were expended. This probably represents the highest efficiency, as measured in results achieved per dollar invested, of any telescope presently in use, and perhaps of any ever built, with the exception of Galilei's little refractor." His survey set the pattern for many later surveys done with bigger instruments and bigger investments of manpower and money. The newest sky survey, due to begin in 2007 with the name Pan-Starrs, will follow Zwicky in emphasizing rapid and repeated coverage of the sky. It will discover a wealth of short-lived phenomena at all distances, from near-earth asteroids to optical afterglows of gamma-ray bursts in remote galaxies. The gamma-ray bursts are the newest astronomical mystery, monstrous outpourings of energy that are seen occurring all over the universe at a rate of about one per day. They are more violent than supernovae, and much briefer. They are providing further evidence, if any is needed, that Aristotle's serene and tranquil heavens were an illusion.

When all is said and done, the conversation I would most like to overhear as a fly on the wall is not any of the real conversations that I have described, but an imaginary one. I would like to bring Aristotle and Zwicky back to life and listen to them talking about the universe. Aristotle was ignorant but not stupid. Zwicky was brilliant but not deep. Each of them would have had much to learn from the other.

Further Reading

Aristotle, *On the Heavens*, trans. W. K. C. Guthrie for the Loeb Classical Library, with Greek and English on opposite pages (Cambridge, MA, 1939).

John Gribbin, *The Fellowship* (Woodstock and New York, 2007).

Richard Preston, *First Light*, New American Library (New York, 1987).

The German Surrender to Montgomery at Lüneburg Heath, May 1945

Sir John Keegan taught Military History at the Royal Military Academy, Sandhurst, from 1960 to 1986. Since 1986 he has been Defence Editor of the *London Daily Telegraph*. He is the author of twenty books, including *The Face of Battle*; *Six Armies in Normandy*; *The Second World War*; *A History of Warfare*, which won the Duff Cooper Prize; *The First World War*, which won the Westminster Medal; and *Intelligence in War*. Sir John is a Fellow of the Royal Historical Society and of the Royal Society of Literature. He was awarded the O.B.E. in the 1991 Gulf War Honors List and was knighted in 1999 for services to military history.

In his book *The Second World War*, Sir John wrote the following about Field Marshal Bernard Law Montgomery: "Montgomery's debut on the battlefield [at Alamein] had been one of the most brilliant in the history of generalship." In this engaging essay we travel with the author to Lüneburg Heath in northern Germany on May 3 and 4, 1945. There we see a very different side of one of World War II's most famous commanders.

The German Surrender to Montgomery at Lüneburg Heath, May 1945

The surrender of German forces in Northern Europe to Field Marshal Sir Bernard Montgomery, Commander of the 21st Army Group, was one of the most carefully stage-managed occasions of the many that concluded the Second World War in Europe. Montgomery's convoy of command and signal vehicles that transported his headquarters had been following the advance of the 21st Army Group across northern Germany until, on April 30, 1945, the convoy reached Lüneburg Heath and encamped above the village of Deutsch Evern, at a spot commanding wide views over the heath, one of the German army's main training areas. The vehicles were parked in what had become a familiar formation beneath a cluster of birch trees. In the seven months since the landing in Normandy, Montgomery's headquarters had swollen to over two hundred vehicles, but its core was the field marshal's sleeping caravan, his office caravan, and his map truck, over all of which was stretched a wide camouflage net. The vehicles were parked close together and camouflaged; twenty-five yards in front of the caravans a portable flagpole was erected, from which the Union Jack was flown.

It was known that the German high command was trying to establish contact with the field marshal, presumably to arrange surrender terms. Until that day surrender had not been possible because Adolf Hitler, though incarcerated in his command bunker under the Reich Chancellery in Berlin, was still alive and had set his face against giving in. With Russian shells falling on the Reich Chancellery garden and Russian infantry only a few yards from its entrance, it was obvious that Hitler might shortly fall into enemy hands, a fate he knew he dared not risk. On April 30, after a farewell lunch with his entourage, he and his newly married wife, Eva Braun, withdrew into their private quarters, where they together committed suicide. Such leading members of the regime as survived, including Hitler's nominated successor, Grand Admiral Dönitz, had already fled to set up a rump government at Flensburg on the Danish border in Schleswig-Holstein, in the buildings of the German naval academy at Mürwik. It was from there that Dönitz broadcast to the German people the news of the Führer's death.

That death unblocked the political process inside what remained of the Third Reich. For curious reasons, the successor government at Mürwik would be allowed to remain at liberty until May 13, when Allied troops at last advanced to take the Nazi leaders prisoner. As soon as the news of Hitler's death was broadcast, however, Dönitz set about contacting the Western Allies to arrange a formal surrender. He made no contact with the Russians, for, insofar as Nazi Germany still practiced a policy, it was to keep the Russians at bay so as many German fugitives as possible, both soldiers of the surviving military forces and the millions of refugee civilians fleeing before the Russian advance, could find refuge inside what the German leaders knew would be the Anglo-American zone of occupation. General Eisenhower, Supreme Allied Commander in Europe, had set up his headquarters in Rheims, in France. There emissaries from Dönitz made their way, in the hope of postponing surrender until more fugitives had fled to the west. Their leading emissary was Colonel General Alfred Jodl, Chief Operations Officer of the Wehrmacht.

Local surrenders were also being arranged. In Italy, General Albert Kesselring had already surrendered all his forces to the Allies. In Northern Europe, the surviving German formations,

German Army North, the Twenty-first Army, and the Parachute Army, which were still fighting and which provided the garrison of occupied Denmark, were seeking to make contact with the British, whose zone of responsibility it was. That meant dealing with Montgomery, whose staff was aware that they might shortly expect a German delegation to appear. On May 2, Montgomery signaled to the Chief of the General Staff in London that General Blumentritt, the Commander of the Parachute Army, was "coming in tomorrow at 1130 hours to offer his surrender. It may well be that he is plenipotentiary for some bigger commander, and we shall not know this until tomorrow. We have had a remarkable day today and tomorrow may become more so."

It is on that next day that I would have wished to be present. The surrender of an army is a momentous occasion, almost always marked by solemnity, formality, and the rituals of final victory and defeat. But this one was very different, perhaps even unique in the annals of warfare. As the field marshal had predicted, May 3 was to be a remarkable day, and it was in large part thanks to Montgomery's considerable powers of showmanship.

Although his public reputation was as a man of short temper and icy temperament, Montgomery was in fact a considerable actor. He greatly enjoyed creating and conducting dramatic episodes. He was to show his talents at their full on May 3. At eight o'clock that morning, Montgomery's military assistant, Colonel Dawney, heard from General Dempsey, commanding the British First Army, that he had received a delegation of four German officers who were seeking to arrange a surrender. The news was released to Montgomery, who ordered that they should be sent on to him. Meanwhile, he set about arranging the mise-en-scène. Colonel Dawney and another officer were to put on their pistols and line up about twenty-five feet in front of his caravan and between it and the Union Jack. Everyone else was ordered out of sight.

Soon after eight, escorted by Allied military police, four German officers appeared, all in long overcoats, two naval officers, two soldiers. They lined up under the Union Jack and stood at attention. After a pause, the door of Monty's caravan opened to disclose the Field Marshal wearing battledress and his celebrated beret, a black beret of the Royal Tank Regiment, to which he was not entitled, with its two badges, that of the regiment and a general's gold badge (soon to be replaced by a field marshal's).

Montgomery began by barking at no one in particular, "Who are these people? What do they want?"—rather as a bad-tempered landowner might address his butler at the sight of trespassers on his estate. Having returned their salutes, in a decidedly casual fashion, he began to question each of them individually. "Who are you?" he said to the first, who answered, "General Admiral von Friedeburg, Commander in Chief of the German navy," a post to which he had been appointed by Dönitz the day before. In a loud voice Montgomery said, "I have never heard of you." He then treated each of the others in similar fashion. First it was General Kinzel, Chief of Staff of the Germany army. Next, Rear Admiral Wagner, flag officer to the Commander in Chief of the navy. The last identified himself as Major Friedel. Montgomery shouted, "Major! How dare you bring a major into my headquarters."

This was knockabout comedy of a high order. Colonel Warren, Monty's Canadian liaison officer, whispered to Colonel Dawney that "the Chief was putting on a pretty good act." Dawney whispered back, "Shut up, you S.O.B. He has been rehearsing this all his life."

Montgomery now barked, "What do you want?" Friedeburg answered that they came from Field Marshal Busch to offer the surrender of his three armies between Rostock and Berlin, which were withdrawing in front of the Russians. Montgomery answered, "Certainly not. The armies concerned are fighting the Russians. If they surrender to anybody, it must be to the Russians. Nothing to do with me." But he conceded that he would "naturally take prisoner all German soldiers who come into my area with their hands up." He then issued his own demand: that the delegation surrender all German forces in Friesland and Heligoland and Schleswig-Holstein, and all forces in Denmark.

The delegation refused to agree but said that they were concerned about the German civilians in these areas and asked if it could be agreed to arrange some provision of care for them. Montgomery now lost his temper. "Do you remember," he asked, "a little town in England called Coventry, which six years ago was blown off the face of the earth by your bombers? The people who took the brunt of it were the women, children, and old men. Your women and children get no sympathy from me—you should have thought of all this six years ago." He then proceeded to describe to the delegates what he had seen in the concentration camp at Belsen, liberated by his armies very recently.

Monty had decided by now that the delegation was likely to agree to his demands and that some softer treatment was called for. He ordered the preparation of a good lunch with wine and brandy, by which the Germans were very impressed, saying that they had not eaten so well for months. Then he had the luncheon tent transformed into a conference room and had the Germans sit down at the dining tables again, now covered with gray blankets on which situation maps were displayed. After the Germans had finished lunch, they were taken to the Field Marshal in his own mess tent, where he showed them the marked-up maps and made it clear to them the hopeless situation of the German armies. He then called Friedeburg, who had been unaware of the reality of the situation, and asked him if he would sign. Friedeburg, clearly shocked by the evidence of the situation, agreed. He then left to be escorted back to his headquarters by Montgomery's staff officers. Before they left, he promised to be back next day, May 4, to sign, and he took with him a letter describing what had passed at Montgomery's headquarters. Montgomery then withdrew to compose the surrender document they would sign. It was quite brief and absolutely clear. All the German forces in northern Germany would surrender to Montgomery personally.

Colonel Warren, who accompanied the departing Germans to their lines, parted from them on the understanding that they would meet at the same spot next day at 1400 hours and that Warren would wait only two hours. Next day Warren was back, with Colonel Ewart, who had been given special instructions by Montgomery to ascertain that the Germans had authority to sign. They did not appear until 1630, but the British party had waited and took them to see the Field Marshal.

Preparations had been made for press coverage of the ceremony. While waiting, Montgomery spoke to the press in absolutely typical Monty style, schoolboyishly triumphant. "The General-Admiral will be back about five. Ha! He is back. He was to come back with the doings. Now we shall see what the form is."

The waiting correspondents watched the German party, which was very despondent, approach Monty's caravan. The Admiral went up the steps to meet Montgomery. Montgomery later described what happened when the two men were alone. "I asked him if he would sign the full surrender document as I had described. He said he would do so. He was very dejected and I told him to rejoin the others outside."

They were then taken across to the larger mess tent. Montgomery described the scene. "The Germans were watched by

The five German delegates listen intently as Field Marshal Bernard Montgomery (seated at the right end of the table) reads the surrender terms to them at the headquarters of the 21st Army Group in the Lüneburg Heath. The document of German surrender in Northern Europe was signed here on May 4, 1945.

groups of soldiers, war correspondents, photographers, and others. They were all very excited. They knew it was the end of the war. I had the surrender document all ready. The components in the tent were very simple—a trestle table covered by an army blanket, an inkpot, an ordinary army pen that you could buy in a shop for two pence. There were two BBC microphones on the table."

Salutes were exchanged. Montgomery, as befitted the occasion, saluted punctiliously. He then read out the surrender terms. He announced that unless the Germans signed the document, hostilities would at once be reopened. He then said that the Germans would sign in order of seniority and handed the pen to Admiral Friedeburg. "Major Friedel will sign last," a concluding Montyesque dig. When all had signed, Montgomery announced, "Now I will sign on behalf of the Supreme Allied Commander" and did so, also dating the document and adding his rank to his signature. "That concludes the surrender," he said, and he retired to his quarters. It would be another three days before representatives of the German high command and government signed at Rheims. A simultaneous signing took place with the Russians and representatives of the Western Allies in Berlin.

For all the solemnity on which Montgomery had insisted, the ceremony at Lüneburg Heath was a secondary and local event. It was what happened in Rheims and Berlin that mattered. Nevertheless, Montgomery, once the reprobate Sandhurst cadet, had had his moment of glory. He would insist on its commemoration. During the years of the British occupation of Germany, a memorial stone was erected on the site of the surrender at Lüneburg Heath. In the following years it was so often vandalized by indignant Germans that it was eventually removed and reerected outside the officers' mess at Sandhurst, in which the Field Marshal in his retirement used often to dine with cadets of Alamein Company. Sandhurst companies are all named for British victories. The old Field Marshal, sharp and waspish as ever in his declining years, used to announce to the Academy's Commandant that he would dine on such and such a date with "my company, Alamein Company, my Company." After dinner he would address the cadets. Montgomery was a natural performer, with a taste for self-mockery, the only form of mockery he tolerated. The climax of his performance never varied. "My company commander," he said, "my company commander said to me, 'Montgomery,' he said, 'you will do no good in the army, no good at all.' Well, gentlemen, I became a field marshal and *he did not.*"

Montgomery, in a way, relished slights because they provided him with an opportunity to counterattack. In retrospect, I have concluded that he regarded the sending of an admiral, instead of a general, to negotiate surrender terms as an intended slight, as it may well have been, and that his performance at Lüneburg Heath was revenge for disrespect, the naughty cadet showing his face again above the field marshal's collar. "Who are these people? What do they want?" He knew perfectly well. His blitzing of the unfortunate major was part of the pantomime. "How dare you bring a major to my headquarters." The Field Marshal must have welcomed him as a useful walk-on part.

Further Reading

John Keegan, *The Second World War: An Illustrated History* (New York, 1990).

Alistair Horne and David Montgomery, *The Lonely Leader: Monty, 1944–1945* (London, 1995).

ACKNOWLEDGMENTS

The editors' greatest debt is to the gifted authors who have contributed to this volume. Most are friends or acquaintances of one or both of us, some we knew only through their published work. Despite busy schedules and heavy commitments, all have been responsive to suggestions, have been congenial to work with, and have made their deadlines, which is unusual in a project of this kind.

Sabine Russ, managing editor of American Historical Publications, has selected and acquired the rights to the illustrations with her usual combination of efficiency, imagination, and good taste. Our thanks to Barbara Leavey for her invaluable support during the preparation of the book.

We are grateful to Katie Hall, whose enthusiasm for the idea of *I Wish I'd Been There* books brought the project to Doubleday, and to our thoughtful and supportive Doubleday editor, Gerry Howard. We also appreciate the warm support of Georgina Morley at Macmillan, London, who has helped to make this publication a true transatlantic endeavor.

Map of Alexander's conquest route: Planetary Visions Limited (basemap), Marleen Adlerblum/Sabine Russ (map overlay).

The Triumph of Alexander, or the Entrance of Alexander into Babylon: Oil on canvas by Charles Le Brun (1619–90), ca. 1673 © Louvre, Paris, France/Peter Willi/The Bridgeman Art Library.

Hannibal and his war elephants crossing the Alps: 19th-century lithograph, English School, © Private Collection/The Stapleton Collection/The Bridgeman Art Library.

Coronation of Charlemagne by Pope Leo III: 14th-century lithograph, French School, after a miniature in Chronicles of St. Denis © Private Collection/The Stapleton Collection/The Bridgeman Art Library Nationality.

Alexander III and Frederick Barbarossa: Painting by Francesco Salviati (1510–63), Sala Regia, Vatican Palace, Vatican State. Photo credit: Scala/Art Resource, New York.

The Magna Carta of Liberties, Third Version, issued in 1225 by Henry III: Vellum, English School (13th century) © Dept. of the Environment, London, UK/The Bridgeman Art Library.

"Wat Tyler for his insolence is killed by Walworth and King Richard puts himself at the Head of the Rebels": Etching, English (19th century). Photo credit: The Granger Collection, New York.

View of Florence in 1490, called "della catena": 18th-century reproduction of the map of Catena, tempera, detail, Museo di Firenze Com'era, Florence, Italy. Photo credit: Alinari/Art Resource, New York.

Piero de' Medici, son of Lorenzo the Magnificent: Painting by Agnolo Bronzino (1503–72), Uffizi, Florence, Italy. Photo credit: Scala/Art Resource, New York.

Portrait of Charles VIII (1470–98), King of France: Oil on panel attributed to Jean Bourdichon (1457–1521) © Private Collection/Lauros/Giraudon/The Bridgeman Art Library.

Chart of the course of the Spanish Armada, 1588: Reproduction of an English engraving of 1739. Photo credit: The Granger Collection, New York.

Queen Elizabeth I with Robert Devereux, second Earl of Essex, in council, 1586: Cartoon, print by Richard Doyle (1824–83) © Victoria and Albert Museum, London, UK/The Bridgeman Art Library.

Charles I as Prince of Wales, ca. 1624 by Daniel Mytens (1590–ca. 1648) © Private Collection/Philip Mould Ltd, London/The Bridgeman Art Library.

Parade in the Plaza Mayor, Madrid: Painting by Juan de la Corte (ca. 1585–1660) © Museo Municipal, Madrid, Spain/The Bridgeman Art Library.

Portrait of Edmond Halley: Photo credit: Image Select/Art Resource, New York.

Isaac Newton: Mezzotint by John Smith after a painting by Godfrey Kneller (1646–1723). Photo credit: Victoria and Albert Museum, London/Art Resource, New York.

George Frederick Handel: Oil on canvas by Philip Mercier, 1733. Photo credit: The Granger Collection, New York.

Portrait of Queen Anne (1665–1714): Oil on canvas by Michael Dahl (1656–1743) © Private Collection/Philip Mould Ltd, London/The Bridgeman Art Library.

Coronation of King George I at Westminster Abbey, October 31, 1714: Engraving, b/w photo by © Bibliothèque Nationale, Paris, France/Giraudon/The Bridgeman Art Library.

Frederick II the Great of Prussia as Crown Prince: Painting after Antoine Pesne, Villa von der Heydt, Stiftung Preussischer Kulturbesitz, Berlin, Germany. Photo: Juergen Liepe. Photo credit: Bildarchiv Preussischer Kulturbesitz/Art Resource, New York.

Parmentier presents the potato to Louis XVI and his family: Color lithograph by Albert Chereau (19th century) © Musée du Val de Grâce, Paris, France/Archives Charmet/The Bridgeman Art Library.

Battle of the Nile: Wood engraving, 19th century. Photo credit: The Granger Collection, New York.

Le Déjeuner sur l'herbe: Oil on canvas by Édouard Manet, 1863 © Musée d'Orsay, Paris, France/Giraudon/The Bridgeman Art Library.

Symphony in White, No. 1: The Little White Girl: Oil on canvas by James McNeill Whistler, 1862, Harris Whittemore Collection, 1943.6.2. Credit: The National Gallery of Art, Washington, D.C.

First Blood in the Revolution: Repulsing the Strikers with Sword, Whip, and Gunshot opposite the Admiralty Building, St. Petersburg, 1905: Oil on canvas by H. W. Kockkock, b/w photo © The Illustrated London News Picture Library, London, UK/The Bridgeman Art Library.

Die Grundlage für den Völkerbund: 1919, cartoon by Thomas Theodor Heine (1867–1948). Library of Congress (LC–USZ62–22634).

Pablo Picasso and workers creating the curtain for the ballet *Parade:* DP 40, photo: Coursaget, Musée Picasso, Paris, France. Photo credit: Réunion de Musées Nationaux/Art Resource, New York.

Curtain for the ballet *Parade:* Painting by Pablo Picasso, 1917. Photo: Christian Bahier. Location: Musée National d'Art Moderne, Centre Georges Pompidou, Paris, France. Photo credit: CNAC/MNAM/Dist. Réunion des Musées Nationaux/Art Resource, New York.

Albert G. Wilson and Walter Baade: Photo by National Geographic Society/Palomar Observatory Sky Survey, Courtesy of the Archives, California Institute of Technology.

Fritz Zwicky at the 18-inch Schmidt telescope at Palomar Observatory, ca. 1936: Edison R. Hoge Collection, Courtesy of the Archives, California Institute of Technology.

Field Marshal Bernard Montgomery dictates surrender terms to German delegates, Lüneburg Heath, May 4, 1945: Photo: Malindine (Cpt), No. 5, Army Film and Photographic Unit, Photo # BU 5207. Used with permission of The Trustees of the Imperial War Museum, London. Crown Copyright. Reproduced by permission of the Controller of Her Majesty's Stationery Office.